A Shepherd's Heart

"And I will give you shepherds according to My heart, who will feed you with knowledge and understanding."
Jeremiah 3:15

A SHEPHERD'S HEART

Sermons from the Pastoral Ministry of J.W. Alexander

James Waddel Alexander

Solid Ground Christian Books
Birmingham, Alabama

SOLID GROUND CHRISTIAN BOOKS
PO Box 660132, Vestavia Hills, AL 35266
205-443-0311
sgcb@charter.net
http://www.solid-ground-books.com

A Shepherd's Heart:
Sermons from the Pastoral Ministry of J.W. Alexander

by James Waddel Alexander

From the 1860 edition by Charles Scribner, New York, NY

Published by Solid Ground Christian Books

Classic Reprints Series

First printing of paperback edition September 2004

ISBN: 1-932474-53-6

Special thanks to Ric Ergenbright who gave kind permission to use the beautiful photograph that graces the cover of this book. It is with a great deal of gratitude that we have listed his titles and contact information on one of the back pages of this book.

Manufactured in the United States of America

PREFACE.

THE appearance of these Discourses is due to the kind importunity of the Publisher, once my pupil and since my esteemed friend, who has for several years asked this contribution. Diligent inquiry of the Trade has informed me, that while the recent depression of business has lessened literary demand in general, the proportion of religious books sold has strikingly increased.

There are, as every one knows, several clever sayings, which set aside the Sermon as a species characteristically dull and unreadable; and this has tempted not a few, in giving the matter of their preaching to the world, to use some disguise as to the original form. Yet the testimony of booksellers is, that some of the most widely spread publications of the day are collections of Sermons.

Printing is only preaching in another shape. Provided, then, that people will read, a minister of Christ needs no more apology for putting his instructions into type, than for going into the pulpit. If he is sincere and zealous, his intention will be the same in both. He is only giving vast increase to the circle of his influence, for good or evil.

The affectionate and often fondly partial hearers of any preacher, are apt to desire the publication of what has been blessed to their spiritual strength and comfort; and such derive a profit from the printed book which cannot be measured by its intrinsic quality. It is with this view that these pages are more particularly dedicated to the beloved people of my charge.

After all, the controlling reason for publishing as well as preaching, should be a desire to glorify God in the salvation of men, by communicating as widely as possible the truth of the Gospel. When we have done all, we leave millions unreached by our endeavours; and if by any means we can add even one to the number of learners, it is worth the labour. Each messenger has some peculiarity in his way of influence. Every man who thinks long and deeply upon the plan of grace has certain favourite views, which have cost him something, which he cherishes with delight, and in which he strongly desires that others may participate. Even truths as old as Christianity itself strike him in such a way that he flatters himself he can bring them home with a kindred freshness to his neighbours and brethren. Let me avow that there are doctrinal statements in the following pages, which, though in no sense novel, are such as conduce to the very life of my soul, and such therefore as I am exceedingly desirous, in my humble measure, to rescue from misapprehension and inculcate on my children and friends. No speaker or writer is likely to leave a deep mark upon other minds, or in any degree to mould the thinking of his contemporaries, except by the utterance of principles, which not only are held by him in sincerity of belief, but are dear to his heart and operative on his character, as being inseparable from the current of his daily and nightly thinking. They may be true, or they may be false; but of him who holds them they are the weapons of warfare. Hence we are sometimes fain to do homage to the earnestness of a man, whose reasonings do not bring us over. For the doctrines here set forth, I claim only this: whether with or without reason, they are my belief. Years fly apace, natural vigour wanes, and opportunities of personal influence become fewer; but my profound conviction of the verities here proposed waxes stronger and stronger, with a corresponding earnestness to diffuse and impress them. No concealment or compromise has been attempted as to the tenets; which belong to a scheme of belief, ancient, intelligibly distinct, even singular, long contested, read and known of all men.

Yet if there is aught here which shall disturb any evangelical mind, it has crept in without a polemical purpose. The field is immeasurably large, in which we may expatiate, without setting foot upon the minor controversies of the schools; and some who are immovably attached to certain theological distinctions, would be the last to lay them among the foundations, or erect them into terms of communion, or set them forth as tests of grace. It is hoped, meanwhile, that humble experienced believers will find here in due prominence those central truths concerning Jesus Christ and Him crucified, by which all theology and all sermons must stand or fall.

None of the articles which make up this book belong to the class of Occasional Discourses; one only, intended for the young, was delivered by request; all are such as came up in the routine of a common ministry. They are intentionally miscellaneous, and several of the number are recent, as having been preached during the late blessed awakening.

It is my humble and hearty prayer, that God would vouchsafe, by his Holy Spirit, to make them useful.

NEW YORK, *November*, 1858.

CONTENTS.

	PAGE
PREFACE	3

I.
OUR MODERN UNBELIEF	11

II.
THE DIVINE PERFECTIONS IN HARMONY	49

III.
THE PROVIDENCE OF GOD IN PARTICULARS	73

IV.
THE INCARNATION	93

V
THE CHARACTER OF THE WORLDLING	125

VI.
THE SCORNER	149

CONTENTS.

VII.
SALVATION TRACED TO GOD THE FATHER . . . 169

VIII.
DYING FOR FRIENDS 187

IX.
THE BLOOD OF SPRINKLING 207

X.
THE THIRSTY INVITED 225

XI.
THE INWARDNESS OF TRUE RELIGION . . 245

XII.
NEW DISCIPLES ADMONISHED . . . 263

XIII.
LOVE CASTING OUT FEAR 283

XIV.
THE YOUNG AMERICAN CHRISTIAN . . . 321

XV.
DAILY SERVICE OF CHRIST 341

XVI.
MIRTH 361

XVII.
BELIEVERS ARE WITNESSES 379

CONTENTS.

XVIII.
THE CHURCH A TEMPLE 399

XIX.
STRENGTH IN CHRIST 423

XX.
YOUTH RENEWED IN AGE 443

I.

OUR MODERN UNBELIEF

OUR MODERN UNBELIEF.*

2 Cor. ii. 11.

"For we are not ignorant of his devices."

I. If Satan has the guile, the experience and the enmity which we commonly ascribe to him, he may be expected not to confine himself to one mode of attack on Christianity, but to bring up new forces and lay siege to new points in each successive age. And if the defenders of Truth have been as successful as we allege, they must make up their minds to see fresh reserves of argumentation, satire and obloquy taking the places of those which have been resisted and overcome. These antecedent probabilities are exactly realized in the actual strategy of our powerful antagonist. Christianity has been assaulted in every age since the beginning, but with a continual change in the object of the onset and the weapons and manœuvres of the foe. The objec-

* New York, February 8, 1852.

tions of Porphyry and Celsus seemed formidable in their day, and called out early writers in those Apologies, as they are named, which still exist in the libraries of the learned; but their objections would scarcely disturb the faith of a Christian child in our times; and they have long been laid asleep. A tremendous force was brought to bear against the Church by the English deists, and their successors, the philosophers of France. From the literature, the elegance, the occasional wit, the numbers and the skill of these opponents, an undeniable shock was given to the belief of thousands, as we may see in the period anterior to the French Revolution. There were not wanting men to predict that Christianity would speedily yield before such talent and daring as those of Voltaire, Rousseau, Hume, Gibbon, Diderot, and D'Holbach. The work wrought by these fascinating scholars, in academies, courts and drawing-rooms, was carried on lower down in society by such men as Paine, in clubs and pothouses. All these attacks of the eighteenth century had a common character. Whether sceptical, deistical, or atheistical, they all belonged to what has since been known as Rationalism. All denied the Bible, and many of them treated it with scorn, sarcasm, and blasphemy; all set up human Reason as the sole origin of Truth on the points in question. Materialists and immaterialists, sober theists and blank atheists, they agreed in this family likeness. There was no elevation, or enthusiasm, or mysticism. Every thing in religion was brought to the test of cold calculation.

The pretence of close logic was never more vauntingly put forth. It was by critical dissection and links of reasoning almost mathematical, that all these unbelievers undertook to demonstrate the falsity of our alleged revelation. This was the form of infidelity which prevailed in France, Prussia, Scotland, and in certain circles in America, during the youth of our fathers. It may be seen in its best colours in Volney and in the letters of Jefferson. What a sweep it made in France, even of the Romish clergy, is known to all who have ever contemplated the career of a Talleyrand, a Sièyes, or a Fouché. Some of the worst of the bloody actors were unfrocked priests. It was against this form of opposition that Divine Providence called forth such writers as Watson, Beattie, Campbell, and Robert Hall.* Some of our most valuable treatises on the Evidences of Christianity are the fruits of this warfare. Voltaire predicted that in twenty years Christianity would be extinct, and Mr. Jefferson seemed to smile in anticipation of an age in which superstition should be no more. Once in a while, and generally among the least educated, especially artisans and operatives who come to us from Great Britain, we find a knot of antiquated scoffers, who pore over these exploded books and shed libations upon the carcass of Paine. That grand army is as thoroughly disbanded as was Napoleon's at Waterloo; but Christianity still survives, and some of its greatest triumphs

* See Hall's celebrated Sermon on Modern Infidelity.

have been made since this very epoch. We have beheld, not the enthroning of the goddess of Reason, but the era of the Bible Society, of Missions, of mighty Revivals, and of increased Protestant union. If the citadel of Christianity is to fall, it must be by other weapons than those which lie black and rusty around the fortification, like the spiked cannon and stray balls which mark the spot of former engagements. That campaign of the antichristian war has reached its close; and he who would bring forth against us the armament of an age utterly left behind, only betrays the simplicity of ignorance. But are we, therefore, to conclude that Satan has desisted from his attempts? By no means. He has only availed himself of the pause, to levy forces for a new campaign, and assault positions heretofore unattempted. And it is a most interesting and needful inquiry, in what shape the infidel incursion of our own day is to be expected; for the whole line of our defences must be conformable to the dispositions of the enemy. It is my desire, therefore, to ask your attention to some characteristics of the infidelity which we have most to fear for ourselves and our children. And here there is danger lest we make the field of observation too wide, and thus content ourselves with a superficial view. We ought therefore to exclude, however important in their place, all those forms of error which claim for themselves a part in the church foundation, and which name themselves Christian. It is not heresy, however noxious, which we would now examine, but infidelity. Nor must we err so grossly as to assert that all infidels belong to a single class. Their name is legion. It has been admitted that here and there a specimen may be found of the old-fashioned calculating unbeliever of the French or Jacobin, that is, the rationalistic school. Among the remainder there are also various degrees. No one is ruined all at once. In the awful descent each apostate finds "beneath the lowest deep a lower deep;" and the precise shade of blackness and darkness which we meet in him must depend on the stage of this downward progress at which we make our observation. Yet the infidelity of the nineteenth century has characteristics as discernible as that of the eighteenth; and if these are occasionally less distinct, it is because the unbelief of our day is forming, but not formed; the process is incomplete; the development is still going on. We have to examine tendencies rather than results; yet as naturalists can detect the poison fruit even in its blossom, and the viper in its egg; and as the premonitions of the earthquake or volcano give inarticulate warnings before the earth is cleft and the lava boiling over, so we have a right to sit in judgment on the falsities beginning to prevail, even though we know but in part whereunto they shall grow.

1. The beginnings of this contemporaneous infidelity were with a show of great learning and science. Assumptions of this sort were indeed made by the Encyclopedists and French atheists; but their attainments were limited and often superficial. Several great sciences,

in their new forms, have been born since their day. We have only to read the "Jew's Letters" to learn the ignorance of Voltaire as to some of the most ordinary matters of Biblical science; and the veriest schoolboy would scout the claim of probability for Volney. In our times, if one country more than another has the boast of learning, it is Germany; and there, if anywhere, Infidelity has made its wildest ravages. It was Lessing who led the way in violent warfare against Christ; Lessing, the poet, the man of taste, the almost universal genius. Goethe and Schiller are claimed by the infidels; yet the last age has produced no greater masters of the human heart. The philosophy which takes its name from Germany, and which has penetrated France, and entered largely into the public institutions of America, was born and nurtured and matured in the bosom of noble universities, founded for the upholding of Protestant religion. The new sciences have been invoked to prove the Bible false. Astronomy has been placed on the rack, to testify that Creation at the scriptural date is absurd. Geologists, scarcely at the threshold of their discoveries, unsettled in their very nomenclature, and unwilling to wait till they can agree among themselves, have so read the strata of the earth as to give the lie to the books of Moses. Ethnography and Ethnology, puffed up in new-born strength, have uttered oracles showing that the negro and the white man cannot have had common progenitors. All have boasted superior letters and philosophy. But above all, the metaphysical reasoners, one after another, have, spider-like, spun a thread out of their bowels, wherewith to entangle and crush the doctrines of the Gospel. With a show of erudition and acumen never surpassed, one of the most prominent infidel theologians of Germany uttered a "Life of Jesus," undertaking to show that all the miraculous histories and most of the ordinary narratives in our four Gospels are poetic figments, mythic fables, innocent or heated inventions, like the story of the labours of Hercules, or the nursery legend of Jack Frost; pleasant personifications and instructive apologues, with scarce a line of real fact at the bottom. Whole libraries have been ransacked to give basis to this absurd structure, the mere statement of which ought to be its confutation. Let it be my apology for alluding to this poisonous book of Dr. Strauss, to say that it is circulated in English in many editions, and that it has, to my knowledge, entered the house of one of our own persuasion, and perverted the soul of one trained under the truth. Our popular literary men have in some cases drunk this poison. Certain portions of the Unitarian body, unable to keep foothold on the narrow edge between their attenuated Christianity and Deism, have cast themselves into the gulf of Germanism. If you would know what I mean, consider the teachings of Theodore Parker, Emerson, and their confederates. This is, as you perceive, no longer the vulgar infidelity of the last age; but it is not less destructive.

2. The Infidelity of our age affects to be religious.

This could hardly be said of that which prevailed before. The attempt was, in most, to scout every thing like devotion, enthusiasm, or inward affection, as superstitious. It was found that this was first impolitic, and then impossible. It was found that man as a religious being must have some outlet for the spiritual sentiments, and would make religions for himself, such as the French Theophilanthropism, or betake himself to the beautiful idolatries of Greece, as both Gibbon and Schiller seemed half disposed to do. It was found that man, despoiled of all the religious emotions, became a Marat or a Paine, a tiger or a swine. It was necessary therefore for the arch-enemy to remodel his devices, and bring in a religion which was better than that of the Bible. This, my brethren, this above all things else, is the grand characteristic of infidelity, in its present most dangerous form. Your sons and your daughters may be breathing the fatal chloroform of German transcendentalism, when they seem to themselves surrounded by the familiar air of Christianity. They may hear much from popular lecturers of the ideal, the spiritual, the divine, even of God incarnate in humanity, of resurrection, of faith, of Christ himself, when the subtle deceiver, annexing to these terms his own antichristian meanings, is slowly and deliciously, but surely and fatally charming from them all that can renew and save the soul. Most of all dangerous is our spiritual enemy when he thus transforms himself into an angel of light.

You have need to be warned against this new form

of error, because it employs almost every term of theology and experience in a false and deceptive sense, often applying the most sacred words of gracious truth to matters of literature, scenery, the fine arts, love, and alas, even to sinful indulgence. Some of the foremost poets of our day are chargeable with these insidious tactics; so that a father has need to look well to the books which lie upon his daughter's table, as splendid presentation copies. I do not mean merely the avowed Atheist and convicted blasphemer, Shelley, who maligned Jesus and argued against marriage; but many seemingly pure and undoubtedly gifted authors, who sing beautifully of Nature and of God. And here we must remark, that while under the former phase of Infidelity, much was said of Nature, under its present phase as much is said of God. Yet be not deceived, my brethren. If frequent repetition of the Sacred Name could sanctify a cause, theirs would be hallowed indeed. But their God is not our God; not the God and Father of the Lord Jesus Christ; not the God of the Saints; not even a personal God. With many varieties of expression, and many modes of veiling their horrid purpose, their inward thought is to remove all that we mean by God. The more they talk of God, the less they believe in him. In their disguised atheism the term implies the sum of all things, or the everlastingly unfolding process of causes, or the universal Reason, as existing in all minds. Sometimes, in their glorification of humanity, they utter the scriptural phrase, God is man;

but their inward meaning is that man is God. Man is the object of their adoration. The highest manifestation of God, say they, is in the human mind. This they dishonestly name, at times, the Incarnation. Indeed, there is scarcely a precious term in the vocabulary of grace, which they have not stolen and defiled by their abominable prostitution. This is the form of atheism which now threatens the world, and which has been called Pantheism. Few have gone the length of holding the system in all its parts; many differ as to minute tenets and explanations; but towards this vortex all the popular and poetical unbeliefs of the age are rolling themselves. This maelstrom has already sucked in and engulfed several sickly and half-living heresies, among the rest a goodly portion of the Socinians. The bloodless humanitarianism of Priestley and Belsham was too cold, too reasoning, too deathlike; their churches were too sombre and empty; their very ministers could not be kept from becoming authors, statesmen, or diplomatic agents; their creed was too near Deism. This was discovered by many of the shrewder sort. Hence the new method of reconciling opposites which had been discovered in Germany was seized with avidity; and from this arises the modern philosophical, poetical, pantheistical Christian. For a reason above given, such a one may, by dexterous use of scriptural terms, give his discourses a sound which is all but orthodox. But the more sober and rational Unitarian abhors these extravagances scarcely ess than we. Never before has the world seen so large a body of infidels, really denying every thing like a proper revelation, yet full of great swelling words about the Spirit, the God of History, the union of Virtue and Beauty, and the excellence of Religion.

3. The Infidelity of our age connects itself with freedom and social progress. So far as the infidelity of France was a reaction against hierarchy and the pope, it had the same colours. Hence the very men who murdered the priesthood in the September massacres, were loud in cries of liberty, equality, and fraternity. But this policy of modern unbelief is much more boldly marked. Hence the cry, on every side, that Christianity is a failure; that the Church has not made men happy; that whatever good the Bible has accomplished, its work is done, and we must have something better. It is a part of this scheme to glory in humanity as such; to assert the independence and self-sufficiency of man; to deify the creature, and pushing the rights of man to a jacobinical and impracticable extreme, to instal lawless Freedom in the pulpit. There is something so attaching and gracious in the first aspect of a levelling system, that any scheme of this kind gains multitudes of converts among the oppressed, the suffering, the discontented, the aspiring, and the greedy. Even in our own free commonwealth, where every man who deserves to rise may succeed in it, so far as outward restrictions are concerned, there begins to be more and more every year, a half-suppressed hum and murmur among certain large classes; as if all ranks must be brought to a com-

mon level; as if the capitalist and the transient worker must share alike; as if the accumulations of industry must become a spoil for the idlest; as if labour with the hands were the only title to enjoyment. This being openly and diametrically opposed to the letter of Scripture, these teachers, however they may begin, are pretty sure to end in discovering that the Bible is false. Thus, strange as it may seem, philanthropy, unsanctified, may lead unsound minds to unbelief; and there are no more reckless and bitter opponents of Christianity than a number of writers, lecturers, and editors, whom we once knew or heard of as ministers of Jesus Christ. The truth, however, must be told: just as with European grain we have brought into our fields the weeds of agriculture, so with the unheard-of emigration from foreign countries, we have imported infidel socialism and communism. It is no longer the books and arguments of false teachers, only, we have the men themselves, the ready-made disciples, clamouring in our public assemblies, and inflaming a peaceful population from the press. I leave, as not pertaining to the pulpit, the question how far this influx from corrupt sources may be expected to modify our political institutions.

The device of Satan is most apparent in all this. The excesses towards which infidelity drives, are counterfeits and caricatures of the very blessings which we owe to true religion. For, is not Christianity the religion of the poor and the oppressed? Is it not the religion of philanthropy? Does it not teach the common origin and spiritual equality of all men, in the sight of God? Does it not seek, and at the safest moment procure, human freedom and social rights? Must it not be named pre-eminently the system of true progress? Yea, yea, in despite of Garrison and Proudhon, forever yea. But when God has launched his vessel, infidelity would board and master it, and, tearing its noble timbers apart, would frame a thousand fantastic and perishable rafts out of the dismembered hulk. Nay, circling around the ancient ship, she would claim for her crazy floats, of stolen material, all the safety and all the glory of the original structure. The press of the day, deeply surrendered to the half-religions and mock-religions of the time, is ever and anon jeering at the Church and at Christianity, as not doing so much for mankind as these reformers would do, as jacobinism would do, as common property and unmarried alliance would do. Thus antediluvians laughed at the Ark. Hiding from view the fact that whatever philanthropy irrigates the desert of humanity, is the product of this very Church and this very Christianity. They calumniate the mountain spring, and claim all its flowing lakes and rivers as their own. But you will agree with me, that the prevalent infidelity assumes to be the benefactor of mankind.

4. The infidelity of our time is extending itself among the less cultivated classes. Begun in learning, it was almost proverbial in ancient times that Chris-

tianity was gladly received by the poor, while it was rejected by the learned. Something of this was true a century ago. The virus of French unbelief was generated among scholars, and fomented in courts and academies. During the progress of the anarchy which preceded Napoleon, the leading spirits were men of education; the brutal masses, it is true, maddened by long oppression, feverish with the thirst of freedom, and confounding Christianity with the despotism of the priesthood and the confessional, abjured the Redeemer, and well-nigh offered up the idea of God. This was more from false political notions however, than from any deliberate theory of religious unbelief. And when Deism, or, perhaps, Atheism, came over sea into many minds in America, it was principally among speculative men, who aspired to be philosophers. But our own day has seen a very great increase of this tendency in antichristian systems to popularize themselves. The most capable observers tell us concerning Germany, for example, that the language of unbelief and blasphemy is no longer confined to the schools and universities where it lingered long. The upland waters have broken themselves away, and are flooding the champaign. There is reason to fear that in central and northern Europe the masses of the people are rapidly becoming corrupt in regard to the essentials of religion. In lands where it is difficult to find a boy or a girl who cannot read, thousands and myriads are growing up to neglect all public worship and all private prayer. I grieve to say it—but a great number of the foreigners who emigrate to America are grossly infidel. It is the solemn and sorrowful testimony of most respected clergymen of their own race. It is attested by the radical, and often antichristian avowals of the numerous newspapers published among us in that language. Nor is the evil confined to one country. The contagion has spread widely among the working-classes of Great Britain, many of whom bring over their scepticism or their impiety. It may be safely asserted, that wherever we find a club, society or institute openly and loudly infidel, we may detect a large infusion of transatlantic people. Yet we must not flatter ourselves that our native population, especially in cities and large towns, enjoys an exemption. While the great body, through Divine favour, remains untouched, the new generation has many growing up without any Sabbath, indifferent to public worship, schooled without the Bible, a ready prey to false religionists in the first place, and thus prepared to take the further step into denial of all revelation. The means of grace do not any longer reach our population in its length and breadth. Churches rise in great numbers, where the truth is preached and honoured; but other places of religious teaching, in equal numbers, draw crowds into Universalism, Socinianism, enthusiastic and fanatical heats, and insane pretensions to mysterious influence and spiritual revelation. And then, what numbers in civic populations frequent no house of worship! A late writer, of much observation and detail, speaking of the street-people of London, assures us that thirty thousand of this single class never enter any place of religious instruction. We have not reached this extreme; but are we not on the way? It is matter of observation, that our churches are generally filled with at least well-doing people. But where are the vastly greater numbers of those who still more need the consolations of the gospel? I bring no charges, brethren; indeed, I have the sickening faintness of one who beholds a great malady, but is not prepared to announce a specific remedy; revived Christianity being the only real cure. For my present argument, it is enough to point to this state of things, obviously increasing, as a proof that the modern irreligion is widely prevalent among the humbler portions of society.

5. The Infidelity of our times is strikingly immoral in its tendency. All falsehood in religion is by its very nature opposed to virtue; but in varying degrees, according to the presence or absence, and according to the degree, of the causes already enumerated. Satan does not always display the cloven foot. The minister of darkness does not at once disclose himself in the colours of the pit. It is the policy of unbelief, while working its way upward into public favour, to assume the garb of purity. Hence, there have been many avowed infidels who, out of the very pride of sect, have led lives of scrupulous outward virtue. Lord Herbert of Cherbury is not the only Deist who has seemed to outshine many a Christian professor. But in our day,

the evil tree is hung all over with its proper loathsome fruit. The prevailing forms of unbelief in revelation are accompanied with manifest deterioration of morals. When men begin to go astray in conduct, and to indulge any great vice, they gladly embrace such errors as may stupefy conscience, and so enable them to sin unchecked. And then, the effect in turn becomes a cause; and by an inverse action the falsehood breeds irregularity and crime. Go where you will, among families, neighbourhoods or communities, where there has been shipwreck made of faith, and you observe a correspondent injury of the moral sense. It is almost an unfailing index of the modern infidel, that he inveighs against the perpetuity and sanctity of marriage. By an easy process, the sanctions of property are worn away. Inoculate any large class with antichristian opinions, and the contagious influence becomes horridly rife. An angry, relentless spirit of discontent, mutual distrust, lust of change, revolutionary fire, and general disquiet, plays on the features and inflames the language. The great and invaluable gift of freedom furnishes no safeguard here, unless it be coupled with true religion. Freedom is only a condition, under which men's principles act. If those principles are destructive, freedom is but an open door to ruin. The absolute freedom of a thoroughly immoral people, " hateful and hating one another," would be nothing short of hell. Indeed, the instinct of self-preservation does not allow men to remain long in any state approaching this;

for, in dread of one another, they are fain to take refuge under the protective shadow of military domination or imperial tyranny.

Blessed be God, the religion which fled to this new world for an asylum is still spared to us; and there are wide agricultural districts which have not been reached by more than the rumour of philosophic infidelity and disorganizing wrong. Yet, so far as this religious guard has been impaired, the consequence has been a relaxation of public morals.

It is not perfectly easy to declare, how far we may trace to this source the increase of crime, which is matter of every-day complaint. Some think that breaches of mercantile confidence are less rare than fifty years ago. The journals of every morning familiarize us to the record of murder. And suicide, the special crime of those who deny a future retribution, is committed with a frequency which often robs the gibbet of its prey. I might note other crimes, but your memory and observation will supply what it might be inconvenient to describe from this place. It admits no denial, that while individual exceptions occur, the usual result of disbelief in the Evangelical Scriptures, is an open declension of morality, and that this result is especially remarkable at present.

II. In the opening of these remarks it was admitted that the period of Infidelity in which we are living has not reached its term, and that to judge it fully we must wait till the causes now in action shall have worked out their full results. For there is a growth in opinion as truly as in the rise, progress and end of a human being; and though in both cases there may be further consequences, it is rather by lineal descent than by the continuance of individual life. There is, moreover, a wide extent in the prevalence of great falsehoods. Beginning in one corner of the world, they spread themselves from country to country; and just as the harvest comes at a different month in Canada, in Maryland, and in Mississippi, so the full crop of infidelity is not seen at one and the same time in all lands. In some it has begun to scatter its narcotic seeds, while in others there is but the tender blade emerging from the furrow; but this very gradation enables us to study the character of the growth. If in certain places we find the mature plant, with its poisonous juices thoroughly concocted, we thereby learn what we may expect from the young and perhaps attractive flower which blooms among ourselves. There are countries where infidelity may be said to have run its race and displayed all its stages of insidious promise and eventual desolation. Such was France under the Revolution. There are others in which it is only beginning. Dreadful as it is, it is nevertheless true, that the presses of New York and Philadelphia have issued thousands of copies of the last century's infidelity, in the works of Voltaire, Volney, Rousseau, and Paine, in Spanish translations for the South American market. And, as if the malignity of Satan could have no rest, some of these same books have been laboriously and widely circulated in the native languages of the East Indies, to corrupt the ignorant and besotted Hindoo, and to close his mind against the gospel. Such states of opinion are widely different from that which exists among ourselves, as indeed our own state differs from that of some European nations, where vaster strides have been made towards the denial of all moral distinctions and of God himself. Thus the giant pestilence of our day, which circumnavigated the globe, began in Asia and traversed Europe before it showed its ghastly visage on our western shores twenty years ago. But this gradual accession of the plague allowed and encouraged medical skill to examine the nature of the disease long before the treatment of it became a practical question. We have been considering a more fatal malady which is traversing the earth, and of which the symptoms are not deathly coldness and spasms of bodily pain, but mental delusion, palsied conscience, and a heart ossified by godless falsehood. We have seen it seizing men of learning, taste and civilization, and then stealing like an infection into the crowded haunts of labour and the hovels of want. We have descried in it a type differing from the infidel deceptions of a former generation. We are old enough to remember its beginnings under this new form among ourselves; and we open our eyes to its more consummate virulence in countries where it has more deeply corroded the vitals of Christianity. We are alarmed at daily indications of its stealthy but effectual expansion in the literature and society around our doors. We begin to tremble for our children and successors. Unless the whole picture has been overcharged, we read in all this a lesson, which may cast a sober hue over the thoughts of even the most selfish and worldly.

1. We are loudly admonished to be on our guard. When pestilence is in the air, wise householders look well to the symptoms of their family. When enemies are in a land, true generalship throws out its parties of reconnaissance, and keeps a sharp eye on every suspicious wayfarer and every sign of treachery and ambush. When the freedom of a kingdom is endangered, patriots are awake to every sign of increased power. These are not tremors of cowardice, but salutary precautions of prudence and benevolence. It is because we are not ignorant of Satan's devices, that we maintain an equal vigilance against our spiritual adversaries. Snares are harmless when discovered, and "in vain is the net spread in the sight of any bird."

But it is not enough to be aware of danger in general; we must know from what quarter and in what particular form to expect it. If infidelity made its first demonstrations in all the dark and bloody colours of downright atheism and licentiousness, it would never show a convert. It is the very insidiousness of the approach which magnifies our peril. Hence our first duty is to know the enemy, and if possible to know his most covert advances. We must learn to pull off masks and see through disguises, to distrust honeyed words, and fear our foes even when they come bearing gifts. This implies a sufficient acquaintance with the whole system of positive truth to know when any part of it is attacked, and then information as to the ways in which those attacks are likely to be made. Among the multitude of books, public journals, orations, lectures, sermons, poems, and common talk, in which we live, there are every day some which propose antichristian opinions. As truth is one and error manifold, no human faculty can foresee the precise mode in which falsehood will be presented by a wily foe; and therefore the grand safeguard, as we shall see, is a knowledge of the truth. But subsidiary to this is a watchful scrutiny of every principle which assaults or undermines any particular doctrine of God. These false teachings often begin far away from the point at which they really aim; but such is the contexture and harmony of the Divine system, that it begins to give way upon the surrender of any leading propositions. Those wretched persons who, from being speculative Christians, have become atheists, arrived at this catastrophe by a series of acts. *Nemo repente fuit turpissimus.* Hence the need of watching the earliest, slightest symptoms of the disease. Our danger is all the greater in proportion as we have allowed the close and thorough religious instruction of households to fall into desuetude. There are many among us who read abundance of books, but among them so little of Christian theology, that they do not even recognise the deadly sentiments of the worst systems, if offered to them with prettiness of diction, cant phrases, pretension to philosophy, and the rounded voice of a popular lecturer.

The devices of falsehood are Protean. Let me cull out of a wide field of tares a handful for a sample. And for reasons already given we must include errors which echo from pulpits as well as from liberal clubs. Be on your guard then, brethren, against the doctrine of man's irresponsibility for his belief. As soon as you have opened your mind to this pregnant tenet, you have admitted within your walls a Trojan horse, fraught with enemies to consume both hearth and altar. For such is the blinding influence of sin, that you have only to make a man wicked enough, to make him capable of believing any thing, even that there is no harm in murder and voluptuousness, or that there is no God. Yet this is a popular doctrine of the age, the entering wedge which shall rend the entire evangelical fabric. Keep a watch against the absurd dogma, that man is the creature of circumstances; so that every human soul is in opinion and character just what the things around him necessitate him to be, and hence not responsible for the vileness or the crime which he could by no possibility prevent or remove. In this article of current unbelief, we have fatalism with a vengeance.

Shun, as you would sugared arsenic, the slightest suggestion that there are no essential moral distinctions. Your arch-poisoner is too crafty to tell you outright that there is no difference between right and wrong. But he will sweeten the cup of death with such forms as these, that Virtue has no essence but its tendency to promote happiness; or that sin is a very different affair when viewed from the side of man and from the side of God; or that God can no more make a universe without sin, than two mountains without a valley between; or that vice is no otherwise vice than as it is judged such by the conscience. Though the unsuspecting youth often receives these, from incapacity to reason far enough, he is actually preparing himself for the denial of eternal morality.

Recognise your antichristian enemy, though in gown and bands, when he whispers to you that there is no punishment after death, a doctrine which is spreading like a contagion in city and country. We may trace to it the relaxed morals of millions, and the manifest increase of self-murder, since many a villain would fly to the rope if he were delivered from the dread of a hereafter.

Guard your soul against the fallacy that there are no mysteries in religion, or that no man can believe what is above his understanding. In another place, it might be proved that this is as contrary to philosophy as to religion; but here we are simply denouncing traitors in our camp.

Above all, fix your eye with detestation on every attempt to deny or impair the Inspiration of the Scriptures. This it is, in which all schools of infidelity, ancient and modern, join hands. So long as a man admits the plenary inspiration of these books, we have some ground common to us and him, and some admitted medium of proof; and even though he be in grievous error, we may hope to reclaim him. He may be a Papist, but so was Martin Luther; he may be a Socinian, so was Thomas Scott. While a man listens to God speaking in this Word, the case is not desperate. But how can we argue from Scripture with one who holds only so much of Scripture to be authoritative as he could have discovered himself, who selects the parts which he shall reject as fable, and who is a Scripture to himself? When these, or any of these, or any like these, present themselves for your belief, know ye, that your enemy is at your door; be on your guard, and be not ignorant of his devices.

2. The existence of such snares should urge us to seek protection against the invasion of falsehood. It is not enough to know our enemy even in his feints and subterfuges; to this we must add positive means to escape from his devices. All these means come at last to a single one, belief of the truth. This, being the exact opposite of Infidelity, is incompatible with it, and exclusive of it. Large and intimate knowledge of divine verities, and strong faith in the same, are the only protection; and this is infallible and sovereign, which ought to be comforting to those overtasked, feeble, or unlettered disciples, who cannot read many books, and who might otherwise be confounded at the sight of an enemy spread on every side, changing his martial columns at

every instant, and seeking entrance at every avenue. Thanks be to God! in order to be an instructed and firm Christian, it is not necessary to answer all the objections of the freethinker, or even to know them. You are not required to soar into the metaphysic of Hegel, or plunge into the sty of Epicurus. Divine Truth is its own defence. Its system is so compact, ordered, symmetrical and harmonious, that it proves itself; and the more you learn of it, the more you find each portion demonstrative of every other. "He that believeth hath the witness in himself." But for this, the humble, unschooled believer would be left to the implicit faith of the Papist, for it is obvious he could not traverse the encyclopedia of scientific evidence. The engines of defence are sublime and impregnable, and have proved mighty in the hands of teachers and learned champions, to stop the mouths of adversaries. But they are not indispensable to the private Christian. His demonstration lies nearer home. Cowper felt this, when he contrasted Voltaire with the pious lace-weaver, a happy, humble woman, who

> "Just knows, and knows no more, her Bible true,
> "A truth the brilliant Frenchman never knew."

The divine method of arming the soul against sceptical attacks, is to shed into it belief of the revealed word by the Holy Ghost sent down from heaven. This is accomplished every day in those who never so much as spelled out the names of the great unbelieving authors. Indeed, even in the case of accomplished theologians, who are called professionally, and often with great pain to themselves, to turn over volumes of sophism and impiety, in order to frame a reply, the solid confidence of which they are conscious is not founded so much on these replies, as on that inward demonstration of the Spirit which is common to them and the most unlettered hind. Every experienced Christian has proofs of the truth of Christianity, which no external science can shake. He is more sure that this Bible is the very word of his redeeming God and Father, than he ever can be that such or such an assertion of Geology or Astronomy is true. And to this interior citadel he continually resorts, under all the temporary shocks produced by the ever changing tactics of infidel discovery. The same is true of objections founded on doctrinal difficulties, on Scriptural interpretation, on alleged absurdities or contradictions in the revealed Word. His conviction and assurance of the great mass of divine truth is such, that he can wait for the resolution of particular doubts, as being certain that they admit a solution even if unknown to him. True piety teaches him, as clearly as does true philosophy, to acquiesce in that golden maxim of all healthy minds, not to let doubts about what is difficult disturb his belief of what is plain. Some indentations of the coast he may never have surveyed, he may have found them laid down on no chart; but those great lights and forelands which have guided all his voyage, he will not surrender or deny, because they cannot be descried through the clouded glass of the scoffer. Such is the protective power of faith under infidel assault.

Confirmation of this is afforded by a fact, known to all who are familiar with conversions of unbelievers, that these transformations are not commonly wrought by the slow process of taking down the infidel structure doubt by doubt, and building in its stead the Christian structure proof by proof; but that the scoffer is pierced by conviction of his guilt, like any common sinner, and led to the Lord Jesus Christ in childlike faith. It is often long before his doubts, in their entire series, are severally resolved, but the blow has been struck which prostrates the capital unbelief of the heart.

A deep and thorough acquaintance, therefore, with the positive truth of Scripture, followed by cordial and evangelical acceptance of it, is the sure bulwark against the operations of antichristian error on our own hearts.

There are, however, as was suggested before, some subordinate precautions to be observed. If it is necessary to have the mind possessed by the truth, it is all-important for this end to shut out the inroads of error. There is such a thing as foolhardy adventure into an enemy's country. Religious falsehood sometimes comes in such a shape as to stimulate the curiosity of the unwary, as the fruit of the Tree of Knowledge tempted Eve. Sometimes it is the vehicle which is attractive. It may be elegant style, it may be romance, it may be closely-knit argumentation, it may be popular eloquence. The union of several such fascinations may invite the youthful student to taste the poisonous clusters, and acquire the taste for doubts and cavils. The most seductive and cunning argument against future retribution, which our age has produced, is contained in a poem of high talent, which you will find in every shop. The name and fame of some great heretical preacher, or some orator who delivers infidel sermons under the guise of lectures to the people, summon numbers of half-instructed people, who admire and acquiesce, and go again, not knowing, in their simplicity, that the new doctrines which they drink in will presently unsettle all the religious belief of their childhood. Happier far is the faith of the vulgar, than literary advancement, bought at such a price. It is a plain maxim of common sense, not to tamper with infection; and he is a fool who, for the mere sake of proving his boldness and freedom from bigotry, rushes uncalled into the miasmatic influence of false teaching. "Cease, my son," says the wise man, "to hear the instruction that causeth to err from the words of knowledge." Prov. xix. 27. "Take heed," said Incarnate Wisdom, "what ye hear." The caution which is good for yourself, is good for your children and dependents. A little mineral admixture in their daily bread, a little morbific quality in their daily milk, would be justly dreaded, as tending to wear away the health; yet the daily journal enters your doors, distilling by little and little false, latitudinarian and radical opinions. No marvel if you find your old age surrounded by sons who have made shipwreck of the faith. Christian parents and teachers, it is impossible to watch too affectionately the literature which comes into the hands of the young. If you desire them to be guarded and manly Christians, their pabulum must be truth. It is as certain of the mind as of the body, that whatsoever is taken into it should tend directly to its growth or strength; all that is otherwise, is noxious. Nutrition, moreover, is a gradual process, the result of repeated acts. If, then, the mind and character are to make progress, and acquire firmness, there must be not slight and occasional, but regular and extensive study of God's revealed will. Nor is there a household among us which does not need reformation in this particular. Thus, by promoting knowledge of truth, and discouraging familiarity with falsehood, we may, under God's blessing, do much to protect ourselves against abounding infidelity.

3. In such a time of prevailing error, it becomes us to prevent its diffusion in society. Let me not be considered an alarmist. There are ten thousand good things of which we are altogether undeserving, and for which we ought to be giving thanks; and among these we must reckon numberless Christian churches, comprising a host of God's people. Yet I tell you no new thing, my hearers, when I repeat that there is a mixed multitude, especially in our towns, who have made terms with the enemy and sacrificed their faith. If frank Deists and open-mouthed Atheists are less common than they were about the beginning of the century;

if, as is undeniable, it is disreputable for a man to attend no place of worship ; if society shudders when one distinctly condemns or ridicules the Bible; it is still true that disbelief in revelation prevails among a large part of our people, including men of letters and science, journalists and authors. And the danger is not lessened but much increased, when such persons, by a new device of Satan, profess to war by our side under the standards of Christianity, and even affect to preach that Jesus whom they disbelieve and despoil of all his glory. Nay more, few who have not made the inquiry a special business, have any adequate conception how many of another class are professed sceptics or real infidels ; how many cherish a low and brutal materialism and atheism under some names of social reform ; how many associations and meetings for debate are kept up by these so-called liberals ; how many cheap volumes go to swell the black sewers of this underground torrent; and how many newspapers, in German as well as English, are more or less characterized by abuse of the church, the ministry, and the Bible. Various methods may be proposed for stemming, averting and drying up this river of death, and no one of them is to be regarded with coldness. But after all, the great method, in accordance with principles already laid down, is to preach the gospel and gather the church. Other means, with incidental benefit no doubt, tend to diffuse themselves, and to be lost by too wide dispersion. The evangelic method tends to permanency and settlement. Every missionary effort, rightly conducted, fixes a centre, plants a standard, designates a rallying-point, draws in one and another, and at length a group, a society, a multitude, builds on a foundation, and binds together in a structure which shall abide. Every single church gathered in the truth and moved by the Spirit, is a permanent and energetic organ for the destruction of infidelity around it. Especially true is this among the more rude and ignorant, to whom the preacher's voice is the instrument of instruction in divine truth, in place of printed books, reviews, magazines and religious newspapers. One bold and sustained effort to keep up gospel means at a fixed point, though among the worst dens of a great city or suburb, shall do more to root out impious unbelief in its precincts, than a thousand random assaults on the individuals who are misled and corrupted. Such has been the experience of all who thus laboured in the mighty work under Whitefield and Wesley. This is our chief hope for populations like our own. A single good beginning, in a small circle, does a certain amount of this warfare against error, by establishing a lasting spring-head of truth and grace. But let these isolated posts become only numerous enough, and the widening circle of one will touch the widening circle of another, till whole districts will be so far occupied, that the unconquered interstices will be absorbed, just as the clearings of the new countries, at first mere patches in the forest, few and far between, grow and multiply and touch one another, and coalesce into the wide continuous civilization of agricultural territories and states. We find, therefore, in the prevalence of infidelity a new motive to attempt gospel effort. Even the freethinking and unbelief of the educated and tasteful will feel the impression of a wide-spread piety among the masses. Precisely in the way which has been indicated did Christianity make its conquest of Gentilism in early times. Precisely in this way was the Reformation extended among our forefathers.

But you need not be told, brethren, that Christians possess other weapons for the demolition of Infidelity. The invention of printing has endowed the silent volume with a voice which is heard not only by the assemblage of a single edifice, but by tens of thousands at once. And when we allude to books against atheism, deism, and all varieties of unbelief, we cannot refrain from naming one which ought to be known and circulated. It has converted more opposers than any other; it answers every counter argument, and displays the entire force of Christianity. I have it here; it is the BIBLE. Safely may it be said, that the best possible way to be reclaimed from doubt and persuaded of divine certainties, is to give a serious and candid perusal to this portable volume; just as the surest mode of being aware of light is to open the eyes upon the sun. The devil, among his arsenal of devices, has this for a masterpiece, to abstract, close, lock up, forbid, exterminate the Bible. Sometimes under a red cap of anarchy, and sometimes under a black cowl, he steals away or tears away the sacred Scriptures, from nations, from schools, from individual readers; but we are not ignorant of his devices. Let infidelity and superstition and hierarchy, change their tune at pleasure from wheedling to fury, we will clasp this book to our hearts, we will send it to our neighbour. We will multiply and cheapen copies; we will translate them into every tongue; we will despatch them on the wings of every commerce; we will carry them as angels of salvation into every willing house. Yea, "this will we do if God permit!" And so doing, "we will not fear, though the earth be removed and though the mountains be carried into the midst of the sea. There is a river, the streams whereof shall make glad the city of God."

Yet, churches and Bibles depend for their efficacy on the direct influences of the Holy Spirit, an agency which it is part of the reigning infidelity to disbelieve, but for which we will pray, as the chief hope of our salvation. Who can tell how far the revolutionary atheism of France might have become the established irreligion of America, if it had not pleased God to make our country the theatre of mighty and extensive revivals? Perhaps I address some who love to recall these awakenings, as the scenes in which they were made to know Christ. Such will join in testifying, that the progress of convincing and converting grace did not wait for the tedious preparative of philosophic reply and formal argument, but went forth to consume at once and forever the difficulties of the sceptic and the cavils of the deist, as the flame of a conflagration reduces combustible obstacles in its rapid and blazing career. All other means together will not do so much to rid our land of antichristian scoffing, as would one general communication of power from on high. Increased prayer for this fresh dispensation is the duty of the Church. This is the defensive means which Satan and his hosts dread, while they cannot emulate. They can blaspheme, they can argue, they can fight, they can write books, and, if need be, quote Scripture for their purpose; but pray they cannot. Our word should be, "Let God arise, let his enemies be scattered; let them also that hate him, flee before him." Ps. lxviii. 1. The more we recognise the devices of the enemy, the more should we gather around the footstool of Him who will shortly bruise Satan under our feet. "In meekness, instructing those that oppose themselves; if God, peradventure, will give them repentance to the acknowledgment of the truth; and that they may recover themselves out of the snare of the devil, who are taken captive by him at his will."

II.

THE DIVINE PERFECTIONS IN HARMONY.

THE

DIVINE PERFECTIONS IN HARMONY.*

---

2 Tim. ii. 19.

"He cannot deny himself."

It is of God that these words are spoken; and they constitute one of those divine maxims which lie among the very foundations of truth, and are fitted to be our guide and corrective in every part of theology. The apostle Paul argues, that however we may disbelieve, God remains faithful, because he cannot deny himself, that is, he cannot be untrue to his own nature. This seems plain enough at the first statement, needing no demonstration, a self-evident proposition, almost a truism; yet it admits of being pondered over and unfolded; and it is the more needful to enlarge upon it,

* New York, December 17, 1848.

because in many of its practical applications it is constantly denied.

The Being and Attributes of God are the basis of all theology. We can never be right on lesser points, when we are wrong here. This makes it greatly important for us to have some clear and settled belief respecting Him whom we worship. Every religious error may be traced up more or less directly to some misconception and unbelief respecting the character of God. And we need the less marvel at the prevalence of such errors, when we consider how few deliberately and lovingly think of God at all, and how even the best and holiest of men faint in their contemplations, finding it easier to study creatures than the Creator; which makes it a concern of every one of us to attain some adequate notions on a subject which is fitted to arrange, preserve and regulate all our other knowledge. Let no one complain of us as adducing what is abstract, recondite, and far from the track of ordinary thought and duty. For what can be nearer to us than He who formed us, in whom we live and move and have our being? Or what can be more profitable than that which has its direct bearing on every other part of the Christian scheme? We shall not therefore lose any time, if we wisely meditate on this consistency of God with himself, or the adorable harmony of all his perfections.

The subject will become more distinct, if we consider the truth, that we are constrained to think of God as an infinitely perfect Being. In this the true

God separates himself by an immeasurable gulf from all the divinities of polytheism. He is One, and he is absolute. When we think of that which has any imperfections, we are not thinking of God. Much of our conception of God is arrived at by a negative process; that is, by denying of the Most High every thing which is faulty or imperfect. We take those qualities, for example, which are included in our idea of God, and lift each of these up to an infinite sublimity. Is it Being? We immediately, justly, and by a sort of logical instinct, think of that Being which has no imperfections. It is therefore unlimited being, for all limitation implies weakness, dependence, or subordination. It is immensity of being. For the same reason it is independent being; because, on whom or what can it depend? It is necessary existence; God cannot but be, and be what he is. In like manner, when we conceive of God as a Spirit, and arrive at the apprehension of him as an Intelligence, the mind naturally and irresistibly proceeds to divest this idea of all the defects and limitations which belong to creatures. It is infinite Knowledge, supreme Reason, absolute Wisdom. The laws of our very thinking demand this. Any thing less than this falls short of God. The same mode of illustration might be derived from each of the Divine attributes, which for this very cause we are accustomed to call perfections. For if we worshipped a being who had any even the least imperfection, then would he not be Supreme, not the Highest and Best; yet every man is conscious that when he is searching for God, if, haply, he may find him, he cannot rest content, except when supposing the acme of excellence. Take away any the least ray of glory, and it is no longer the deity you seek, for above and beyond this limited and imperfect divinity you can conceive of one all perfection; and this is what reason demands in the true God. So true is this, namely, that the idea of God includes that of infinite perfection, that we perpetually employ it as a medium of investigation and a corrective of our conclusions. Having found out a little concerning the dread Supreme, we render that little valuable, by denying of it all imperfection and removing from it all boundaries. Let me not be considered abstruse; for the principle alluded to is both important and very precious, and is, I am persuaded, level to the ordinary hearer, who will yield his attention. We might illustrate it by any one of the Divine attributes. Suppose we take one of the most undeniable. As soon as we conceive of God as the Creator and Preserver of all material nature, we attribute to him a presence with all his works. But the invincible disposition, just stated, to remove all limits and imperfections from God, causes us at once to make this presence Omnipresence. There is no point in his dominion where he is not. But the same mode of reasoning leads us further still. The presence of creatures is divisible; that is, each is partly in one place and partly in another; and the vaster they are, the more divisible. For example, the solar system is present in a certain dimension of space; but part is here and part is there, and between the extremes is a distance which, to our poor measurement, seems infinite, as it is certainly immense. Not such is the presence of God. This mode of presence which we ascribe to the stellar universe, has two imperfections; one from being matter and the other from being creature. God is not present in any divisible sense, because he is indivisible. He is not partly here and partly there; there is not one part of God in heaven and another here and yet another in the planet Saturn; because God is without all parts. We are forced, therefore, by a necessity of reason, to fall upon a new kind of presence, a presence which is unique, without example or parallel, to meet the conditions of Omnipresence. God is then all-present at every point of the universe, at one and the same time. All there is of God (I speak reverently) is fully in every place in his dominions, at one and the same instant; and this because we attribute to him the absence of all imperfection, such as division would be. So strong is our rational determination to abstract all fault and all limit from our idea of the Most High. This Omnipresence of God has its difficulties. Would we desire a God whose nature should have no depths? It is a mystery. It transcends our discursive understanding; yet we believe it; all but Atheists believe it; we cannot but believe it: sound reason compels us to believe, however difficult it may be, that of which the contrary is self-contradictory or absurd. And let me step aside from the direct line of inquiry to say, that sound reason in the same way allows us to believe other mysteries which we cannot fully comprehend, such as the Trinity and the Incarnation. But we return to observe, that everywhere in theological science we hold fast to the first principle, that nothing must be affirmed of God which does not belong to the idea of an infinitely perfect being; which brings the subject directly under the general proposition of the text. He cannot deny himself; he must be true to his nature; nothing can be asserted of him which is inconsistent with absolute perfection.

We advance hardly a single step, when we say, that all the Attributes of God are in perfect harmony with one another. If any one were discordant with the rest, or with any other, God would therein deny himself. Our best and clearest views of the Great Supreme are poor and inadequate. There is a sublime and absolute simplicity in God, which we, from weakness, must take severally and by parts. Thus, when we survey some heavenly orb, no astronomic skill enables us to behold it at one view. We wait for its motion, and watch how it revolves before us, and catch a glimpse of side after side. The ray of light is one; but in the prismatic spectrum and in the rainbow, we see it parted into hues; while the violet, the indigo, the blue, the green, the yellow, the orange, and the red, seen dispersed in the showery arch, are one sunbeam. So of the infinite and primeval Light, all the perfections are glimpses of the same indivisible unity. All the attributes are phases of one and the same Divine orb. The seeming variety, and still more, the sometimes seeming contradiction, arise from the incapacity of our vision. All are in perfect harmony, and whatsoever violates this harmony, by exalting one attribute at the expense of another, wars with the maxim, that he cannot deny himself. This modification in the statement of the great principle allows us to apply it to a diversity of interesting particulars. Let us briefly make the attempt. And for a beginning, we need not go further than the suggestions of the text itself. He cannot deny himself. What! the inconsiderate will rejoin; and is there any thing which God cannot do? He can do all things; for is he not Omnipotent? Of a truth, God is Omnipotent. At this truth we arrive, even by natural religion, and on the principle already adopted by us, which removes all limits and asserts all perfection. So soon as we admit a Creator, that is, one of power sufficient to make and sustain the Universe, we run on by a happy necessity of reason, and ascribe to him all conceivable power. Every sane mind, in its reflective moments, does so. Here the Christian agrees with the serious Deist. Every thing included in power, in infinite power, belongs undeniably to God. This is a fixed point, and whatever denies this, errs, by making God deny himself.

But, does it therefore follow, that in respect to the Most High, there is nothing that can be called impossibility, in any sense? How prone is poor human understanding to play tricks upon itself, and to involve its limited faculties in the meshes of entangling words. This was the fault of the Schoolmen, or Latin theologians of the Middle Age. Never were there minds more keen and subtle, but they dulled the edge of their nice faculties upon questions which are impracticable. They debated, for example, whether God could cause the same thing to be and not to be, at the same time; whether he could cease to exist; whether he could create two mountains without a valley between, or a triangle with more or less than three sides. These are the riddles of childish understanding. When we ascribe power to God, we do not mean an attribute which is at war with his other perfections; we mean, as aforesaid, nothing incompatible with the sublime and infinite idea. God can do all that is properly an object of power. Those absurd and contradictory suppositions include no object of power. They demand no might, greater or less. He who should do them, would be neither stronger nor weaker for the achievement. They imply no excellence and savour of no perfection. They are inconceivable; the mind can frame no notion of what they are; a jargon of words without a sense. . There is, therefore, that which God cannot do; because he cannot deny himself.

But some, while they avoid the folly of such demands as these, fall upon another, less ridiculous, but equally full of danger. Because God is almighty, say they, he can destroy all the sin and misery in the Universe; and therefore, he will eventually save all mankind, and make all creatures happy. I would not introduce this, if it were not one of those suggestions which, at one time or other, find lodgment in every human mind. Here is a strange mixture of truth and falsehood, which must be carefully dissected apart. God can do all things; in this we are perfectly agreed. But it is not a just inference, that he will do all that he can. Whether, and in what cases, he shall exert his omnipotence, is to be determined by other perfections, which he will not and cannot deny. Looking to the future, do we venture to predict, that an Omnipotent Creator and Governor will make every creature happy? But if we take a point before the creation of man, and suppose an angelic spirit to be speculating on the probable fortunes of our race, is it not certain that he would have predicted a world without sin and without misery? Would he not say, the Almighty can prevent the introduction of sin, and he will! Yet, how false would have been such a determination! The answer is in the fact. Sin and misery do exist. Our earth has been scarred, and burnt, and drenched, by crime, and war, and famine, and pestilence, and earthquakes. Our faculties are too scanty for the resolution of such high problems. That it was within the power of God to create a universe into which sin could not enter, no sound reasoner can deny. Yet, he did create a universe into which sin has actually entered. He is in no sense the author of that sin; and yet he did not prevent it. Such is the fact. No man has ever denied it. Must we not conclude, that there are limits, not to the power, but to the exercise of power? The Wisdom, the Holiness, the Justice of God, all perfections which must be honoured, came in with awful majesty, to produce results which poor, short-sighted man cannot comprehend. He cannot deny himself.

Let us look again at the text, and in regard to the same attribute. There are those things which God cannot do. As, in another place, " God, that cannot lie." Why not? Because he is infinitely holy, and infinitely true; because falsehood would militate against these attributes; because he cannot deny himself. The inability arises from his moral nature. He cannot be untrue or unholy, because this were to cease to be God. Every thing within us rises up against such a supposition. The infinite Jehovah, then, has no capacity of evil; and this, from that very perfection of his nature, which we love to assert and press. We must beware, therefore, how we lightly ascribe to God those things which may suit our narrow prepossessions, lest unwittingly we offend against some of his blessed attributes. And hence we learn how closely we should adhere to the teachings of Scripture, in respect to what God will or will not do, in his government or his grace, since we know little of his plan and purpose, except what he has vouchsafed to express in the Scriptures. Secret things belong unto God, but such as are revealed unto us and our children. And we must continually cherish a reverent determination to indulge no thought of God, which shall be discordant with his glorious and often inscrutable perfections. Let it stand high inscribed on our whole fabric of derived truth, that he is eternally and immutably consistent with himself.

There are other applications of this cardinal truth, which will at once occur to the thoughtful mind. As God cannot deny himself, we must shun the error of derogating from his Wisdom, Holiness, Truth, and Justice, under the pretext of adding lustre to his Mercy. A neglect here has led many into grave errors with regard to Atonement, Satisfaction, and Justification. If God were all mercy, no Atonement would be necessary. But, " a God all mercy were a God unjust." He is full of mercy, and out of this fulness flows the tide of redemption; but in such wise as to preserve the honour of his law untarnished. He cannot deny his law; he cannot deny his justice; he cannot deny his threatenings of truth. Of his infinite compassion, he will save the lost; but it shall be in such a way as shall make his other glories more illustrious. It is the sublime necessity of harmonizing these otherwise conflicting traits of Divine majesty, which calls for the exercise of that grace, " wherein he hath abounded toward us in all wisdom and prudence;" " to the intent that now unto the principalities and powers in heavenly places might be known by the Church the manifold wisdom of God." He cannot deny his Wisdom. It is made to subserve the vindication of the law. Does a blind and condemned rebel ask that sinners should be pardoned without a satisfaction? Such is not God's method. This were to prostrate Justice and the Law in the very dust. How different a course does infinite Wisdom prescribe! How different a lesson do we read in the crimson spectacle of the Cross! Mercy is gratified, but Justice triumphs, "to the praise of the glory of the grace wherein we are accepted in the Beloved." God denies neither his Justice nor his Mercy. And why? Because the Word is made flesh, and the Only-Begotten of the Father dies upon the tree. "Die he, or justice must." And around this awful, fascinating, transforming sight, we behold all the attributes in perfect harmony, and God immutably true to himself. The principle of the text shines illustriously in the whole work of redemption; and the more we study the character of Jehovah, the more shall we learn that the divine consistency of this character made it impossible that sin should be pardoned, unless Christ should bear "our sins in his own body on the tree." But the same union of perfections in the Divine nature presents itself in an alarming view, when we consider the condition of those who reject God's chosen plan of salvation. The soul that passes into eternity without an interest in Christ's atoning work, faces the unmitigated blaze of vindicatory law. The Cross being neglected, there remains no more sacrifice for sin. Justice, no less than mercy, has its place for appropriate triumph. God will fulfil his utmost threatenings; for he cannot deny himself. On whatsoever side, then, we look, we observe the beautiful and inviolate harmony which subsists among all the perfections of God. In conclusion, I would point out a few lessons which may be derived from the truths on which we have meditated.

1. The subject aids us to compare and settle our minds, in regard to what may be called the difficulties of Scripture and theology. These all arise from our ignorance, and our inability to fathom the mysteries of the Divine Nature. As in our best estate on earth, "we know in part," and see through a glass darkly, some of these enigmas must remain unexplained, so long as we are in the body. The only part of wisdom is to bow with profound reverence to whatever is revealed, even though we may be incompetent to reconcile it with other truths. 'Thus saith the Lord,' ought to allay all doubts. Philosophy has wearied itself for ages, in the attempt to reconcile the existence of physical evil with God's holiness and goodness; but not the slightest advance has been made in the explanation. 'Why did God permit the fall?' is a question which can never be answered, but by humbling our minds before the general consideration, that divine reasons of state are beyond our ken; that some of God's attributes may demand a course of government beyond all our expectation; that his wisdom is infallible as his love is immense; and that whatever he ordains or allows, is agreeable to the concord of those perfections which we at awful distance revere and worship. The same is true with regard to the fearful doom of the wicked. The finally impenitent shall go

away into everlasting fire, prepared for the devil and his angels. The smoke of their torment goeth up forever and ever. We are incompetent to decide on the grounds of this undeniable sentence; just as we are unable to explain the incalculable amount of sin and misery now actually existing on earth. We do not comprehend the infinite depths of evil there are in sin; we cannot estimate the glory which shall redound to God from the never-ceasing display of his inflexible justice; we know not how far such an exhibition of wrath may tend to the increased sum of happiness, in all the remaining intelligent universe. The problem will one day be solved. What we know not now, we shall know hereafter. This and all inscrutable facts and doctrines shall be seen to have their ground in some perfection of God, or in the harmony of all his perfections. We may safely leave the matter in such hands. God is love; and there is no one of his decrees which is not prompted by infinite benevolence. We may not see the connexion or consistency, in all cases, but this is conclusive—He cannot deny himself.

2. The truth we have been considering, may encourage us to commit the whole matter of our salvation to God with implicit confidence. A man needs a strong foundation on which to lean his everlasting interests. Ordinary securities will not avail here. When storms assail our hope, and unnumbered sins arise to irritate our conscience, and the dreadful justice of God is arrayed against us, especially if all this happens when death

is in view, we need something more than vague expectation or mere probability. The true basis of trust is found in the character of God; and this is all-sufficient. It is the part of revelation to make this known to us. It is the part of faith to rely upon it. The constancy and immutability of God are the ground of our security. If he were changeful, the Universe would be a hell. How ready we should be to fly into despair or madness, if the God in whom we trust were uncertain and capricious, like the divinities of the Gentiles? But he says, "I am Jehovah, I change not, therefore ye sons of Jacob are not consumed." * So changeable and capricious are we, that if our salvation depended on our abiding constant for an hour, we should inevitably be lost. But though we "believe not," or are unfaithful, he is faithful. Especially may we rely on his covenant engagements, from which he will not draw back. His truth is confirmed by repeated asseverations; "wherein God, willing more abundantly to show unto the heirs of promise the immutability of his counsel, confirmed it by an oath; that by two immutable things, in which it was impossible for God to lie, we might have a strong consolation, who have fled for refuge to lay hold on the hope set before us." How refreshing is it, to look away from the endless vicissitudes of our own hearts, which ebb and flow like the sea, and wax and wane like the moon, to Him who is immutable, and whose decrees of

---

* Mal. iii. 6.

love are as firm as his very being. In disheartening hours, our greatest repose is obtained, by lifting the soul to One who in Jesus Christ is the same yesterday, to-day and forever. I put it to Christian hearers, above all, to such as are habitually prone to write bitter things against themselves, whether they are not more ready to ascribe constancy and immutability to God's justice, than to his grace. Yet, he can no more be unfaithful to one than to the other. Only make sure of an interest in his covenant, by connexion with the Lord Jesus Christ, and your salvation is as firm as the throne of eternity. We read the threatenings, and quake because He is unchangeable. Let us read the promises, and believe that heaven and earth shall pass away, before one jot or one tittle of his gracious engagements shall fail. He cannot deny himself; he cannot deny his Son. We have a Surety, in his nature and in ours, who shall make good every article of the eternal treaty. And how resplendent will this glory of grace shine forth in " that day," when the elect jewels shall be made up, without one loss, even of the faintest creature who ever believed, and when every vault of the heavenly city shall ring to the honour of Him who is forever true to his own nature !

3. In every moment of life, we learn from this subject to look up to the harmonious attributes of God, with profound adoration and lively affection. The object is glorious, and, above all others, deserves our contemplation. He is one and the same. The changes of

time and creatures are but the trifling waves which keep up their noisy flow at the base of this Eternal Rock. He was infinitely true to himself before time began; such will he be when time shall be no more. Every one of those adorable perfections remains in plenitude of majesty, and all in blissful concord with each other. "He is the Rock, his work is perfect : for all his ways are judgment : a God of truth, and without iniquity : just and right is he!" There are times when the wavering soul needs recourse to such thoughts. There are wars and tumults among the people. Nation rises against nation. Iniquity abounds, and the love of many waxes cold. The cause of truth and righteousness seems to tremble; and unbelief suggests that the plan of heaven has changed or been frustrated. But all these mutations are but a faint ripple on the surface of the sea of things. "The Lord reigneth, let the earth rejoice." The principles of his government are more settled than the everlasting mountains. "The Lord sitteth upon the flood; yea, the Lord sitteth king forever." Great calamities startle a whole population. A gallant ship is labouring in the tempestuous deep. Stout-hearted men quiver with apprehension; veterans who have stood at the cannon's mouth yield to awe before the raging elements, and the cry of panic-struck women and children ascends amidst the crash of timbers and the ruthless brawling of the storm. The mountain billow makes its clear sweep over the deck, and whole bands plunge through the wintry, strangling surge, into eternity.

Has God closed his eyes upon his creatures? Nay, blind insect of yesterday; it is He who orders all. He is true to his justice, and true to his mercy. "Thy throne is established of old, thou art from everlasting. The floods have lifted up, O Lord, the floods have lifted up their voice; the floods lift up their waves. The Lord on high is mightier than the noise of many waters, yea, than the mighty waves of the sea." However he may send the stroke of death, which he sends to all, "just and right is he!" He cannot deny himself. Be this our anchor, when in regard to our own little personal affairs, the billows threaten to overwhelm us. They cannot reach the throne of our God, nor change the settled purposes of his love. Clouds and darkness are round about him, but righteousness and justice are the habitation of his throne. Sometimes, if we could look into his heart, we should discern paternal compassion behind the lifted rod. Let us rejoice that he is, and such as he is. Let us glory that he changeth not. Let us summon our thoughts away from all creatures and all second causes, to dwell on the throne that cannot be moved. Though all else fail, it is well with us if God remains. See to it that he is yours. Hazard not the consequences of being found in the way of his advancing vengeance. His covenant of grace is sure, but his justice is as irrevocable as his love is fathomless. Now, in this temporal state, the offer is made, to change our relation, and from enemies to become friends. But presently, a trumpet shall sound, to tell that parley is over, and that what remains is arrest, adjudication, doom! O, saint! O, sinner! in that hour, it is near, heaven will stand vindicated, thy destiny sealed, thy heaven or hell made eternal. For he cannot deny himself!

III.

DIVINE PROVIDENCE IN PARTICULARS.

DIVINE PROVIDENCE IN PARTICULARS.*

MATTHEW x. 30.

"But the very hairs of your head are all numbered."

THE subject to be treated from these words is that of a particular providence. And by a particular providence, we mean a divine care, unceasingly bestowed on all creatures and all their actions; on things heavenly and things sublunary; whether small or great, whether good or evil; whether natural or moral; whether necessary or free; so that nothing can occur in the universe which is not immediately governed by Omnipotence. The Epicureans feigned a deity who takes no cognizance of creatures. The followers of Aristotle seem to have confined the divine regards only to celestial things. The Pelagians withdraw from the rule of

* Princeton, January 2, 1855.

God all free actions of moral beings; and men of the world, professing no philosophical creed in particular, entertain a vague notion of some general oversight which the Supreme Intelligence exercises since creation, while they practically deny any such special care as we have just asserted. It is of vast importance that our minds be firmly settled on this fundamental point. Generalities will not suffice, when we sustain the shock of great and sudden afflictions. As the doctrine of chance is the most absurd and cheerless of all human tenets, so any approach to it, by withdrawing a part of all events from the circle of God's plan, tends to hesitation, darkness, and misery. For which part shall we so withdraw? What objects and what acts shall we abandon to the fortuitous concussion of circumstances? Or if this could be determined, how shall we be assured that the particulars in which we affirm God to have no concern, are not the very ones on which our highest happiness hinges? In opposition to all such irrational hypotheses, we maintain that he who firmly believes in a universal providence, extending to every hair, and who feels accordingly, has arrived at the true secret of a happy life.

We argue a particular providence from a particular creation. That which God has deigned to make, he will condescend to care for; and that which he has made in all its minutest details, he may, without derogation from his infinite majesty, continue to sustain and govern even in its least members and motions. The instance chosen by our Lord is among the most light and impalpable of all objects connected with the human frame. Yet, under the glass of the microscopic anatomist, the single hair presents wonders of structure and adaptation which no human hand can reproduce or imitate. Indeed, the further down we go into the interior recesses of nature, all invisible to the naked eye, the more amazing become the revelations of power, and skill, and goodness. So that the very antennæ of the fly that annoys our slumber, the dust of the downy fruit, and the volatile pollen of the lily or the rose, awaken new adoration of Him who is *maximus in minimis*, greatest in that which seems least. Take any inch-square of the ground we tread on; and to the eye of reverent science, it is a world teeming with wonders. Nor do we observe any tendency to a termination of these wonders, or any limit of this creative ingenuity, though we press our investigation to the utmost length which adventurous observation can reach with its most elaborate, costly, and recent appliances. The finger of Omnipotence is still before us; tracing contours of beauty, adding lustrous hues far beyond the reach of human gaze, weaving tissues, conveying tides of circulation, and adjusting forces with mathematical exactness, in the filament of the tiniest floweret, and the organ of the evanescent animalcule. Now, that which it was not unworthy of creative power to make, it is not unworthy of providential care to uphold and govern. Our scale of measurement on this subject is arbitrary and partial. We know little of great or small, as applied to the works of the Almighty. In his eye, there may be as much value in the living mote, that scarcely darkens our vision, as in the leviathan of the hoary waters. And here, let me deviate, if it be not in the direct line of our argument, to expose the emptiness of that flippant reasoning of half-philosophy, which sometimes makes bold to jeer at our doctrine, that all things were made for some good end. These laughing sages demand of us for what purpose the contemptible insect, which flits across our path or alights on our persons, was created. Let it be a successful and triumphant reply to ignorant and impertinent scoffing, that an infinitely benevolent Creator, besides other reasons unknown to us, has had sufficient reason for the production of wondrous living mechanisms, in the securing of happiness to the being itself, which thus stands forth as a small but animated argument of the divine goodness. On this point, I gladly borrow from the sometimes erroneous, but, here, incomparable Paley: "The air, the earth, the water, teem with delighted existence. In a spring noon, or a summer evening, on whichever side I turn my eyes, myriads of happy beings crowd upon my view. 'The insect youth are on the wing.' Swarms of new-born flies are trying their pinions in the air. Their sportive motions, their wanton mazes, their gratuitous activity, their continual change of place without use or purpose, testify their joy, and the exultation which they feel in their lately discovered faculties. A bee amongst the flowers in

spring, is one of the most cheerful objects that can be looked upon. Its life appears to be all enjoyment: so busy and so pleased; yet it is only a specimen of insect life, with which, by reason of the animal being half domesticated, we happen to be better acquainted than we are with that of others. The whole winged insect tribe, it is probable, are equally intent upon their proper employments; and, under every variety of constitution, gratified, and perhaps equally gratified, by the offices which the Author of their nature has assigned to them."—
"Walking by the sea-side, in a calm evening, upon a sandy shore, and with an ebbing tide, I have frequently remarked the appearance of a dark cloud, or rather very thick mist, hanging over the edge of the water, to the height perhaps of half a yard, and of the breadth of two or three yards, stretching along the coast as far as the eye could reach, and always retiring with the water. When this cloud came to be examined, it proved to be nothing else than so much space, filled with young shrimps, in the act of bounding into the air from the shallow margin of the water, or from the wet sand. If any motion of a mute animal could express delight, it was this; if they had meant to make signs of their happiness, they could not have done it more intelligibly, Suppose, then, what I have no doubt of, each individual of this number to be in a state of positive enjoyment, what a sum, collectively, of gratification and pleasure have we here before our view." *

* Natural Theology.

In conformity with this, we believe with pleasure that whatsoever God has made, even to the smallest details, he continues to preserve and regulate. Providence has sometimes been considered as a continued creation; but more properly, as the constant will of God to maintain the being of that which he has created. For there is no innate power of self-sustentation in the creature; and if God were to withdraw his power, all that he has made would collapse into its original nothing. Being is too sublime an endowment to own any other source, even for an instant, than that which first gave it. We are to look on nature in its minutest varieties, and having God perpetually standing by it, upholding and guiding. In this there is nothing low and nothing wearisome. Omnipotence is equally unexhausted in driving whole stellar systems through their awful incalculable trajectories, and in supporting the gossamer that floats over our autumnal fields. The reason of creation thus becomes the reason of providence, and we exult in the truth, as sublime as it is consolatory, that the hairs of our head are all numbered.

After this preamble, we argue particular providence from the express teachings of Scripture. Here it will be necessary to use selection. First, we open upon passages which ascribe to God the wielding and governance of all things in general. As where Nehemiah prays: ix. 6, "Thou, even thou, art Jehovah alone; thou hast made heaven, the heaven of heavens, with all their host, the earth and all things therein, and thou preservest them all." As when Paul, at the Areopagus, challenging the assent of even a heathen auditory, says, "Though he be not far from every one of us; for in him we live, and move, and have our being." As when, Heb. i. 3, the Son of God is represented as "upholding all things by the word of his power." But passages of this sort are numerous and familiar. Next we meet with places where this very particularity of providence is explicitly asserted. Thus the smallest as well as the greatest objects are referred to his care; as in our text, and in that beautiful and parallel instance, "Are not two sparrows sold for a farthing? and one of them shall not fall on the ground without your Father." Or, where he chides the distrust of disciples as to food and raiment, by pointing to lilies and birds, arrayed and fed by God; in other words, the objects of his careful providence. The very insects, used by the sceptic for his ill-timed jests, were fearfully employed in vengeance among the plagues of Egypt; and at a later day, the locust, the palmer-worm and the caterpillar, are marshalled by him in battle-array against a guilty land, while he says, Joel ii. 11, "And Jehovah shall utter his voice before his army; for his camp is very great."

But this Providence of God includes in its range a nobler class of creatures, even those which are rational and immortal. These, with all their thoughts, affections, and acts, are parts of his marvellous plan. Indeed, if these were excluded, there could be nothing in the doctrine of Providence which could afford us any contentment. It were a mockery to tell us that we should have safety by the hand of Omnipotence, in regard to the powers of irrational nature; but that in all that concerns the free or the wicked actions of men, we must rely on ourselves or on chance. It were a crippled and insufficient providence which should guard me against the serpent or the tornado, but which should leave me to myself the moment a moral and responsible agent came upon the stage. Yet, this is the strange, uncomfortable doctrine which prompts the language heard in many a Christian circle. Which of us has not listened to such words as these? "I could bear this trial, if it were ordered of God, but it proceeds from man. It is not providential, but from wicked human beings." There is in this a sad confusion. Such a government as is here assumed, would be no providence at all; and would render all rule impossible, as excluding those very agencies which are most important. And I return to say, that the Bible teaches no such doctrine. While it abhors the thought of making God the author of sin, it does not exclude sinful acts from his wise and holy plan. While it evermore denies God's participation in the evil of wicked deeds, it still asserts, that in the directing and governing of such deeds, there is a sovereign providence, working out its own wise and holy ends. "Man's goings are of the Lord; how then can a man understand his own way?" "A man's heart deviseth his way, but the Lord directeth his steps." The wrath of man shall praise him, and the remainder of wrath He will restrain. Let it be clearly fixed in our minds, as the only true philosophy of this subject, that an act may be wicked, as to the intent of its agent, and yet its result may be really intended by God. Were it not so, we could have no relief under our worst sufferings, namely, those which we endure from depraved and malignant human creatures. But these also are providential. Joseph's brethren committed a great sin. This none can deny, so far as they were concerned. Yet was it strictly and particularly providential: "So now it was not you that sent me hither, but God." "God did send me before you to preserve life." "Ye thought evil against me, but God meant it unto good." Here is particular providence, in regard to free and wicked acts. Other instances in point will occur to the memory of the scriptural student. Especially the great and striking case of our Lord's arrest and death; intensely wicked as to its free perpetrators, yet a part of God's providential scheme for the salvation of mankind. We cannot on any principle of reason escape from this great and most consolatory truth. The dependence of the creature upon the Creator enforces it. As man is suspended absolutely on God for his being and his life, so also is he dependent on him for his power to act, and for the acts themselves. If for the body, then yet more for the soul, the nobler part. Conceive of a being independent of God in acting, and you infer a being independent also in essence. But if he is dependent, then is he in all his actions brought within the circle of providential ordering. And surely there can be derived neither peace nor profit from the doctrine, that a large part of human acts, many of which most nearly concern us, are performed without God's knowledge, which were to deny omniscience; or, without his caring for them, which were to deny his love; or, without his power to prevent them, which were to deny his omnipotence. Yet, this is the doctrine of the Epicurean, of the world, and of many who suppose themselves to be Christians.

As none but infidels deny all providence outright—a truth which forces the assent of the sober Deist—the usual method of error is to admit some general care of the universe, but to deny such care as extends to minute particulars. And this misconception is widely prevalent among superficial thinkers. Now, not to repeat what has been already urged, that in the sense intended there is with God neither great nor small, and that there is to the Almighty no degradation, nor weariness, nor waste of power, in caring for the sparrow, the hair or the atom, I would bring it before the serious consideration of doubters, that their tenet is destructive of all providence whatever; and that if there is no particular providence, there can be none at all. General providence infers that which is particular. For, surely these deniers do not mean to tell us, that God singles out the great acts of the universe and the world's history, and neglects the small. In this case, the small must after all be considered in the divine prescience, in order that they may be left out. The meaning, perhaps, is, that Divine wisdom fixes and decrees the grand and momentous events in history, but fixes not minor and intermediate points. But look a little more closely, and you will perceive, that those momentous points are caused and determined by these which are smaller. The most astonishing changes in human things, which have rent empires, and made the world ring for ages, have depended on the most trifling occurrences, and but for these would not, and could not have been. Did Providence then secure the great event, and leave its proximate causes to be settled by chance, or not settled at all? The rise and fortunes of Moses occupy a just eminence, as connected with the destiny of a people still subsisting. Was there, or was there not, a providence in the fact that the princess of Egypt, at a certain hour, spied that wicker cradle upon the Nile? It was a grand event, that Christianity should be carried to Ethiopia. Was there any providence in the meeting of Philip and the treasurer of Queen Candace, on the road to Gaza? The death of Julius Cesar is one of the capital events in human annals. Was there a providence in the great man's failing to read the scroll of papyrus, handed to him in the crowd, and which would have revealed to him the conspiracy? Nay, each of us, in his own little life, can recount incidents, trivial in themselves, yet directly conducive and even necessary to the occurrence of what has given colour to our whole subsequent existence. The truth is, general providence is only the sum of particular providences, as every whole is but an aggregation of its several parts. And he who speaks of a providential plan, so general as to exclude details and minutiæ, utters he knows not what, and professes what he cannot expound even to his own conceptions. Let us, therefore, reverently and delightedly, come back to the doctrine of our childish days, which is at the same time a conclusion of the profoundest philosophy, that all events, even the smallest, fall out according to the comprehensive and well-ordered plan of a sleepless benignant and all-wise Ruler, who doeth his pleasure in the armies of heaven, and among the inhabitants of the earth.

How beautifully this shines out in the records of the Scriptures; making them herein differ strikingly from all other annals! This clew will often guide us through the mazes of an otherwise inexplicable narrative. This will often explain to us, why some things are given in great detail, while others are passed over in silence. For, the accounts given in Scripture are the history, not so much of the intentions of man, as of the plans of God. Especially in the vernal sunshine of patriarchal days, we behold God's hand, we feel his presence, we admit his agency, at every turn. And all the way through the tangled web of Judaic history, it is Jehovah who is the planner, it is Jehovah who is the hero of the story. Well were it for each of us, if we could transfer this spirit of the Bible to the explanation of our own lives. It would clear up many a day of clouds, and solve many an enigma. In this belief, I dare not close without certain practical conclusions from truths, I trust, sufficiently established. We may sin against the doctrine of a particular providence in several ways.

In regard to the past, we may offend by repining, or quarrelling with providence. It is one of our daily and most heinous transgressions, excluding the thought of God's wise and beneficent rule from the events of our common days. The sin of murmuring was the fatal iniquity of Israel in the wilderness. It should be enough to reconcile us to every event, that it befals us agreeably to the wisdom and justice and mercy of God. What misery, what weakness, what consumption of health, what decay of spirits, what paralysis of effort, what sourness and morose care, might have been avoided, if we had learnt to live in a continual submission to Providence, as to every particular of our lives. ." Lord, increase our faith!"

Akin to this is despair, when there seems to be no outlet from our troubles. It may befit a Cain, a Saul, or a Judas; but not a child of God. If time had allowed, I might have shown how Providence, under a special covenant, concerns itself for those who shall be heirs of salvation. The lessons of our Lord, already cited, go to forbid this undue despondency. Hard as it may be for unaided nature, it is the prerogative of grace, when the night is darkest and most dreary, not only to submit to what is sent, but to trust and hope in God for the future; and there is a blessing on such exercises of soul. Distrust of Providence implies an actual disbelief of God's rule and disposal of the events which concern us.

Another sin is the imputing of our sins to God, which is a horrible abuse of the doctrine of Providence. The metaphysics of this subject may be difficult, and we are not called upon to resolve all the doubts which may be raised by an ingenious and perverse reason; but a few undeniable truths stand out in fire, like lighthouses flaming along a tempestuous coast. Whatever we know not, we do know that the Judge of all the earth will do right; that God cannot be tempted of evil, neither tempteth he any man; that while he permits sin, bounds it, and overrules it, he is infinitely remote from being its cause, and from participating in its malign quality; that, as all good is from above, so all the evil of our misdeeds is from ourselves. These plain and admitted truths should rise fully before us, when at any time we are tempted to charge God foolishly.

Again, there is a perversion which turns providence into fate, and professes to hope for results without using means. Whatever is to be, will be—is the familiar maxim of the profane and superficial fatalist; often upon the lips of those who have no real belief in providence. Wise men know that he who orders the end, orders also the means, and that the means are made necessary to the end by the decree of God himself. Providence is itself a system, regularly working by a chain of means, in the order of cause and effect.

Providence does not ensure the result in spite of neglects and omissions, but by ensuring the means required. Where any man, whether from fatalism or indolence, omits the performance of his part, providence then goes on its stately march to produce the failure of the end. Hence the sin of presumption is chargeable on such as rush on dangers, uncalled, in the profane expectation of safety or deliverance. "Thou shalt not tempt the Lord thy God." In things temporal, and in those which concern our personal salvation, we abuse providence when we neglect the diligent use of those instrumentalities which God has ordained.

Prone to extremes, however, sinful human nature sometimes speeds to the very opposite, and relies implicitly on second causes. This is the reigning sin of the busy world. It becomes flagrant in many, who, after long prosperity, come to ascribe all their success to their own endeavours, forget the hand which has sustained and supported them, and mentally expel the God of Providence from his own dominions. Such are the sons of wealth, who fear no reverses, give no thanks, expect largely from self, or, as they speak, from luck, and mean to be happy in spite of God. There may be cases in which they have their good things in this world, feel no bands in their death, and expire as they have lived. But it is very common for a holy and just God, by some stroke of his judgment on body, reason, family, reputation, or estate, to show such persons, as he did Nebuchadnezzar, that "the Heavens do rule."

We shall best avoid these various errors, by establishing our minds on a thorough persuasion of God's all-pervading, all-embracing providence. And happy should I be, my brethren, if the words now spoken should prove seasonable to any one who has come to this house overburdened with care. To such a heart the blessed assurance of the text, carried home by the Spirit of grace, will become a sovereign balm. The bitterness of our griefs arises from our denying or forgetting, that whatsoever lies heavy on our lot is laid there by the hand of Him who is ordering all things for our good. However vexing may be the annoyances of our pilgrim state, the loving soul can bear much from the hand of a compassionate Creator and Redeemer. These unwelcome visitations are intended to bring us to right views of God's government of all things for his people. Is the trouble past? It is the Lord who hath done it; let him do as seemeth him good! Be still, and know that he is GOD. Is it present? Own the chastening of a present God, who doeth all things well, and who is near you, to bring good out of evil. Is it future? Take no anxious thought for the morrow. He who plans in wisdom and executes in power, is your Keeper, your Shield, and your exceeding great Reward. Nothing is too hard for his might; nothing too little for his condescension. The very hairs of your head are all numbered. Apply this to the circumstances of this very day and hour; apply it to those second causes, which, to a vainly-wise unbelief often seem too insignificant to be brought to the foot of the infinite throne. You may use a child-like confidence in coming to your Father in heaven; you may unbosom before him your smallest disquietudes. The thorn in the traveller's foot is sometimes grievous as the sword of an adversary. The strongest Christians are those who, from holy habit, hasten with every thing to God. Summon this doctrine to your aid, not merely when the weightier class of calamities oppress you; but amidst the perturbations of ordinary life, the collisions of business, the perplexities of the household, the mutations of health and spirits, nay the clouds of the sky, which too often carry darkness into the windows of the shrinking and sensitive soul. The very moods which make our wheels drag slowly through the daily task, the tempers of those around us, the petty disappointment and chagrin, the slight, the cross, the look of unkindness and the silence of rebuke—all are dispensed in season and in love. Happy is the soul which, having secured an interest in providence by securing acceptance in Christ, can roll its burden on the Lord and lie down secure amidst the tempest, because its Father is at the helm.

IV.

THE INCARNATION.

THE INCARNATION.*

---

1 Timothy iii. 16.

"God was manifest in the flesh."

"The Catholic faith is this, that we worship one God in Trinity and Trinity in Unity; neither confounding the persons, nor dividing the substance."

"Our Lord Jesus Christ, the Son of the Father, is God and man; God of the substance of the Father, begotten before the world; and Man of the substance of his mother, born in the world. Perfect God and perfect Man; of a reasonable soul, and human flesh subsisting; equal to the Father as touching his Godhead, and inferior to the Father as touching his manhood. Who, although he be God and Man, yet he is not two, but one Christ."

* New York, February 11, 1849.

These are formulas which some will not pronounce, who nevertheless vaunt their belief of " God in Christ." Our present task is not to prove or even to illustrate the Incarnation, but only to look at one of its aspects, to wit, the manifesting of God. In plainer terms, the question is, How God's becoming man brings God any nearer to our understandings and our hearts. And in this inquiry we shall be led to the result, that by the humanity of Christ the Divine Nature is brought more within the reach of our understanding and our affections. But as these two branches of the subject are large and distinct, they may be properly treated in succession. Accordingly, our first topic is this, that by the Incarnation God is brought near to our understanding; and the second, that, by the Incarnation, God is brought near to our affections.

I. By the Incarnation, God is brought near to our understanding. We know more of God, by this means, than we could ever have known without it. We are no more able than before to grasp the infinite, or comprehend the incomprehensible, or measure the immense, or see the invisible; yet these divine and unapproachable perfections are brought into such connections with humanity as to furnish us with some steps by which to climb up towards the height of these glories; to acquire some ideas, though inadequate, of what would otherwise entirely elude our research. All creatures together could not by searching find out God, yet one may know more than another; and many, more at one time than at another; angels more than men; saints more than sinners; and every believer much that he could not have discovered without this gracious intervention. Look at it as we may, there is a wonderful mystery in God's willing to be known of creatures. The whole creation is fruit of such a will. God might have spent eternity in blissful silence, in the all-satisfying glory of his own perfections. But his infinite benevolence chose to impart this excellence, which is what we mean by God's declarative glory or his glorifying himself. This is the key to all the successive manifestations of God, and especially of the creative manifestation. In the work of the six days, including all the beauties and utilities of the earth and all the regulated immensities of heaven, Jehovah was only giving us a sparkle of his grandeur; and when we now look at the heavens and the earth in their vast generality, or, taking any one particular, as an insect or a leaf, descend into its infinitesimal minuteness of detail, we are studying just so much of God. The common expression is just, we read the Book of Nature. But no external manifestations could ever bring us to the chief of what we need to know of God, his moral perfections, his mercy and his love; and God had regard to this, in making man.* I do not mean merely that it was necessary to make a rational creature, in order to see and know God's glory, which is true indeed; but over and above this, that the creature, thus rational, should be so made as to have within himself some facilities for knowing his Creator; some analogy, some resemblance to him, some ray of Godhead which might guide him back; some image and likeness of the Invisible; and therefore in this image and likeness was he made. If man had been made without this conformity, I do not see how he could ever have come to any understanding of the Divine perfections. Unless man were intellectual he could have no notion of God as truth; unless man had conscience, he could have no notion of God as righteousness; unless man had volition, he could have no notion of God as power; and unless man had affections, he could have no notion of God as love. But because he is made in God's image in these respects, he is able to gain glimpses of the Divine attributes, of which he gets the best ideas when he removes all limits from his own powers, and conceives them as enlarged to infinity. For example, if a being were found, with intellect, memory, will, and affections, but with no moral faculty, we could never, even by centuries of reasoning, convey to such a being the slightest notion of virtue or holiness, or of God as morally pure or holy. And there is no absurdity in supposing that there are in God a thousand perfections, of which the very kind is unknown to us, because, among all endowments, we have none even generically resembling these perfections. Lower animals, possessed of but one sense or of but two, can by no possibility arrive at the sensations of higher senses; no absolutely blind man can conceive of colour, or deaf man of sound. There are animals probably which possess senses unknown to us; and among higher created spirits there are angels who possibly have faculties of mind as inconceivable to us as colours to the blind. But what shall we say of Divinity? All comparison is lost in the boundless glory! Yet immeasurably as God transcends our powers, he has placed in us certain germs of resemblance, whereby we may come to know him; and this was gloriously true of man in his primitive integrity. But why, you will be ready to say, does the preacher go back to the original creation of man, when the subject is, the manifestation of God by Jesus Christ? For this reason, brethren, that the original man was the first Adam, and that Christ is the second Adam; for this additional reason, that in the wonderful parallelism between the first and the second, there is a common element of humanity in both, by means of which, as like to God, man is able to come nearer to God, than would have been possible otherwise. Just as the image of God in Adam placed him in a situation to know his Divine exemplar, just as in humanity we see somewhat of divinity, so in the perfect and more glorious humanity of Christ we are enabled to know more of God than by all other means, even when we consider it as mere humanity; but infinitely more when we consider it as the containing tabernacle of the Godhead. For, be it ever remembered, we are not to hold that the only divinity revealed in Christ is his godlike humanity; but that this humanity, thus like God, and more like God than that of the first Adam, affords a vehicle for divine communications, and a channel for divine revelations, infinitely suitable and complete, when the Godhead becomes one with the manhood. Here, therefore, is an analogy between the first and the second Adam, which might otherwise escape us. An additional reason for the communication by Christ is found in the dreadful fact, that since the fall man has in a great degree lost this image of God, though certain broken traces undoubtedly remain, so as to form the basis of further knowledge.

Let us proceed, then, to the application of these principles to the case of the second Adam. We at once perceive his infinite superiority to the first. Even in Christ's humanity, the divine image shines with a splendour unknown in paradise. "The first man is of the earth, earthy; the second man is the Lord from heaven." The wisdom, power and holiness of Adam were unimpaired, but limited. They did not attain even that mark which they would have reached, if the covenant had been so fulfilled as that Adam should have been confirmed in perpetual indefectible goodness. For Adam, though erect, was not established; though not an infant, in Eden, as Socinianizing divines teach, he was but infantile as compared with the Lord from heaven. The Lord Jesus Christ was possessed of glorious perfections, even in his humanity, altogether unknown to our first progenitor. He was the medium of conveying divine wisdom. The Spirit was given him without measure. He was not only sinless, but insusceptible of sin, and thus immeasurably sublime. Though we cannot comprehend the union of the ever-present Deity with the man Christ Jesus, yet we perceive at once that it must have exalted every power; and that, while humanity was still humanity, and there was no confounding of the two natures, the human was all glorified by the indwelling of the divine, even as a globe of crystal, by an internal fire, is made all light. Nor can we think of the infinite God as united personally to a manhood which was other than sublime. O, my brethren, what marvels dwell within that Son of man! Even as the tabernacle in the wilderness was a homely structure, without presenting a rugged covering of the skins of beasts, but within radiant with gold, and inhabited by the visible glory, between the cherubim above the ark, so under that body which was worn with weariness and pain, and within that face which was "marred more than any man," there abode the sublimated glory of humanity, in a divinely-sustained knowledge, holiness and power. Sometimes these rays shot forth. "We beheld his glory; the glory of the Only-Begotten of the Father." In authority over tempests and evil spirits; in power to heal; in creative miracles; in searching of the heart; in amazing endurance, forgiveness and love; we behold more of God than all the universe beside reveals; and the point is, that it is revealed to man by man. Perhaps you inquire, how this is a revelation of divinity, since the subject of these excellencies was truly man? How can the excellencies of a man, however exalted, show us the excellency of God? My dear brethren, this is a hard question, and there are difficulties in it which I should dread even to approach; yet we may coast around a continent which we dare not penetrate and cannot survey; and there are some fixed points here, where we may take our position amidst a sea of uncertainty. This is more remarkably true of the moral perfections of God. In respect to these I would offer two remarks, intended to show that the revelation of the excellency in Christ Jesus is a revelation of God.

1. Virtue and holiness, with lowly reverence be it spoken, is the same in God as in man. Virtue is not simply a relation of temporal things, but an eternal quality; because it is a quality of the Eternal God. His command of virtue does not derive its excellence from God's mere power or arbitrary order, but from his eternal nature. God is himself the foundation of virtue. Could we believe the grovelling doctrine of expediency, or that there is nothing in virtue but its tendency to produce happiness, we might think otherwise. But then we might also believe that the highest happiness of God and the aggregate happiness of the universe, require our vice and misery. No, my beloved hearers, it is a fixed point, equally in morals and divinity, that holiness in God, though infinitely removed above holiness in man, is still one and the same holiness. The

truth of God, the righteousness of God, the mercy of God, and the love of God, are not different qualities called by the same names, but the same qualities existing in their highest power. So that when, in the God-man, Jesus Christ, we observe the beautiful and touching manifestation of feelings, habits and volitions, residing in a human subject indeed, but in a human subject personally one with the divine, we are really beholding the very excellencies which reside in God. And by this means we are brought higher in the scale of morals and nearer to a contemplation of divine holiness, than would be possible by any or by all other means. In every word, act and gesture of Jesus Christ, we see the invisible Godhead breaking forth.

2. Although the nature in which obedience was rendered is the human nature, yet it is human nature in such union with the divine, that the two constitute but one Person; and this adorable Person is divine. Therefore the moral states and acts of the Lord Jesus Christ, even when proceeding from a human will, are nevertheless, so far as we are concerned, the moral states and acts of God. To which we must add, that the human and the divine will, though not confounded, as though there were a divine agent in a new human form, are in perfect consonance; there is no diversity, or struggle. In this sense it is but one and the same Will; and thus the revelation of excellency in Christ Jesus is a revelation of God.

In contemplating the character of Jesus Christ, we

observe one class of virtues, which you will join me in regarding as most affecting, and most fully showing the need of an Incarnation. These are the suffering virtues; or those which are evolved under trial and pain. The first Adam, remaining sinless, would have remained as painless as God himself. There would never have been a sigh or a tear in Eden or in Heaven. But after the introduction of sin into our world, a new class of affections entered; and sin has been, by God's mighty wisdom, wrested against its own nature, to show forth the loveliest aspect of the Redeemer's glory. "For it became him," says the apostle, "for whom are all things, and by whom are all things, in bringing many sons unto glory, to make the Captain of their salvation perfect through suffering." * Dear Christian brethren, could we allow ourselves to be robbed of these delightful, heart-affecting shades, in the picture of our Lord's life, or could they have existed without an Incarnation? These tender, gentle excellencies of Christ, are so numerous that they fill your memories of his ministry. His lowliness, his meekness, his fortitude, his fear, his grief, his patience, his pity, his forgiveness. Which of these lineaments would you dash out of the picture? See him among the sick and suffering; at the house of Peter, the gate of Nain, the plains where he fed thousands, the bereaved dwelling, and the grave of Lazarus. See him weary at the well. See him not having where to lay his head. See him in the upper chamber among the twelve.

* Heb. ii. 10.

See him in the garden, at his trial, and on the cross. Observe the benignant, yet sorrowing virtues and graces of these hours, marked with tears and blood, and say, even though they tell of human weakness, which of these would you relinquish? Yet, none of them could have been manifested to us, unless because " the Word became flesh, and dwelt among us." And, on the principle already laid down, these excellencies are not merely human but divine. The glory of the godhead shines out, not only in the raising of the dead, and the pardon of sins, but in the tears and sighs of compassion, and in the unexampled cry, " Not my will, but thine be done." We may therefore affirm with confidence, that all the human character of Christ, as shown in his ministry on earth, is really a bright disclosure of the character of God, such as could be made only by the Incarnation.

But the mention just made of suffering, leads us most naturally to consider the summing-up of those sufferings in the Cross of our Lord Jesus Christ, and the manifestation of God in that complication of agonies. By the Cross, I mean here the whole series of events in the close of Christ's ministry as a sufferer; his " Cross and Passion," as going to make up one oblation. And let it be specially noted that we are not now surveying this, in its primary intention, as a sacrifice to satisfy divine justice, but in its character of a manifestation of God in the flesh; such a manifestation, moreover, as could be made only in the flesh, or by the assumption of humanity. The Son of God looked steadily to this one termination. In eternal covenant he devoted himself to manhood and the curse. In his own divine intention he was "the Lamb slain, from before the foundation of the world." All the lines of type and prophecy are seen to converge on this one point. When he became a human being, every step was towards this consummation. And at this accursed tree, as at a focal point, all the manifestations of God concentre with a burning effulgence. It is often said, and nothing was ever said more truly, that all the divine attributes harmonize in the plan of redemption, and therefore in the death of Christ. It is not necessary to show this by a formal and laboured catalogue of these perfections. They are all there, as the hues are all in the rainbow; but they are there as constituting a single luminous ray. All there is of God seems to pour down on that spot of earth; and the channel by which it is conveyed is indicated by these words, "God is Love." There, in that bleeding spectacle, all that we behold is in one sense humanity; in another, it is godhead.

> "Here his whole name appears complete;
> Nor wit can guess, nor reason prove,
> Which of the letters best is writ,
> The power, the wisdom, or the love.
>
> Here I behold his inmost heart,
> Where grace and vengeance strangely join,
> Piercing his Son with sharpest smart,
> To make the purchas'd pleasures mine."

THE INCARNATION.

The Christianity of all ages has beheld in the human sufferings of a Divine Person, a manifestation not so much of man as of God. That one thing which was wanting in the first Adam, namely, suffering, is here prominently set forth. This sight of Jesus Christ is the nearest view we can ever have of God. His unapproachable glories forever elude our search, and even though in pursuit we fly on the wings of the morning, we behold the radiant throne forever flying before us; but in the wounds of Christ, and in his dying countenance, we read the great lesson of manifested divinity. The Word was made flesh; called the Word, as being the Revealer, and in this dying scene, revealing more than in all ages previous: " to make all men see what is the fellowship of the mystery, which, from the beginning of the world, has been hid in God." Hence, Eph. iii. 19, to " know the love of Christ," is to " be filled with all the fulness of God."

The Son of God, then, by becoming incarnate, has made a manifestation of the Godhead, more complete than the universe has ever known. It is not merely, as even Unitarians and Deists may believe, that a certain good man, called Jesus of Nazareth, has taught more clear, and full, and accurate doctrines concerning God. This is true, but infinitely more is true. This Jesus of Nazareth, very God and very man, possessing the two natures in one indivisible divine person, has, in human guise, and with a human body and soul, so lived, so spoken, so felt, so acted, and so suffered, as to reveal the divinity through the manhood, as it was never revealed before; and so as to present those attributes which were otherwise invisible and remote, in near, palpable action. Henceforth, it is not merely Truth, Wisdom, Power, and Love, in distant abstractions, but Incarnate Truth, and Wisdom, and Power, and Love. Suppose, my brethren, that we were to remove out of the Scriptures all *that* knowledge of God, which has come to us through the Lord Jesus Christ, what would be left! How would our Christianity be shorn of its brightest rays! No; when we would behold divinity, we look for the light of his glory as it shines in the face of Jesus Christ. In him dwelleth all the fulness of the Godhead, bodily. So he taught his disciples that the sight of himself was the sight of God. "Have I been so long time with you, and yet hast thou not known me, Philip? he that hath seen me, hath seen the Father; and how sayest thou, then, Show us the Father?" John the Baptist knew this, and testified it in his last recorded speech. His morning-star "paled its ineffectual fires" before the rising sun. "He that cometh from heaven," said he, "is above all; and what he hath seen and heard, that he testifieth." All the time that Christ was upon earth, he did not cease to be in heaven with God. "No man hath seen God at any time; the Only Begotten Son, who is in the bosom of the Father, he hath declared him." Hence, the Apostle John, in language otherwise unintelligible, speaks of the Word of God, as if subjected to the scrutiny of the senses, 1 John,

i. 1; "which was from the beginning, which we have heard, which we have seen with our eyes, which we have looked upon, and our hands have handled of the Word of life." It is Christ who is the great Revealer, even to our understandings; and no man cometh unto the Father, even intellectually, but by Him. He is not simply the Teacher; he is the Word. He is God himself in revelation. And, as incarnate, he is God in the flesh : the mirror, the luminous manifester of God; the "brightness," or radiant effulgence, or outshining of his glory, the express image, or sealed character of his subsistence.

Remembering that it does not become us to intrude into those things which we have not seen, we must not undertake to say by what methods God will reveal himself to us in the future world. We know that Christ will still be Immanuel, God with us. We know that he will still bear our nature, forever, in heaven. We know that the absolute perfections of the Godhead will never cease to be inaccessible. We know that our Redeemer will still possess that same love which has led him to make all previous manifestations. We know that our own human nature shall then be brought unspeakably nearer to the human nature of the Lord Jesus Christ, than it has ever been on earth; since it will be freed from all sin and imperfection; and since we can scarcely form ideas too high of what the Lord shall confer on our souls, when he shall change even " our vile body, that it may be fashioned like unto his glorious body, according to the working whereby he is able even to subdue all things unto himself." Phil. iii. 21. And hence, it is surely within the modesty of Christian conjecture, that when our humanity shall be brought so much nearer the glorified humanity of the Lord Jesus Christ, we shall enjoy communications from his divine nature, proportionably surpassing all that has fallen to our lot here.

In this world, therefore, and in the other, we know more of God, by the Incarnation, than we could ever have known without it; and this is the first point to be established.

II. By the Incarnation, God is brought near to our Affections. This, my brethren, is a part of the subject which involves less of theological argument, but which comes home more nearly to our hearts. Religion dwells much in the affections, and all intellectual views are important as tending towards emotion and action. Stoical philosophy tried in vain to expel human passions. Our very life is made up of them, and so far as we succeed in banishing them, we reduce existence to a condition such as that the world would be, if all colour were removed from the objects of nature. But, thanks be to God, it is in a very small degree that we are capable of destroying sensibility. Though, by so doing, we prevent some pain, we still more certainly prevent all pleasure; and God has wisely constituted us so as to fear, to hope, to desire, to love, to rejoice and to grieve.

Who is there that needs to be instructed in the power of human domestic affections? These it is, which make the charm of home. A hundred pictures rise to your mind, the more delightful, because they are the product rather of memory than imagination. There are some things of which fancy may brighten the hues, and which may be lovelier in fiction than in real life; but it is not so with the affections of warm hearts. The attempt would be

> "To gild refined gold, to paint the lily,
> "To throw a perfume on the violet."

The love of parent to child, of children to parents, and the conjugal affections from which these spring, are beyond description. Dwell a moment on that which was first named. See the young mother, hanging over her babe, with a new and overmastering affection, which has changed her within a few short months from the buoyant maiden, swimming in the dance of pleasure and admiration, to be the doting, fearing, indefatigable, watching parent, whose whole soul is treasured up in that cradle, and who lives a new life in this experience, which no one could have described to her, and which she cannot hope to make credible save by those who have borne the same burden. Suppose affliction and illness should come, there is bitterness infused into the cup; but the passion has not lost its strength. What picture is more lovely or more familiar than that of two parents gazing upon the little ones whom they have consigned to sleep, as the unconscious objects of their love lie locked in each other's arms? And often have we been called to see the same affection clinging to the languishing and dying child, and hanging over the dead; a faithful watch-lamp among the tombs. Nor are these the only instances of strong attachments: I trust there is not one within the sound of my voice, who is not himself the subject or the object of such love, which goes beyond the lines of blood, and dignifies the field of sacred friendship. Think not, my hearers, that I have alluded to these acknowledged evidences of feeling for purposes of embellishment or entertainment. They serve another and more important end; they bring strongly before your minds the great part which is occupied by the affections, and remind you how much the happiness of life is dependent on them. Staunch the well-spring of love, and what is left of existence that would be worth saving? We might have intelligence, purpose, and animal appetite, but we could have no elevation, and no happiness. No, my brethren; next to the love of himself, God has given us nothing better than the love of one another, as it flows forth in all the mutual relations of society. But, lest you think I wander from my topic, let me hasten to trace out the connexion of what has been said, with the loftier topic which engages us. I have instanced in a single affection, that of love; but while brevity demanded this, I would beg you to observe, that most of what has been offered, has equal application to such other emotions as

THE INCARNATION.

may terminate on a good object. We are now therefore prepared to remark, that God has brought our feelings within the circle of religion; and this in two respects. He has sanctified these affections by his grace. He has turned these instincts into duties; and has made feelings which are delightful in themselves part of our tribute to himself. He has, with his own finger, inscribed on the second table of the Law, the household names of husband, wife, father, mother, son, daughter, servant, and neighbour, and thus made them sacred. He has proposed to us to receive payment of duty in the shape of affections and their fruits, which are themselves a reward. He has enlarged the circle so as to take in all mankind; and has said of good bestowed on the suffering, "Inasmuch as ye did it to the least of these my brethren, ye did it unto me." Christianity has seized upon these natural affections, and enlarged, purified, refined, and sanctified them. The theme is inviting; but I must go on to state a second respect, in which God has brought our affections within the circle of religion; for He has, wonderful to declare, permitted these affections to terminate on himself. This is more amazing than at first appears. God suffers creatures, lately condemned for their sins, to look up to him with hope, desire, pious sorrow, joy, and love. That we can thus feel toward fellow-creatures, we know; we experience it every day, to our solace, relief and enjoyment; but towards God! how is it possible? Surely the thought were impious. Jehovah is too high to be reached by such affections as ours; and such a flight were too daring and presumptuous. Enough were it for us to stand at the foot of Sinai, and look upwards to the distant Majesty, with another class of emotions, with reverence, dread, admiring awe, and solemn fear. Sufficient were it for sinners to know that God will not consume them with a blaze of his wrath. And such indeed are the views engendered by the Law. It can go no further. But ye are not come to the mount that might be touched, and that burned fire, nor unto blackness, and darkness, and tempest, and the sound of a trumpet, and the voice of words; but ye are come unto Mount Zion, unto the city of the living God. The whole relation is so changed, that we approach no longer as servants, but as sons, and are permitted to pour into the bosom of God the very same affections which we bestow on beloved human creatures, only with a greatness of volume in the tide, such as could not reasonably end on any thing finite. God, in infinite condescension, permits us to look on him with a genuine and personal affection. And it is this which brings the whole matter clearly within the scope of the present argument; since our proposal is to show that by the Incarnation, God is brought sufficiently near to be the object of these affections. We have seen how the same glorious event brought the divine perfections within the range of our mental vision; but to stop there, would be but the half of religion. It is not the cold contemplation of certain attributes, even though divine, which accomplishes our work. The first and chiefest commandment, yea, the sum of all, is Thou shalt love. But who can love a metaphysical abstraction; even when named by the name of God? Who can draw nigh to a Deity so abstruse and distant? No contemplation of the glories of nature can do more than excite admiration, and perhaps a modified thankfulness, of the vaguest and coldest sort. It is the Gospel which brings God nigh. We do not deny that in the Old Testament there are many representations of God as a Father, and many views of his character, as long-suffering and of tender mercy, and forgiving transgression, such as awaken tender emotions towards him. But all these are so many anticipations of the Christian era; Christ, my brethren, is in the Old Testament as well as in the New. His name was on every altar, laver, pillar, vail, and censer, on all the golden imagery, and all the cunning work of the tabernacle; but it was there in hieroglyphic device and cipher, such as required a key, and a practised eye; and these were read backwards by the legalists of Israel, for want of the knowledge of Christianity. When the Messiah came, he found them with this law in their hands, yet devoid of all generous, melting, loving affections towards God. A yoke of galling, intolerable formalism lay on the necks of the whole people. The general aspect of the Old Testament unquestionably wears a frown, not in its real intention, but as apprehended by those whose hearts were veiled as to its real meaning. The doctrine of the New Testament was needed to expound the Old. All which is strikingly confirmed, when we survey the condition of the modern Jews, in their rejection of the Lord Jesus Christ. Their service is slavish. With the Old Testament in their hands, and read daily in their synagogues, they nevertheless approach God with attempts at a hard routine of ceremonies, which neither they nor their fathers were able to bear. The grand defect in all their services, and which they have no means of supplying, is the want of spiritual filial love. The total absence of this among the heathen, is a striking fact in their history. Even while their poets say, "For we are also His offspring;" none of their books make any part of religion consist in affectionate regard for their deities, even the chief. No moral duties are referred to any attachment to the gods, as their motive; no law says, Thou shalt love Jupiter or Neptune, or all the gods, or any of them. Whereas, when we turn to the New Testament, or even to the Old as explained by the New, we observe this exercise of the affections on every page. And wherever true religion enters a soul, it works as strongly as do the natural impulses within us towards a beloved circle. The believer looks on God with as real and as personal affection, as on his children or his parent, though with a purer and higher flame. He is not content with the impersonal Deity of the philosopher; the mere power of Nature, or Soul of the Universe, which

"Warms in the sun, refreshes in the breeze,
"Glows in the stars, and blossoms in the trees,
"Lives through all life, extends through all extent,
"Spreads undivided, operates unspent."

Though these words may be taken in a good sense, the believer craves more than this. He asks for a personal God, to whom his soul, as an individual person, may come. My brethren, I am uttering what may seem a truism; but the age demands clear views on this point. The giant heresy of the age is that which makes the Universe God. Many years ago, the greatest female mind of the day said, "The public secret of Germany is Pantheism." That which began in Germany has spread over France and surrounding countries, and has appeared among ourselves, in the extravagant teachings of the transcendental infidelity. And there is a dreadful tendency in such opinions to gravitate from the schools of philosophy downward to the masses, in the grosser form of downright Atheism. These opinions have mingled themselves to a large extent with the political revolutions of the continent. Let me cite one of the latest indications: At one of the great conventions in Germany, lately held, the Hessian delegate, Professor Vogt, used the following language: "I am for the separation of Church and State; but only on condition that what is called the Church be annihilated. The National Assembly must recognise a church of unbelief. The time has come, when a man may have permission in Germany to be an Atheist." * Such are the tendencies of modern philosophy; and they spread more widely than is thought; among professed, and even among real Christians, their taint is felt; and, where they cannot destroy faith, they succeed in disturbing it. Thus, a celebrated Christian author of Prussia said to a friend of mine: "O, that I had your views of God! O, that I could say THOU to him, as to a personal God!" My brethren, the believer can approach his God as a person, and with a real, personal, individual affection, as when a man comes to a friend or father. But in order to this, there must be that approach through a Mediator, which is our principal subject. When Luther said, "I cannot have an absolute God," *Nolo Deum absolutum*, he expressed a great fundamental truth. As he meant it, the doctrine is, that as a God of Justice, Jehovah cannot be approached by sinners, save through a propitiation. But it is true in another sense: we cannot come to God with a tender, bursting, filial affection, until we behold him manifested in the Son. He is distant, towering, abstract; the object of awful dread, and marvelling admiration, but not of confiding attachment. God must be brought nigher. Those attributes of heavenly fearfulness must be translated into the language of the heart. The immaterial and evanescent perfections must be presented in some tangible form. In the former division, we saw the provision made for

* Kirchenfreund, Feb. 1849.

this, in regard to the intellect; the same provision is equally available in regard to the heart. "God was manifest in the flesh;" manifest first to the understanding, which we have considered; and, secondly, to the affections. The problem being, How is human love to such a being as God possible? the answer is, We love God by loving Christ. In these simple words is contained a lesson of religious experience which would, if properly acted upon, change our whole life. It is by faith in the Lord Jesus Christ, that we behold that aspect of God, which awakens tender affection. No man cometh unto the Father, but by him. Till this faith arises within us, God is seen far off, in clouds of angry justice. Faith manifests him as full of love, and ready to pardon and adopt; and all this through Jesus Christ.

But here the question presents itself, whether we may encourage our affections to go forth to Christ, as to a personal object of love. This does not seem difficult to one who has in memory the New Testament narrative. In those scenes, Jesus moved among his creatures as a man, and was the object of tender and generous affections, which are recorded in the book, and are reproduced in ourselves while we read. Is there any believer who reads the four gospels, who does not feel his heart going forth perpetually and increasingly toward the individual character of the Lord Jesus? He who knows nothing of this, in my judgment, knows nothing yet as he ought to know. It is a sympathy with those who surrounded the Son of God when he "was manifest in the flesh." In that narrative, if anywhere, he is "altogether lovely." The eye singles him out from among all the scriptural characters, as he walks by the sea of Galilee; as he opens his lips upon the Mount; as he heals, and feeds, and comforts; as he fasts, and prays, and sighs; as he prepares the disciples for his departure; and as he finally dies upon the cross. It is this "historical Christ," a term used in contempt by Strauss, and his imitators in America, whom we love; even after his resurrection, when he appears to Mary, to Cleopas, to the Apostles, and when he is caught up from among them into heaven. Now, we have only to reflect, that though in heaven, he is unchanged, "Jesus Christ, the same yesterday, to-day, and forever," to satisfy us, that as truly as he was loved by disciples on earth, so truly he may be loved by us; and this, not with a vague approval or admiration of abstract virtues, but with a strong and moving individual affection. And this is not contradictory to the spirit of Paul's words, 2 Cor. v. 16: "Yea, though we have known Christ after the flesh, yet now henceforth know we him no more;" for here the apostle means to condemn and repudiate his former carnal expectation of Messiah, as a temporal prince. In this very connexion, Paul is so far from condemning a spiritual affection of the Redeemer, that he exclaims: "Whether we be beside ourselves it is to God;" that is, "if as our enemies say, we are transported out of ourselves by enthusiasm, so as to seem deranged, let them know we are animated by a zeal for God; for the love of Christ constraineth us;" or, as the word means, 'bears us away like a strong and resistless torrent.' It is therefore possible and lawful to look on the person of our Redeemer with a strong individual regard; loving him for every bright virtue, and gentle word, and beneficent act of his human pilgrimage; and ascribing to him the same excellencies, now that he has ascended into heaven. And experience testifies that this love of the Lord Jesus Christ is as true and distinct an emotion, in the Christian's mind, as any which he cherishes towards children or friends. But here the question meets us, How, or in what sense is this the loving of GOD? How are we hereby brought any nearer to the Great Supreme? In replying briefly to this, I must recall to your mind what has been said under another head. That which we love in Jesus Christ, is not his exterior form, of which the Scriptures wisely give us no details; but the lineaments of his spiritual nature; the moral features; the virtues and graces of his inner life; his humility, faith, devotion, gentleness, meekness, longsuffering, fortitude, courage, benevolence, and truth. These internal beauties are manifested by his words, his works, and his sufferings. The whole Gospel narrative is a record of them, and as we read, we love. We muse upon them when the book is laid down, as we do over the letter of our dearest friend; nay, we must open it once again, and look at the very words. The picture is formed in our mind, and rises before us, as that of a distant husband to the affectionate wife; but it is a moral image, and the sum of the traits is holiness. Now, these spiritual attractions, though manifested to us through a human soul, are nevertheless divine; because Divinity shines through that manhood. The Godhead, yea, the whole undivided Godhead, has its union there with human nature. Nowhere else in the universe is so much of God presented for our adoration, as in the Lord Jesus Christ. With every thought, emotion, and volition of that holy human spirit, there is a present and consenting holiness of the Divine Nature. These virtues and graces have two sides: one toward us, and one toward heaven. Toward us, all that our eyes behold, is human; toward heaven, is the equal and coincident will of divinity. Not only so: while Christ Jesus, as a man, is manifesting toward us these perfections and attractions, he is one with God. Though there are two natures, there is but one person: the glorious person who is named Christ. The constitution of this adorable Person, was for the very purpose of manifesting God. As has been fully said, we behold more of God in the face of Christ, than elsewhere in all the universe. Is not the question answered, then? When we love Christ, we love God. We cannot in any way so intelligently love God, as when we love Christ. And therefore, we need not be afraid to let our thoughts and powers go out with all their fulness toward the Son; we need not be apprehensive lest we defraud the Father of his glory.

Christ is God, in human manifestation. The Word was made flesh. God is incarnate, and as incarnate is made ours: the Only Begotten Son, who is in the bosom of the Father, He hath revealed him. The reverse method is not so safe. There are some who are full of high expressions towards God, in general, but who make little of Christ. Having not come by the only way, such persons have no true apprehensions of God. "Whosoever believeth that Jesus is the Christ, is born of God; and every one that loveth him that begat, loveth him also that is begotten of him." "He that hath the Son, hath life; and he that hath not the Son, hath not life." This is a great mystery to the world; but it is understood by the people of God. It is indeed the great principle of Christianity. But it never could have entered into human minds to conceive it. How new and impossible to be foreseen! This is the reason it is called a mystery, that, having long been hidden, it is now made known. How influential! Religious views are no longer cold and inoperative. They are brought within the circle of our heart-affections. The Lord Jesus Christ, so to speak, sits by our fireside. All our natural emotions are brought in as auxiliaries to our love of Christ; and in loving him, we are performing our great duty to God. And then how delightful! Here it is, in the love of Christ, that the chief happiness of religion consists. Loving God is no longer an impossibility or an abstraction. We are bound to him by ties of humanity, as by the "bonds of a man;" for, "we are members of his body, of his flesh, and of his bones."

The great proof that this view is correct, is derived from an inspection of the New Testament; for there we see it to be the view of the early Christians. If, on looking at these records, we had found it to be otherwise; if, for example, we had found, either that the Redeemer was spoken of as one to whom no tribute of affection could properly be paid, because he is only a deceased man; or, that the Son of God is too highly exalted, and too far removed, for us to visit him with our affection; then, indeed, we should have had good cause to reject all the doctrine which has been proposed. But this doctrine meets full confirmation in primitive experience. "Our fellowship," says the Apostle John, "is with the Father, and with his Son Jesus Christ." "Whom, having not seen," says Peter, "ye love." He addresses himself to the body of Christians in many countries; it was the common experience of the age. They loved the unseen Christ. They looked for "that blessed hope and the glorious appearing of the great God and our Saviour Jesus Christ." And it was so radical a distinction between the Christian and the world, that Paul, in his zeal, declares, "If any man love not the Lord Jesus Christ, let him be anathema maranatha." And after apostolic days, this personal love to the Lord Jesus was the characteristic of disciples. The expression of the martyr Ignatius is celebrated, in its Latin version: AMOR MEUS CRUCIFIXUS est! I must go further, my brethren, and say, that this is the great lesson of evangelical Christianity. Wherever vital piety decays, this decays. It takes its flight long before the alteration of creeds or the denial of doctrines; for there may be an age of cold orthodoxy unenlivened by one beam of love to the Redeemer. But when this affection has fled, sound doctrine soon prepares to spread its wings likewise. For a time there may be accurate metaphysical discussion, controversy about tenets, and even persecution for differences. But by degrees the Cross is thrust into a corner; and at length the propitiatory work of Christ is extenuated or forgotten. The Atonement being tarnished or exploded, the Godhead of Christ is soon found to be superfluous. There is no need of a divine Redeemer under that easy system of liberal Christianity in which every man is his own saviour. This may account for the known fact, that among those who reject the Trinity, small account is made of personal love towards the Lord Jesus Christ. The too frequent allusion to his double nature and to his redeeming blood becomes offensive, and the people are in a fair way to forget that there ever were such spots as Gethsemane or Golgotha. Whereas, in direct opposition to this, whenever vital piety revives, there is a marked revival of love to Jesus Christ. It was so at the Reformation, and it will be more gloriously so in the centuries of light which are to come. Wherever a genuine convert is made from heathenism, his heart is expanded with a new affection, love to the crucified Redeemer. In their best moments, Christians of every age and country have risen in love to God manifest in the flesh. This is witnessed by the thousands of hymns and spiritual songs in which Christian affection has poured itself forth in all the languages of Christendom. We need not except the Greek and Latin hymns of the early church, before the rise of papacy: some of which have providentially been retained even among many corruptions. The lyric effusion of some favoured moment of unwonted transport in an individual saint, being consigned to the care of poetry and music, thus became part of the worship of the whole church. At the Reformation, songs in an unknown tongue were suddenly exchanged for those in the vulgar tongues, and thousands of hymns to Christ burst forth over Germany, Switzerland, Holland, France, and Britain. The piety thus reviving continued from century to century, and for the same object. So far from shunning the death of the Lord, it was Christ on the cross that, above all things, attracted their hearts, because it was here that most was seen of God manifest in the flesh. How many a night of affliction has been brightened by this vision! How many a dying lip has made the name of Jesus its last articulation!

V.

THE WORLDLING.

THE WORLDLING.*

Philippians iii. 19.

"Who mind earthly things."

The pencil of inspiration, by one rapid sweep, often depicts a whole class of human souls. In the present instance, the view given of ungodly men, in a single fearful aspect, is important enough to be severed from its most interesting context, and made the object of our profound consideration. The apostle, with deep Christian feeling, is here describing the people of the world. He closes this description with the hint which I have selected. It is the portrait of all unrenewed persons, however widely they may differ in other respects. They mind earthly things. The word is peculiar in its force; they set their minds upon earthly things, think of

---

* New York, October 3, 1852.

them, think much of them, yea, constantly and supremely. Earthly things, and not heavenly, fill their minds and occupy their regard and affections. And this charge, which to careless, unenlightened souls may seem quite a trifling one, is so grave in Paul's estimation, that it moves him to tears, and he weeps while he writes. It is this minding of earthly things, as characteristic of unbelieving men, which we are about briefly to consider.

Readers of the Scriptures have observed that two great opposing spheres are often held up to view; one as engaging the hearts of the ungodly and one of the godly. They are the earth and heaven, verses 19, 20, this world and the world to come; things visible and things invisible; the present and the future; the world and Christ; Mammon and God. All these are the same in substance; and the contrast or opposition is complete and irreconcilable. According to these two sets of objects, or two worlds as we may call them, the whole race of men is divided into two portions; the World, an expressive term for all that is opposed to God and the Church, or people of the living God.

It may as clearly be presumed that the noble creature whom we call man, was not made to spend his powers on passing sublunary things, as that he was not made to browse with the ox or grovel with the serpent. A consideration of his powers shows that he was destined for eternity and for God. Revelation has for its great end to set before him the objects which are suited to these capacities. Their residence in the present life is a period of grace, in which men under the gospel are invited to rise from earthly towards heavenly things; and it is the principal work of the Holy Spirit to invite, win and attract men to the pursuit and enjoyment of spiritual realities.

Notwithstanding which, we have before us the continual spectacle of the majority of mankind worshipping the creature, forgetting God, and living for the present fleeting hour. For them, heaven and hell, the law and its satisfaction, eternity and God, are as though they were not; sending forth no moulding influence. For them, the present world is heaven enough, if they could only make it sure; and they would rejoice in a decree, which should fix their abode here forever. Let us look a little more closely at this side of our common human nature.

It requires but a glance at the busy crowds around us to perceive that the great things of the soul and of eternity do not absorb their chief interest. Whether you judge them by their words or their company, by what they do or leave undone, you find them to be "of the earth, earthy." This is the more striking, when you contrast with it their high-wrought zeal in all that concerns the present life. When personal honour and applause or family distinction are in view, no labour seems too great; and under the goad of fashionable rivalry, they expend language, time, and even thousands of money, which proves too well how much they are in earnest. In this race they will suffer none to leave them behind; and we have lived to see high professors in the church, whose manner of household life, equipage, and entertainments, leave us marvelling what those pomps and vanities of the world can be, which they have renounced as followers of Christ, or where we are to look for cross-bearing, godly simplicity, and self-denial. Our Lord certainly had a meaning when he set forth the imminent peril to the soul, which comes from worldly riches; and I suppose the wealth against which he warned his followers, was less than that of many who hear me, but who feel no danger. The way in which worldly possessions jeopard the soul, is by occupying the affections, leading the heart away from God and divine things, to take its contentment in the good things of this life. This is serving Mammon; making a god of present things; giving the supreme regard to that which is perishing; and it is declared to be inconsistent with the love of God. The minister of the gospel, as one "who must give account," must not shun to exhibit this danger to those who are possessed of worldly goods. Whether they will hear or forbear, his commission is explicit: "Charge them that are rich in this world, that they be not high-minded, nor trust in uncertain riches, but in the living God, who giveth us richly all things to enjoy." The trusting in riches, here intended, is the setting of the mind on them as the source of comfort; making them a staff and stay; relying on them, as a provision against trouble; indulging a secret complacency in them, as making us better than others, who have lost them or have never attained them; and flattering ourselves at the supposed security of our own acquisitions, as compared with the precarious fortunes of others. Those who so live, whether in the church or out of it, are minding earthly things and estranging their hearts from the living God, who giveth us all things richly to enjoy.

But it would be unwise to limit our view of the earthliness of worldly riches to the use which is made of them while actually possessed. A large part of the human family is engaged in the hot pursuit; some with success, and many more with disappointment. This variety in the result makes no difference, however, in the temper of mind with which the seeming goal is sought. We need only open our eyes, at mid-day, in any great commercial city, to learn that this is the prime mover in all the complex and indescribable commotion of human business. Mistake me not; I am not denouncing activity in business, or even the pursuit of wealth, simply considered. As a chief instrument of happiness in this life, it may be sought in different degrees and from different motives; moderately or immoderately; selfishly or benevolently; with an entire absorption in the creature, or with an hourly reference of all to God. But I will affirm, and none will soberly deny it, that, as a matter of fact, the multitude, the majority, the mass of men thus engaged day and night with impetuous, feverish, often delirious haste, are actuated by no impulses but those which spring from the creature, and thus that they mind earthly things. This is what they live for; for this they make their sacrifices and run their risks. This occupies their thoughts, at rising, and as they hurry through the great emporium, at desks and places of trade, in the retirement of the evening and the intervals of night. It is this which excludes prayer, meditation, the Scriptures, the care of the soul, the seeking of Christ's kingdom and righteousness. The desire is not quenched by successes. No philosopher has discovered the point at which insatiable avarice can consent to admit that it is rich enough. We know of no principle recognised by the world on this point, but this, that every man must be as rich as he can. Great accumulations do but stimulate the appetite for more, and the close of life, instead of being devoted to quiet preparation for death and eternity, is frequently harassed by more vexing cares of acquisition than its youthful dawn. The point of the charge is, that God is shut out. For this no reasonable and immortal creature can frame an apology. He drives a hazardous bargain who barters away his opportunity of salvation. "For what shall a man give in exchange for his soul!" Yet look abroad, and behold the face of society. The broad and thronged avenue is filled with human beings, rushing towards the gates of death, all engrossed in that which perishes even while it is obtained. We need no longer wonder that the church dwindles, and that few are added to the company of

God's people. There is a contagion in the evil, and every day fresh thousands yield themselves to the same impulse. Unless God break the spell, unless he seize upon them by the strong hand of the Spirit, these deluded beings will die as they have lived, and, plunging into a state whither they can carry no earthly gains, will learn by experience what it is to gain the world and lose their own souls.

The brief description of the text includes the lovers of pleasure. Either in the pauses of business, or as their whole employment, great numbers of persons spend their time in seeking amusement, recreation, the satisfying of curiosity, appetite or passion. This host includes most who are in youth, but many also who tread on the confines of age. It needs no laboured argument to show that these mind earthly things. They are living as though they had no souls. They are lovers of pleasure more than lovers of God. It is common to speak of such as amiable and good-natured, or as injuring none but themselves. But no persons are more intensely selfish, than the confirmed devotees of pleasure. Their motto is, Who will show us any good? What shall we eat, and what shall we drink, and wherewithal shall we be clothed? There are none more bound to the earth. There is no temper more incompatible with religion, or with the serious pursuit of it. Hence the reiterated injunctions of our Lord to those who would follow him, to leave all, to deny themselves, and to take up the cross daily. Hence also the striking admonitory pictures of the rich man clad in purple and fine linen, and faring sumptuously every day; of the young ruler, who went away sorrowful; and of him who said to his soul, "Take thine ease; eat, drink, and be merry." The entertainments and pleasures of an easy life destroy tens of thousands, who nevertheless never fall into open and flagrant vices. Satan's end is sufficiently gained, when, by immersing them in thoughts of the present world, he can keep them away from all consideration of eternal things.

What a horrid fraud Satan is practising on the church, in regard to the daughters of the covenant! In fashionable circles—dare I name them Christian— the years where girlhood merges into maturity are frequently sold to the adversary. The young American woman is taught to deem herself a goddess. If there be wealth, if there be accomplishment, if there be beauty, almost a miracle seems necessary to prevent the loss of the soul. Behold her pass from the pedestal to the altar. The charming victim is decked for sacrifice. Every breath that comes to her is incense. Her very studies are to fit her for admiration. Day and night the gay but wretched maiden is taught to think of self and selfish pleasures. Till some Lenten fashion of solemnity interrupt the whirl, the season is too short for the engagements. Grave parents shake their heads at magnificent apparel, costly gems, night turned into day, dances at which Romans would have blushed, pale cheeks, bending frames, threatened decay; and yet they allow and submit. And thus that sex, which ought to shew the sweet unselfish innocency of a holy youth, is carried to the overheated temples of Pleasure. Thus the so-called Christian verifies the apostle's maxim, "She that liveth in pleasure is dead while she liveth."

But it is needless to classify worldlings. Their number is so great that we can scarcely move without encountering them; and it is well if we do not find ourselves infected with the same disease. The god of this world has brought them under his incantation, by blinding their minds. He magnifies to their apprehensions the gains and exaltations of sensible things; he colours the pleasures of life; he shuts out the future, the spiritual and the divine. That ardour with which they run their short career, would be worthy of a better object. Alas for them! they are building on the sea-sand, and the tempestuous waves will soon overwhelm their confidence.

Let me very earnestly put it to the mind and conscience of every hearer, whether he belongs to this class or not. The Scriptures divide the aggregate of all that the human soul can pursue with desire into two great worlds, the earthly and the heavenly. Every man living is intent on one or the other; and no man can attain both. There can be no compromise. Ye cannot serve God and Mammon. Ye cannot mind earthly things, and at the same time mind heavenly things. If any man love the world, the love of the Father is not in him. Nay, he that loves the world is at enmity with God.

So much is at stake, that you cannot be too earnest in the self-examination. Here you may bring your inward character to a test. Ask not whether you have at some former period been admitted to the external church; thousands have been thus admitted, without any change of nature. But ask, which of these two worlds has your heart? Are you living under the power of the world to come? Does its awful shadow fall across your path, and give solemnity to your purposes? Do you go about the business of every day under the deep impression that all these things are perishing, that this is not your rest, that presently God your Judge, whose penetrating eye is always upon you, will call you hence, to give an account of the deeds done in the body? Are you seeking a home and kingdom which cannot be moved? Is your treasure laid up in heaven, and is your heart there? Do you look for your choicest gratifications in divine things, in heavenly truth, and in communion with God? Are you jealous of every thing, however usual or valuable among men, which removes your thoughts from the great invisible world in which your true possessions lie? And do you feel yourself a pilgrim, who can enjoy no settled and satisfying rest till you reach a world from which sin is to be forever absent? These are questions which admit of an answer.

Or, on the other hand, are your thoughts at waking wholly upon the things of time and earth? Do these things occupy your most active endeavours and employ your words? Are you bent with all your energies on the acquisition or preservation of gain, pleasure, ease, or fame? And is this so fully your turn of mind, that you seldom pray, or seldom with any engagement of heart; seldom think of God; seldom meditate on the eternity to which you are hastening; and seldom feel your sins to be such a burden as to force you to flee to Christ for relief? Such is the case of many, of most; and if it be yours, then know assuredly that you mind earthly things.

But I am not permitted to leave you with the bare conviction that this is your state. A superficial persuasion of this, as an undoubted fact, has often come over you, without producing any change in your way of life. Consider with me, I pray you, the quality, character and end of this your chosen course.

1. To mind earthly things, as the great paramount object, is degrading. It is unworthy of an immortal intelligence. You were made for better things. You were no more framed to fill your boundless capacities with these fleeting vanities, than to take the pleasure of the beast, bird, or insect. That nature of yours was once in the image of God, and still sighs for a restitution, which, through grace, is attainable. The course you pursue belies and repudiates your immortality. Your animated breathless chase of these temporalities, when translated into its true import, speaks thus: "Let us eat and drink, for to-morrow we die." You are prostituting a noble instrument to an ignoble use. This is the secret cause of those disgusts

which you often feel. Earthly things have not done for you that which they promised. They have not made you happy; they have often left you weary, sated, disappointed, and smarting. Some of your earlier pleasures have already lost their exquisite zest. Increase of years has brought weakness, repining, and bitterness. Accumulation of worldly goods has failed to give you comfort in proportion. Nay, if you will own the mortifying truth, you are less tranquil and satisfied than in former days. Many things on which you relied, have been taken from you, and for many that remain your appetite has died away. The foam of your brimming cup has been blown away, and you are endeavouring to cheer yourself with the dregs. Confess it, O my earthly hearer, and add the solemn consideration, that you are a spiritual, immortal, and accountable being, who will before long be hurried into the presence of Eternal Judgment. In reference to this, your great and certain destiny, the objects which interest you have no weight, except to condemn you. Having lived so long, you have not yet begun to live in view of your endless existence; and painful as is the charge, it is nevertheless just, that your whole course thus far has been such as to lower the true dignity of your nature, as one of God's immortal creatures.

2. To mind earthly things involves incalculable loss. Men are prompt to avoid losses in that which concerns worldly possessions. But those who live altogether for this life, lose an entire class of pleasures and benefits.

To them one avenue of happiness, and that the greatest, is closed. The higher faculties of the soul are unemployed. The gifts and consolations and delights of religion are unknown to them. Communion with God —a wide, expressive term—is all a mystery. They lose the pleasures of holy truth, and the witness of a conscience pacified by the blood of Christ. They lose the intercourse of faith and devotion with an unseen world and a benignant Saviour; the calm, hopeful anticipation of death; and the rapturous contemplation of glories yet in reserve. They lose the sense of God's favour and the consciousness that they have entered on a progress of discipline and improvement which shall never end. In a word, they lose all that we mean by religion.

To some of you, my hearers, this seems no great loss. So wedded are you to the world, your idol, that you can look for happiness to no other source; no, not even to God. Yet I am bound to protest to you, that Wisdom's ways are ways of pleasantness; and that you forsake them to your infinite loss.

3. Hear me yet further, when I solemnly declare to you, that to mind earthly things is to incur fearful guilt. It is sinful. It is contrary to God's holy will, and to his express commandment. It is wounding to your conscience, which still makes you feel the difference between right and wrong, and rebukes and punishes you for this habitual sin of your life. You admit to yourselves, that you were not made for this world

only; that you are the creatures and subjects of God, bound to do his pleasure, and that he demands of you to love him with heart, soul, strength, and mind. No doubt there have been moments in which your worldly pleasures have been embittered by the thought, that you were enjoying them in opposition to the known will of your Creator, Benefactor, and Preserver. Looking back on the long course of years, which you have spent without God, you have no moral complacency in it. It has not been the life which a dependent, favoured creature should have led. To have thus preferred created things to God, and made them the source of your happiness, to the exclusion of the Great Supreme, must appear to you, in any honest retrospect, all glaring with the colours of idolatry. It is ample ground of condemnation, that you have not made choice of God, but year after year have made choice of the world. And the proper consideration of this might bring you to repentance and to the foot of the cross. O that you could be induced to meditate profoundly on this charge brought against the ungodly world, that they mind earthly things!

4. To mind earthly things involves peril of eternal destruction. I use a strong term, because the strongest I can use is likely to leave the worldly mind unimpressed. Yes, the man who deliberately chooses this world sets himself against God; and, oh, how unequal is the contest! He has his reward. In this life he has his good things, and many a despised Lazarus evil

things; but you remember the reverse, indicated by the parallel. The world passeth away and the lust thereof. All that is in the world, the lust of the flesh, the lust of the eye, and the pride of life, all is rapidly fleeing; and when it has fled, the worldling's heaven has fled with it. Here, in this present state, he chose his paradise. No eyes had he to behold any thing beyond. Revelation and its ministers warned him of the unstable basis on which he was rearing his tall and costly structure, and sought to win him or alarm him to take the glass and look towards that city which hath foundations. But in vain. In all this he could make out nothing like reality, nothing to be an actuating motive. Living amidst the things of sense, and alive every moment to their palpable pressure, he took into none of his accounts that invisible state whose awful sweep, comprising God and angels and saints and all that is holy and ennobling, encircled him; nor that solemn eternity into which he was about to make the irrevocable plunge. And when the hour struck, which he so dreaded while he scarcely believed, the hour of his separation and departure, it found him still with clenched hands, striving to retain the things of time, and torn away bleeding and despairing from the earth which he had preferred to God. Read his doom in the brief but pregnant words of the context: Whose end is destruction! It is the lot of those who forget God.

There is reason to fear, that more are incurring this danger than are willing to believe it. The very closeness of their attachment to the objects of sense makes them insusceptible of impressions from divine realities. In regard to these, they hear as though they heard not; listening to the voice of admonition as the antediluvians listened to the forebodings of Noah, or as the men of the plain received the warnings of Lot. For persons thus infatuated, what hope can there be? What shall hinder their dying as they have lived? Nothing human, my brethren, but a bold, sudden and determinate resolution, to give up this world for the sake of another; to distrust the specious fallacies of sense and give credence to the testimony of God. Here, indeed, I am made to feel my own insufficiency. How solemn is the position of a minister of Christ! Placed amidst perishing fellow-mortals, to entreat them to escape from impending ruin, he finds them deaf to all his arguments and solicitations. Year after year he comes to them, with such pleas and motives as his closest research and most earnest prayers can enable him to offer. Yet he finds the same hardness and resistance only augmented, as years roll on and the cords of evil habit are wound about them more indissolubly. One after another drops away, whom we dare scarcely follow in their flight into the worlds unknown. The ranks close upon the vacancies they make, and the battle of cupidity, pleasure, and ambition rages on as before. It is in such circumstances that we lend a wistful ear to the oracle which proclaims from heaven, "Not by might, nor by power, but by my Spirit, saith the Lord of hosts." Our waiting eyes are unto God, for the outpouring of his Holy Spirit. And next to this, and as instrumental of this, our appeal is to the professed people of God, that they would join their prayers for the awakening and conversion of an ungodly world. It was the contemplation of souls thus besotted and endangered, which extorted from Paul the pathetic burst which accompanies my text: "For many walk of whom I have told you often, and now tell you even weeping, whose end is destruction, who mind earthly things!" Beloved brethren, I should hail it as the brightest promise which has ever gilded these feeble labours among you, if there should be apparent in the midst of us a deep, extensive, and tender concern in the hearts of professing Christians, for those who are wedded to earthly things. Suffer me, with all sincerity, to commend this to you as a subject suitable for your prayers; in private, in your families, in social devotion, and in the house of God. For unless it please God to send revival, our outward increase will be but the signal for our inward decay.

If numbers were strength we should be strong. But mere numbers are fallacious. If souls are not brought to God by converting grace, in due proportion, our extension is but a weakening process, resulting in unhealthy plethora. Let me confess it, my respected brethren, the thought often occurs to me, that of this sort of enlargement we already have too much; it may be our temptation and our snare; it may invoke God's chastening. If we are selfish, if we wrap ourselves up in complacency, if we "number the people," if we sum up the wealth represented within these walls, for any purpose except to rebuke our sin and quicken our activity, if we hug our easy privileges, and refuse to break the charm and go forth to the help of weaker congregations; we may confidently expect, first checks and then visitations. When I look fearfully upon this great, compact, and harmonious assembly, and consider its resources and strength, and then around us and near us behold numerous weak and struggling churches, which need money far less than they need men, I cannot resist the conviction, that a considerable body of self-denying men, with their families, ought, by concerted action, to go forth as an evangelical colony; and if the fifty best and ablest of the flock should do so to-morrow, while friendship would weep over the wound, I should give thanks over it, as the best day of my life. But to produce such dispositions we need a new spirit. Christian professors, to whom we look as leaders, will have to learn fresh lessons of moderation, temperance, and regard for weak brethren. They will have to separate the amusements of their children by a more visible line from the amusements of a world lying in wickedness. They will cease to plead for Baal, and to frame excuses for all that their soul lusteth after. Religion will become the grand, paramount affair of life. Heavenly joys over the salvation of the offspring whom you have encouraged to prefer every thing to God, will render needless and even abhorrent the worldly pleasures in which you now inconsistently indulge. How shall this change be brought about? Know ye, that God has manifold ways of effecting it; and among these the way of trial and affliction. If you are his, he will use even this, rather than suffer you to perish. Let our eyes be unto the Lord, saying with intense desire, "Wilt thou not revive us again, that thy people may rejoice in thee!"

VI.

THE SCORNER.

THE SCORNER.*

PROVERBS iii. 34.

Surely He scorneth the scorners."

THAT mode of irreligion which the wisest of kings so often stigmatizes under the name of scorning, makes itself known in every age. It is the derision of that which is good, and has its origin in ignorance, folly, and sin. The contempt, sometimes producing ridicule, which scoffs at wisdom and holiness, is begotten of that pride which "was not made for man," and which is hateful to God. To despise that which is heavenly is not a lower degree of wickedness, but passes the borders of the flagitious. Hence we should regard the very beginnings of such a temper with great jealousy, and should be willing to examine its signs and nature,

* New York, February 21, 1858.

in order to secure ourselves against its contagion. In treating the subject, we shall find it profitable to begin with lower degrees of the evil, and thence to trace its progress. To laugh or jeer in regard to that which displeases us is from a disposition which needs no artificial fostering. The opinion of Lord Shaftesbury, that "Ridicule is the test of falsehood," will find few serious defenders in our day. The laugher's side is not always the side of reason; as we might show by referring to the ridicule heaped upon many a great enterprise and improvement in science and art; the satire lasting in almost every case until it was put to shame by manifest success. That form of impotent contempt which we call sneer, belongs by pre-eminence to those who are to some extent conscious of being least armed with reason. Many a mischievous hand can fling the fire-cracker or the squib, which could neither wield the sword nor aim the rifle. Those were not all heroes who "called for Samson out of the prison-house," that he might make sport for them. All the world over, the derisive portion will be found the weakest; and this upon solid principles. The love of truth and practice of goodness, always allied, have a certain pure simplicity and candid uprightness which disincline the mind to take pleasure in the inferiority of others. Whatever in us is unselfish and benignant revolts against making spoil of a neighbour's delinquency. And, with reverence be it said, the trait is divine, for "God is mighty and despiseth not any." Job. xxxvi. 5. But ridicule cast on our fellows proceeds from contempt, and contempt is a mode of pride. Hence the lower down we go in the scale of morals and civilization, the greater fondness do we find for the language of scornful raillery. Little minds, incompetent to forge or handle massive links of argument, find a petty satisfaction in teazing cavil, and sarcastic irony. The number of such minds is greater than that of powerful reasoners and men of insight, and we must be content to leave them in the enjoyment of their characteristic warfare. Their buzzing assaults on religion are perpetually reminding one of the lesser but annoying plagues of Egypt. And such characters, fond of vexatious sayings, and growing in piquancy as they fall into the "sere and yellow leaf," need much grace to keep them from becoming scoffers.

The evil of ungenerous contempt and acrid censure becomes more imminent where there is some pretension to wit or humour. Very few of a thousand possess wit; scarcely one of the thousand does not sometimes attempt it. Perhaps there has never been an age which so overvalued the ludicrous, in speech and literature, as this of ours. The populace cries out for what is comic on the stage, and on the platform; and the periodical journal is incomplete, unless, like noble houses in the olden time, it maintains its clown. The wise man had this in his eye, when he said: "As the crackling of thorns under a pot, so is the laughter of the fool. This also is vanity." Ecc. vii. 6. We would contentedly leave the jester to wear his motley, if he confined his witticism to his own ring; but when he brings his gibes and grimaces into the sanctuary of God, and seeks to provoke mirth with holy things, we must silence and debar him. And yet how common is it to connect divine subjects with the ludicrous, and even the burlesque. As true wit involves some surprise, some unexpected turn, some sudden apposition of opposites, that which is false finds a certain spurious zest in low, trivial, even vile suggestions, forced into contrast with ideas of Eternity and God. Therefore, as a liar will swear in his common talk to add credence to his doubtful word, and a fool will throw imprecations into the scale to give weight to his feeble reasoning, so your vulgar jester resorts to profane abuse of religious objects, that he may startle the scrupulous, or extort laughter from the stupid. A verse of Scripture, a psalm or hymn, the text of a discourse, or some chance expression in a sermon, serves such a one, even with repetition, as a counterfeit coin serves a sharper. The mental poverty, the irreverence, and even the lewdness, of such pretenders, render them, sooner or later, disgusting to all whose judgment is worth asking. But their folly and degradation are less to be regarded by us than their sin; for we violate the Third Commandment when we trifle with God's name, titles, and worship, or when we profane his Word by associations which are ludicrous. So that I would solemnly charge it upon those who do not wish to destroy souls, that they shun with pious fear all tales, anecdotes, and jests, which defile by their touch any

Scriptural passage, and that they avoid the intercourse of those debased minds who descend to such resources.

The great adversary of souls has so many snares for the feet of pilgrims, that we cannot be too wary in regard to the imperceptible passage from what seems innocent or venial, to what is really wicked. From idle words about God's holy Scripture, youthful heedlessness is beguiled step by step, into by-paths of positive impiety. Satan's emissaries are generally near, ready to help on the error. Seducers try their victims first by milder approaches; and he or she who listens without protest or indignation, is believed to invite further liberties. If your unclean but amusing friend finds you tolerant of his ridiculous parody on a prophet and apostle, or the Lord himself, he will make bold to vent a sneer at doctrine, at principle, at law, at the gospel, at the very Cross of the Blessed Jesus. Beware, my youthful friend, how you cross the threshold of irreverence. The conversation of wicked persons is dangerous, their intimacy is defiling, their settled friendship is destructive. Walk not " in the counsel of the ungodly ;" stand not " in the way of sinners," lest at length you come to sit " in the seat of the scornful."

The beginnings of all transgression are remote, and the descents gradual. The soul would fly back in horror, if those extreme turpitudes were proposed, to which it will nevertheless come at length. Hence the derision of heavenly things must be presented at first under some less appalling form. For example, nothing is esteemed more lawful and acceptable in society, than ridicule of professing Christians. Their preciseness and supposed hypocrisy, their alleged breaches of engagement, their singularities of life or devotion, especially their real failings, backslidings and sins, become almost the stock in trade of the small dealer in church scandal. One might readily think, from the censor's complacent chuckle over the inconsistencies and falls of Christians, that every such delinquent was a scape-goat to bear away his own sins. Every successive generation has had its several crop of disparaging or opprobrious names, by which to designate God's children, in the dictionary of the scorner. They are the 'Zealots,' 'Devotees,' 'Precisians,' 'Puritans,' 'Methodists,' the 'Saints,' the 'Godly.' "They that sit in the gate, speak against me," says the Psalmist, "and I was the song of the drunkards." * The gatherings of ungodly men, in all ages, have been enlivened by the grateful strain of a derision aimed at serious and conscientious persons; and the playhouse, a synagogue of Satan, shakes with vociferous mirth, when the scruples of pure minds are held up to contempt. The prophet declares his separation from such assemblages: Jer. xv. 17: "I sat not in the assembly of mockers, nor rejoiced." If there is any meaning in what Scripture says of God's special regard for those who trust in him, let mockers beware how they choose them, in their religious character, as objects of indignity.

* Ps. lxix. 12.

Ministers of the Gospel, though in a sense public representatives of Christ's cause, are individually as open to criticism as any persons on earth. Not only are they compassed about with human infirmity, they are made by their very post peculiarly conspicuous. It is not wonderful that they have sustained showers of scorning. Especially if they have upheld the majesty of law, if they have denounced vice, if they have run counter to the fashionable, licentious, apostate Christianity of the day, if they have preached the sovereignty of God and the gratuity of salvation, they have had obloquy and contempt for their lot. Many a shaft is aimed at the heart of religion, through the person of the ministry; for he who would be afraid to reproach Christ, may attain the same end by satirizing his servants. Let the ambassadors of God lift up their voice against any prominent abuse, and straightway the journals, which reflect the baser interests and grudges of society, will beset their path with greetings like those which David received from Shimei, the son of Gera, who "came forth, and cursed still as he came, and cast stones at David." 2 Sam. xvi. 5. And if the preachers of the Word were more fully to discharge their function in declaring that gospel which is foolishness to the unenlightened and a stumbling-block to the proud, they would be yet more "filled with the scorning of those that are at ease, and with the contempt of the proud." Ps. cxxiii. 4.

Upon further inquiry, we shall find, however, that

all this opposition to the persons of Christians, has a deeper origin, in hostility to the spirit, principles, and life of religion. The pride, the scorn, the contemptuous laughter, the malignant sneer, which are a sort of persecution, directed against those who uphold Christ's cause, are immediate products of depravity, and of the carnal mind, which is enmity against God. The antagonism is one of ages; nay, it is one pointed out by prophecy: "I will put enmity between thee and the woman, and between thy seed and her seed." Cain and Abel are types of the scoffing world, and the suffering church. The first-born man "was of that wicked one, and slew his brother. And wherefore slew he him? Because his own works were evil, and his brother's righteous." To which the loving Apostle adds the caution: "Marvel not, my brethren, if the world hate you." 1 John iii. 12, 13. A similar allusion to a typical pair of brothers, is indicated by Paul, when he says of Ishmael and Isaac: "But as then, he that was born after the flesh persecuted him that was born after the Spirit, even so it is now." Gal. iv. 29. The mutual repugnance is radical, being between contraries infinitely remote, that is, holiness and sin. The modes of exhibiting this proud hostility are various. One of the most frequent, and that which we are now concerned with, is the arrogant derision of what is good, as evinced by manner, gesture, language, act, or the silence of bitter contempt.

The great standard of right is God's perfect Law, in

which all moral excellence is summed up, as light is gathered in the sun. Holy minds admire and love the law, feeling themselves sweetly and unconstrainedly in union with it. Unholy minds are conscious of a secret opposition between their natural tastes and the intense spirituality of the divine law. Restraining grace, religious training, and the common or special influences of the Holy Spirit, keep this enmity in a certain abeyance, in those cases where sin has not pushed its victim towards the brink of positive impiety. But this brink is often fallen over, or at least looked over, by the thoughtless, the impure, and the abandoned. A large part of the world's sceptical and cavilling attack on the code of Christian morals arises from personal immorality. Proud selfishness kicks against the goads. What though the enemy wears a comic mask? his sardonic laugh is that of hate. The strict requisitions of the holy commandment are so distasteful to the self-pleasing offender, conscious of a crookedness which this plummet reveals, that he tries to laugh off the restless sentiment of obligation; and, but partially succeeding in himself, he makes the attempt with others. Ridicule of God's commandments, or of the just fears, scruples and tender doubts of our neighbour, is a sign that the soul harbours inward hatred of the law. " It was a severe retort which a young man lately made to an infidel, who was speaking against the divine legation of Moses. He had made many objections to the character of that holy man; and the young Christian said to him: 'There is something in the history of Moses that will warrant your opposition to him more than any thing you have yet said.' What could this be? 'He wrote the Ten Commandments.'"* Read parallel proofs of the immoral soil out of which scoffing grows, in the unholy lines of Voltaire, Rousseau, and Paine.

This uneasiness of conscience, in regard to precept and prohibition, when it concurs with self-conceit, haughtiness, and a low talent for impudent reply, constitutes the genuine scoffer of Solomon's photograph. You see his demeanour under criticism, advice, reprimand, and expostulation. Pride causes him to take his friend for an enemy; he is regardless of the truth uttered; inimical to the parent, the minister, the brother, the elder associate, the wife of his bosom; if any one of these dares to touch his sore, he resents the supposed affront with words of bitter ridicule. Behold thy likeness, O, misguided sinner! "A scorner heareth not rebuke." "A scorner loveth not one who reproveth him." "Reprove not a scorner, lest he hate thee." "He that reproveth a scorner, getteth to himself shame."† In all these, and in other places cited, the same Hebrew word is used. It involves the notions of vanity, mocking, treating with mimicry and illusory speeches, satire, sneer, sarcasm, irony, and reckless disregard. The counterpart of this picture is in many a household, as many a disappointed father, many a heart-

---

* Life of Dr. Waugh.   † Prov. xiii. 1, ix. 7, 8.

sick mother knows full well. Up to a certain age, children, unless precociously vile, yield themselves in docile compliance to the parental voice. But, alas! except where Grace has early wrought, there comes a disagreeable crisis, of greater or less duration. Family training arrives at the stage first of shyness, then of forwardness, sometimes of bitterness. The foolish boy, governed more by companions of the school or the street, than by his wisest, dearest protectors, sets up to be wiser than his father. The frivolous, vain, selfish girl, corrupted by the daughters of the ungodly, from whom she takes her tone at some fashionable but heathenish school, turns upon the mother who bare her, and tosses the head, with imaginary knowledge of the world, and disgust at old-time maxims of modesty.

It were well if intolerance of rebuke were confined to childhood and youth; but we encounter it in every stage of life. Though one of the sincerest acts of true friendship is the bringing into the right way of one who has strayed, it is nevertheless true that, in things moral and religious, scarcely any one relishes attempts to lead him back from wandering, or to prevent his flying from the track. Tell your neighbour that his house is too gaudily furnished, that his children are sadly perverse, or that he himself drinks too much wine, and is drowsy and muddled after dinner, and you run the risk of losing an acquaintance for your pains. If to this you should add serious admonition respecting his eternal state, and the need of preparation for death, you would be likely to have in return severe jesting, if not scoffs.

"Fools make a mock at sin." The enemy of souls continually allures them towards the persuasion, that it is a small evil. Who can believe that yonder timid youth, flushing with the colours of Virtue, will one day laugh to scorn the reprovers of his profaneness or his dissipation? Yet we see such changes every day. Society is always suffering from perverse banter and coarse humour, directed against rigid morals. The thefts, defalcations, peculations, forgeries, fraudulent escapes from obligation, full living on other men's money, and filthy purchase of votes and verdicts, which are at once the opprobrium and the rottenness of certain classes in modern society, are fostered and brought into development by what young men hear in the houses where their business lies; by jokes, which imply that a clever operation is worth some moral risk; by pleasantries about lying and stealing, under decent names; and by contemptuous pity of the tortoise-like habits of a former age. Let us in justice observe, that we have, in the highest places in the world of trade, men whose names are unsullied, and whose voice authorized by experience, would, if permitted, chastise the sharper and the villain, under whatever garb of mocking and persiflage he might lurk. Such animadversion is useful to those who look on; as indeed is the detection of every arrogant pretender. "Smite a scorner, and the simple will beware; and reprove one that hath understanding, and he will understand knowledge." And again, "When the scorner is punished, the simple is made wise." The public award is generally right and final, in respect to one who has distinguished himself by sneer, sarcasm, and arrogance; for, as Solomon says, "the scorner is an abomination to men." Prov. xxiv. 9.

It is not easy to stop upon the downward slide of sin; and hence he who begins with trifling and badinage, upon subjects of duty and grace, will descend, unless divinely stayed, to the degree of undervaluing his own danger, and making light of God's threatenings. This is the foolhardiness of transgression. There is a sublime, silent delay about the Divine Justice, which leaves rash sinners under the delusion, that, against a Lawgiver so longsuffering, they may offend with impunity. If every Cain were marked the very instant he shed blood, and every Ananias struck dead upon the utterance of his lie, scoffing at judgments would be impossible. But the awful tread of justice is slow, and so the depraved soul grows bold. "Because sentence against an evil work is not executed speedily, therefore the heart of the sons of men is fully set in them to do evil." Conscience sleeps, and therefore the sinner thinks the sin is not on record. "He hath said in his heart, God hath forgotten: he hideth his face: he will never see it." Ps. x. 11. In Ezekiel's time, the idolaters who polluted the very temple-chambers by secret imagery, said, "The Lord seeth us not; the Lord hath forsaken the earth." The same folly and wickedness bear like fruits in later days; and when these depraved tempers find vent in words, and corresponding demeanour, we have the Scorner named in divine threatenings

Unbelief and unholy daring may attain such a height, as madly to try their strength not only with menaced, but with actual wrath; and creatures have been found, who, amidst the falling bolts of judgment, have stood out against the Creator and Judge in arms. A cheat, of course, is, in such cases, put upon oneself, as if there were a chance of escape after all; or, as if these inflictions were not judgments for sin; or, which is more common, as if infinite mercy would at length remit. When scornful offenders laugh at war, famine, pestilence, and other tokens of divine displeasure against sin, whether national or individual, denying all providence in such events, and baring the head to receive any storm from such quarter, they only re-enact the part of ancient unbelievers, who cried, "The evil shall not overtake nor prevent us." Amos ix. 10.

But on whatsoever side we turn, we find exposures of the fundamental evil, on which all these contempts repose, as all later formations on the primitive base. It is depravity of mind and heart in regard to Almighty God; disbelief of his being; derogation from his attributes; forgetfulness of his presence; disregard of his infinite purity; hardihood towards his awful justice; in a word, it is practical atheism which makes the scorner. " Wherefore doth the wicked contemn God? he hath said in his heart, Thou wilt not require it." Ps. x. 13. Every form of sin involves something of the horrid evils just named; for who could sin under the thorough and constant influence of right views and feelings towards the Divine Majesty? "Thou God seest me," so far as it sinks into the heart, is a preservative against transgression. But sin begets sin; yea, one sin begets numberless sins, and one violation of law and conscience, leads to other violations, and these to more, till the fearful progression ends in open profligacy, insult to the Eternal King, and speedy destruction. No one knows, when initiated into some lower degree of Satan's lodge, whether he may not penetrate to the highest. This makes it dangerous to parley with temptation. Judicial blindness befalls those who voluntarily put out the light of education and conscience. One sin, in God's awful judgment, becomes the punishment of another. The crime which the youthful sinner now looks at with shuddering, as it stands before him in his path, he may one day see behind him, among the dim, cloudy beginnings of his career, the earliest steps of his enormous transgression. It is a greater evil to scoff at the religion of others, than to be simply irreligious ourselves. Many ties must be rent, many walls overleaped, and many guards cut down, before the race of evil attains to open derision of truth and duty. Opposition to God's spiritual agency, and ascription of Christ's words to the Evil One, accompanied with deliberate utterance of the same, in scoffing language, constituted that blasphemy against the Holy Ghost, which hath no forgiveness, either in this world or that which is to come. And he who treads under foot the Son of God, and counts his blood unholy, " hath done " so it is written, " despite unto the Spirit of grace." Heb. x. 29. Those, therefore, who are tempted to make merry with divine realities, with the Word of Salvation, with the work of the Holy Ghost in the revival of churches and the conversion of sinners ; especially those who, from levity, folly, inconsideration, deference to bad example, or temporary gusts of pride and passion, indulge themselves in ridiculing such as begin to seek the salvation of the soul, should beware in time, lest, abandoned to themselves, they make shipwreck of all principle, and find their lot among hopeless scoffers. " Judgments are prepared for scorners, and stripes for the back of fools." Having thus tempted Satan, they may be led by him into an incapacity of believing ; having sneered at all that is pure, august and heavenly, they may, amidst the ruins of their faith, be haunted by spectres of multiform doubt ; having challenged God to forsake them, they may spend their decline in ever learning, yet never coming to the knowledge of the truth ; for, " a scorner seeketh wisdom, and findeth it not." And these are cautions peculiarly needful at times when the Spirit of God manifests his agency in the churches, humbling and melting believers, and convincing the impenitent ; and when, likewise, Satan, in his prime character, as adversary and arch-scorner, is busy, breathing into his children, at the corners of the streets, in the haunts of vice, and alas, in the editorial chair, foul blasphemies, which may turn away men from the great salvation. We have no fear for the church of the living God, from the mocking laughter of surrounding foes; though "they return at evening," "make a noise like a dog, and go round about the city." Ps. lix. The people of God will still rejoice in his power, which shall lead them on to triumph. But, for the scoffers themselves, we tremble; and are ready to address them in the words of Paul at Antioch: "Behold, ye despisers, and wonder and perish; for I work a work in your days, a work which ye shall in no wise believe, though a man declare it unto you." Acts xiii. 41. It is a dreadful fall, from haughty scorning of God's ways, down to grovelling vice and drivelling falsehood: such contrasts have we seen. The freethinker and the heretic, after deriding the mysteries of Scripture and the inspiration of prophets, have sat down to prate of endless, unintelligible dreams, and to sit at the feet of spiritual mediums, so named in their jargon. Safer, my brethren in the Lord, is it to trust in Him, " that frustrateth the tokens of the liars, and maketh diviners mad; who turneth wise men backward, and maketh their knowledge foolish." Isaiah xliv. 25. O pray to God, beloved hearer, that he would keep your conscience tender, and your mind reverent, lest from one degree of profane scorning you proceed to another, and at length reach the point of those who crucify the Son of God afresh, and put him to an open shame. At present, you think this acme of impiety far from you, and so I trust it still is. But consider, I pray you, who it is that holds you back from such enormities, and shrink from every form, or sentiment, or speech, which could grieve that Spirit of grace. "Quench not the Spirit," in yourselves or in others. And that you may make all sure, turn your back upon the world, the flesh, and the devil, and, going to the Lord Jesus, take him as your Saviour, Teacher, and King.

VII.

SALVATION TRACED TO GOD THE FATHER.

SALVATION TRACED TO GOD THE FATHER.*

JOHN iii. 16.

"For God so loved the world, that he gave his only-begotten Son, that whosever believeth in him should not perish, but have everlasting life."

WHAT verse of Scripture is more deeply engraved on our memory? Where is a passage to be found which has been more frequently uttered in Christian assemblies? Is there one which more fully comprises the essence of the Gospel plan? Or could we choose a divine saying of our Lord better suited to guide and elevate our thoughts?

Here is Jesus speaking of himself, and declaring why he came from heaven to earth. Here is the provision of mercy traced up to its eternal fountain, in the

* New York, May 16, 1852.

infinite benevolence of the Most High. Here is the river of compassion widening towards all nations. Here is the door of escape set wide open, from hell to heaven. And here is the direction how any willing soul may gain entrance to that way. My brethren, it is matter which interests us all; for we are all unholy and subject to condemnation; we are all in jeopardy; we are all hastening to death, yet naturally desirous of everlasting happiness. And in these words we have a Saviour offered to all. The subject is God's love, and the method by which this love may become our personal salvation. If God should vouchsafe to carry the truth home to your heart this day, he would thus make it a temple of the Holy Ghost. And I affirm without hesitation, that the words of my text, if received in their spiritual meaning and with firm persuasion, are able to make you wise unto salvation through faith that is in Christ Jesus.

Does God the Father really love the world of sinners? and what is the character of this love? These are the questions which we have to answer. We may vaguely assent to the existence of such love without deeply entering into its grandeur. Accompany me, while we consider, first, the reality of this love, and secondly, its degree. Both are exhibited by means of a great and marvellous gift.

I. THE REALITY OF THE FATHER'S LOVE TO THE WORLD IS SHOWN BY HIS GIVING HIS SON. The words upon which we have come to meditate set forth this great and overwhelming argument for the love of God: He gave his Son. Small words sometimes contain vast meaning. In the solemn act of worship called an oath, and in the form of it so often uttered and heard with lightness and irreverence, So HELP YOU GOD, the immense weight of the imprecation lies in the shortest monosyllable so; that is, may Almighty God so help you, or the reverse, as you now declare the truth. In like manner the text revolves on the same brief adverb, as the principal hinge of its significancy. By what proof or evidence are we convinced that God loved the world? And how great was this love? The answer is, God so loved the world that he gave his only-begotten Son. This is the demonstration of the love in its reality, and the measure of the love in its greatness. And if God so loved the world as to make a sacrifice of infinite value, the love is such that it passeth knowledge.

The heathen had no such being in their crude mythology as a God of pure love. When the philosophers revolted against the incredible and corrupting fables of tradition and poetry, they formed various conceptions of a Supreme Intelligence; but the best of them fell infinitely short of the idea which a young child in Christian households acquires of a Being, infinite, eternal and unchangeable in wisdom, power, justice, truth, and goodness. As soon as we think of One who has all perfections, we think of One who is benevolent.

and if we add the conception of this Supreme Existence as coming forth from the solitude of his eternal majesty to create intelligent spirits, we immediately, as by a necessity of reason, conclude that he loves the creatures whom he has made. If we could stop here, all would be free from difficulty.

If we could truly regard the Most High as not only benevolent, but nothing besides; as loving every object, whether good or evil; as possessing no moral discrimination, as acting only and forever towards the happiness of all he has made; we should look with confidence toward the awful future of eternity, as assured that, whether pure or sinful, we should be made blessed forever. And some take this view; thus founding on a partial idea of divine excellence the destructive scheme of universal salvation. But on this hypothesis we can never explain the enigma of the universe. If God were all love, and in such a sense as to be nothing but love; if God had no end in creation but to make his creatures happy, there would of course be no unhappiness in the world. The proof that such a view is false, stares us in the face on which side soever we turn our eyes. For is the existing earth, to go no further, full of unmingled bliss? Answer ye, who pass lifetimes of sorrow; ye millions of sufferers by disease, war, and a thousand deaths. The fact, as we see it and feel it, disproves the assumption that God has no other principle of government than that of promoting universal happiness. Unless, indeed, we deny his sovereignty, diminish his perfection, ascribe the present state to some rival divinity, and thus upturn the very basis of all religion, natural and revealed. If God's sole object in creation had been to secure the absence of all unhappiness, no sound mind will deny that he had power to effect it. If, as the fact shows, the case is tremendously the reverse, we have no escape from the conclusion, that along with the disposition to make his creatures happy, there were other divine attributes which allowed the possibility of pain. We must affirm this, or else refuse God's permission to the present state, or deny the perfections or very being of a God. As we shrink from these dreadful tenets of chance and atheism, we are forced to bow down and acknowledge that our plummet cannot sound the depths of the divine immensity. We must own, with adoring fear, that the Infinite One has reasons of awful state why even misery should be allowed to enter his dominions. And we justly look for these reasons in those other attributes of Jehovah, which are revealed no less clearly than his goodness.

God is infinitely holy. He is so by the eternal necessity of his nature. He cannot deny himself. He is and must be forever opposed to all sin. It is his very nature, it is of the essence of his Godhead, to stand in eternal opposition to moral evil. All moral good is such simply because it conforms, we need not say to a divine command, but to the divine nature, as its standard. All moral evil is such, because it deviates from this eternal standard. But the two are necessarily and everlastingly opposed to one another. The will of God, which is our Law, is only the effluence of this eternal nature; and hence, creatures remaining the same, we cannot conceive of the law as otherwise than it is, or of a law demanding the opposite of what it now demands, or as demanding less than it now demands; in other words, less than perfection. This tendency of God's nature to demand conformity in moral creatures, belongs to his essential glory, and we call it his JUSTICE. It is not for us to ask why He created man; or why he created him a free agent, or what is the same thing, capable of sinning. He has done so; and shall not the Judge of all the earth do right? We might deem it wiser and holier to make a world in which no sin and no pain could ever exist; but that such a purpose was not necessarily demanded by God's holiness, we learn assuredly from the fact that God actually designed the world which we see. There may be reasons, nay there must be reasons, all unknown to us, why the greatest glory of God is, after all, most promoted by the very irregularities which we deplore.

Still it abides true, that our Lord is a God of love. No one attribute conflicts with any other. When free creatures, and creatures are not moral beings unless free, in the exercise of their freedom sin and fall, the consequence is misery. Let us not quarrel with this arrangement. The connexion of sin and misery may, for all we know, be as necessary as the connexion between the absence of light and the presence of darkness. Many things in our own experience, lead us to believe this to be so. We are never happy when we sin. Suppose a law given, the misery consequent on violating this law fixed as a penalty; the Word of God uttered to declare this connexion; and we at once behold God's Justice and his Truth committed on the side of Holiness, and against the sinner. Thus far we gain no relief by clinging to the assertion that God is good. It is true, eternally true. But how do we know that even Benevolence, on a large scale, may not be glorified by the punishment of obstinate offenders, when, even in civil society, cases occur in which the destruction of one life promotes the salvation of many? But these are mysteries which we are not called upon to resolve. Secret things belong unto God. The Justice and Truth of God are as clearly revealed as his goodness and mercy. They must not be thrown into opposition, but must forever co-exist. And the great all-important deduction which we should make, for the guidance of our thoughts, is, that if Mercy be ever displayed, it will be in such a way as shall hold up Justice and Holiness with undiminished and equal splendour. This is, indeed, the key to the whole Gospel, which is none other than a device of Infinite Wisdom to repair the evils of the fall, and thus show forth all the commingling perfections of God in magnificent and adorable harmony. All hues blend with consummate beauty in the rainbow around the throne. To effect this harmony was the intention of the most extraordinary transaction in the earth's history, namely, that He who made it died upon it. The difficulty must have been great which made so extreme a method necessary. No physical difficulty can be imagined in regard to God, for he is Omnipotent. By an act of sovereign will he could translate all souls from heaven to hell, or from hell to heaven. The obstacle to such a transaction can be none but a moral one. There is a sort of impropriety in asserting any such thing as difficulty, where God is concerned; but human language can do no better. It is only a way of saying, that to do this or that would be for God to deny himself.

Even in our own circle of experience, different principles within us may thus come into seeming conflict. The Judge may have to pass sentence on one whom he pities; here justice has to settle it with compassion. The parent is often called to punish the child whom he loves. It is easy for us to say that God might freely pardon any sinner, or all sinners, without any intervention or propitiation. I prefer at this time to rest on the reply—and it admits of no contradiction—that God has done otherwise, and has so proved that there was no other way. One thing, indeed, the Supreme Lawgiver and Judge might have done. He might have suffered the sentence to become absolute; have shut the door of pardon; and have turned away from the world of sinners, and left them to whirl away into the infinite spaces of increasing sin and misery. No man can say this would have been unjust, unless he is prepared to say that the law was unjust; for this was the demand of law. Especially might the offended Sovereign have so done, when the mode of doing otherwise involved the most stupendous sacrifice. And why not? Why did Divine Wisdom and Holiness pause, and suspend the lifted sword of vengeance? Why did heavenly condescension look upon ruined men? Oh, my brethren, it was because LOVE, boundless Love, stayed the hand of Justice, held the bolt of fiery retribution, and interposed itself between the descending edge and our condemned souls. If God were all Justice, and he is as truly just as loving, no redemption had been possible. If God had been all Love, and he is as truly loving as he is just, no redemption had been necessary. But because He is both Justice and Mercy, and because Justice demanded satisfaction, and Mercy pleaded for remission, " Righteousness and Peace kissed each other;" and Love hung on the arm of paternal severity, while Wisdom pointed out a method to reconcile both.

To our poor limited faculties, this has to be represented under figure of a conflict of attributes; but, in reality, there is no conflict in God. To our apprehension, there seems a series of counsels and a change of plan; but there is neither succession nor mutation in God. Still the highest philosophy commands us to abide by the childlike expressions of the Bible. We shall never comprehend this mystery better than when, as in our early days, we regard God as angry against sin, yet desiring not the death of the sinner. This love for sinners must have been unutterably great, or there had been no such event as the Crucifixion.

And let me with more than ordinary earnestness implore you not to misapprehend this love, by an error which is common among shallow theologians. I intend those, who think of God the Father as less loving than the Son; as more rigorously just than the Son; as in some sort a relentless and implacable sovereign; as originating no tender mercies, and thirsting for the blood of vengeance, till appeased by the Son. Into such extremes some may be led by the inadequacy of all earthly words and figures to represent heavenly realities. No, beloved brethren, the GOD of our text, who gives his SON, is God THE FATHER. He is as clearly the God of Love. There is no conflict between the Father and the Son; and there is a divine harmony in their acts; for whatsoever things the Father doth, those doth the Son likewise. The adorable Son of God is co-equal in infinite justice and hatred of sin. The adorable Father is boundless in love and compassion. From him came the whole scheme of salvation. "For God so loved the world, that he gave his only-begotten Son, that whosoever believeth in him should not perish, but have everlasting life." Thus far have we dwelt mainly on the reality of this love. True, this it was impossible to do, without frequent glimpses of its degree; but now more particularly let us bring this into review, by meditating with you on the extent of this divine love, as manifested in its grand testimonial.

II. THE GREATNESS OF THE FATHER'S LOVE TO THE WORLD IS SHOWN BY HIS GIVING THE SON. Not that you or I, or angels above us, can take the gauge and dimensions of this divinity of goodness. With us they look into the chasm, with folded wings, and murmur, Oh, the depth, the depth! Yet, again, they learn enough to burst forth into chorus, while the shining retinue, reaching from earth to heaven, breaks forth in the doxology, "Glory to God in the highest, and peace on earth, good-will to men!" Love is measured by its gifts and sacrifices. Greater love hath no man than this, that a man lay down his life for his friend. God's love is measured by the gift and sacrifice of his Son. But while we repeat and adopt the words, who will assume to comprehend them! God gave his Son, but who can take the measurement of the gift? for who can ascend to the height of his glory, or descend to the depth of his humiliation? Who hath entered into the dread chamber and pavilion of that eternity before all worlds, in which the Only-Begotten, who is in the bosom of the Father, dwelt in the plenitude of the triune bliss, the Word, which was with God, which was God? Lose yourself as you may in the delightful contemplation of this wonderful glory, you are still baffled in every essay to gaze more nearly into the empyrean majesty, or seize the dazzling lines of that transaction, when it was decreed in council that God should become man. Yet with reverent intentness of adoring thought, we may, through a veiling cloud, discern so much as the Spirit has seen fit to intimate. No man knoweth the Son but the Father, and he to whom the Father shall reveal him. From the recesses of that unapproachable glory, "dark with excessive light," proceeds a voice which syllables the sentence dear to every penitent and thankful soul, "God so loved the world that he gave his only-begotten Son." Here are tones which cause the inmost chords of humanity to vibrate.

The word Son carries its peculiar touching charm to any parental heart. An "only Son," is of all phrases that which wakes affectionate yearning here about our sinful hearths. Faint shadows are these of the things in heaven. He who has chosen to be known as Father, has chosen to reveal the eternal Word as Son, and as "the Only-Begotten of the Father." Divine paternity is inscrutable. Divine love is as far above human love, as God is above the creature. Yet we were made in his image, in order to know a little of his heart; and the sentiment, though vastly unequal, is the same in the points intended to be believed.

God gave his Son. In intention and decree he gave him. In covenant he gave him. Looking on man as helplessly fallen, he gave him, as purposing him to be man's Saviour. In the garden of Eden, now stained with deadly sin, he gave him, and anticipated the words of curse by words of blessing. Throughout the tedious tracts of the long Judaic night, when clouds and transient rays struggled together, in a coloured haze of types and vision, he gave him, the Messiah yet to come.

But fully and actually and with transcendent love he gave him, when the Word became flesh and dwelt among us, full of grace and truth. And then, consummating the boon of eternal destination, he gave him, when, amidst a quaking earth and a shrouded heaven, it pleased the Lord to bruise him, when his sword awoke against the Man that was his fellow; and when Justice, as a weapon of death, steeped itself in the heart of humanity embraced by Godhead, and the Holy One, at the acme of his dying pangs, cried, IT IS FINISHED.

The thoughts need repose after such a contemplation. Sit down, oh believer; sit down with the beloved John, and with the Marys, amidst the effusion of the water and the blood, and tell, if you can, the magnitude of this affection. It is divine. "Herein is love, not that we loved God, but that God loved us and *gave his Son*."

Would you feel it more? Look in that other direction, to the damned world. Measure the sin and sorrow of a state which but for this sacrifice had been yours and mine. That we should not perish but have eternal life, was the motive of this gift. Raise your eyes to that "eternal life," and meditate the glory and the bliss, till you somewhat forget the seductive pleasures of time. All this is signified by the gift of God's only-begotten Son. Once more turn inward and attempt an estimate of your own demerit. "God commendeth his love to us, in that, while we were yet sinners, Christ died for us!" What! still unrelenting! Are no gentle affections stirred within you, this day, by God's chief argument? With what can we hope to move you? Behold here the hell you have deserved and sought; the heaven surpassing your most adventurous imagining; the Cross of Jesus, where the just God becomes the Saviour. This is the great sight which has melted the hearts of all generations of those who have been saved. And I have yet to add, if I would not withhold the principal theme of my commission, that *God the Father gives the Only-Begotten Son this day in the offer of the Gospel.* To you is the word of this salvation sent. The great atoning action was not to be concealed, but to be published to all nations for the obedience of faith. There is no restriction. To whom, do I hear you ask, is this offer tendered? To the world, I answer; to all who hear the "word of the truth of the Gospel." To you who have come hither this morning; to every one of you; from the hoary despiser to the babe who only begins to comprehend the words. By whom may it be accepted? By sinners. "This is a faithful saying, and worthy of all acceptation, that Christ Jesus came into the world to save sinners." If the greatest offender of all the sons of men were to rise revealed as such in this assembly, I am authorised to address him as included in this invitation of abounding grace. This Gospel was preached first at Jerusalem, and made known to those who crucified the Lord of glory. "Therefore," cried Peter to the pentecostal multitude, "let all the house of Israel (the very nation which had committed this sin of sins) know assuredly, that God hath made this same Jesus, whom ye have crucified, both Lord and Christ." The apostle's declaration, and all subsequent preaching, have held forth the same Gospel, or good news of God's love in giving his Only-Begotten Son. By this alone have perishing souls, in all ages of the dispensation of grace, obtained eternal life; and the proffer is now to you. To you, my hearer, however hardened in your sins and however destitute of all right feelings, this way of immediate escape is held out. The fountain which burst forth from the rock smitten at Golgotha continues to follow the march of our desert pilgrimage; and the terms are, as of old, "Whosoever will, let him take the water of life freely."

Before closing the service, I must lay before you, in few words, one provision of my text. It concerns the mode of becoming interested in this gracious gift of God. The mode is by believing; "that whosoever *believeth* in him should not perish," etc. Gospel faith is the cordial believing of this message. Some of you, let me joyfully think, have already believed, do now believe. Your language is, "This is my beloved, and this is my friend. He found me fainting in the wilderness. He lifted my head. He spake words of comfort to me. He strengthened me with strength in my soul. And all this he did by pouring a flood of light on his own person and work, by making this great object stand forth prominent and luminous, that is, by working in me faith."

But there are others whose language is, "Nothing is more mysterious to me than the saving character of faith. I believe these truths; and yet I find no relief for my burden." To such a one I must, in all respect and love, speak a word of contradiction. No, my anxious hearer, you do not believe the Gospel. Or, at at any rate, since there are degrees in faith, you believe but faintly. You have been looking too long and too much at self, and too little at the Saviour. If you believed that GOD SO LOVED THE WORLD, you would see and know that even for you there is room in the bosom of infinite Compassion. If you believed that Christ Jesus came into the world to save sinners, and by specification, the chief of sinners, you would see salvation brought home to your own heart. If you believed that Grace is abounding, free, present, made over by gift to just such as you, in all your hardness and all your guilt, and that the very first saving act is that of acquiescence in this gratuity, you would gaze with wonder and gratitude on the pierced hands and feet and the opened side, and would exclaim with Thomas, MY LORD AND MY GOD! If you believed, you would turn away from the study of your wretched self, and being all absorbed in another object, resplendent, soul-entrancing and divine, would joyfully cry, "God forbid that I should glory, save in this." And it is just because you still refuse to let go your hold of something within you; because you doubt the capacity of Christ's love to embrace you as you are; in a word, because you do not believe, that you persist in perishing with a condemned world.

The difficulty does not lie in any want of atoning love or gracious provision. The sacrifice has been made; it is infinitely pleasing to God; it is accepted; it can never be repeated; it can never be added to; it stands before the universe in immutable, consummate glory. Nor does the difficulty lie in the nature of faith, as though it were complicated, mysterious, or unintelligible; it is one of the very simplest actings of the human soul. But it lies in this, that you do not apprehend in a spiritual manner the precious, the ever-blessed truth to be believed. You see God under a false aspect, as a hard, exacting Lawgiver and a relentless Judge. You look on Christ as coming to you with some legal conditions to be fulfilled in you, before He can be yours. And justly conscious that such conditions are wanting in you, you stay away from the fountain of life, and will forever stay away, till the light of God dawns on your erring mind. Now, my sorrowing friend and hearer, now you have arrived at what is perhaps a critical point in your history. Will you flee to Jesus Christ to-day? Will you perish, or will you believe? Whatever is your determination, note it when you go home; "This day I have chosen Christ," or "This day I have rejected him." For it is noted in heaven.

VIII.

DYING FOR FRIENDS.

DYING FOR FRIENDS.*

JOHN xv. 13, 14.

'Greater love hath no man than this, that a man lay down his life for his friends. Ye are my friends, if ye do whatsoever I command you."

FRIENDSHIP is a sacred word, belonging as truly to Christianity as to morals. It is such a relation of man to man, that from mutual esteem, admiration and attachment, rather than from regard to interest, each contemplates the person of the other with complacency and benevolence, each desires the welfare of the other, and delights in his company ; and consequently each is ready to fulfil the wishes of the other and to make sacrifices for his pleasure. It is a flowing of soul to soul. It is—so says the Roman adage—to will and to refuse the same things. Wretched is he, who cannot go to experience for his definition ; for " poor is the friendless

* New York, March 13, 1853.

master of a world!" We need not go to the Damon and Pythias of Gentile story, or even to the touching records of David and Jonathan in the Old Testament. The Gospel assures us, that in the circle around our Lord, there was one disciple whom Jesus loved. Friendship never rose to so sanctified an exaltation. We do well, therefore, against certain perverse philosophers, to include friendship among the Christian virtues, and to practise it in the daily intercourse of life. Even in common society, its triumphs are sometimes beautiful and ennobling, but it is nowhere so pure and unearthly, as where it subsists between souls which have been touched by the Spirit of God. Then it is a fountain which wells forth from the Cross of the heavenly Friend. But we are this day to ascend a yet loftier eminence, and to contemplate a friendship which exists between Christ and the believer. The word seems to acquire a new and heavenlier acceptation, when we apply it to Him who is above all blessing and all praise. And this we shall do, in meditating on the delightful words of the text.

This relation then of friendship is sustained by the Lord Jesus to his people. His whole life was a series of blessed friendships. There are no pictures of attachment like those of Bethany and the upper chamber. The Twelve, the Seventy, the holy women who companied with him, the thousands of less distinguished disciples, all stood to him in the relation of friends. It was not merely John, who reclined on his bosom, or

James and Cephas who shared his more sacred retirements, or Lazarus whom he loved, or Mary and Martha who ministered to him; but all who hearkened to his words and sought his companionship. He was so unlike us who preach his gospel in degenerate times, that he associated visibly and at the banquets of the Pharisaic great, with persons who had lost their character, and was designated as the friend of publicans and sinners. To every diversity of people he showed himself accessible; as indeed he is, still the most accessible being in the universe. The most abject offender against purity felt reassured by his forgiving rebuke, and the very leper cast out of human habitations, and the demoniac haunting tombs and charnel-houses, ventured to accost him. How much more near, and delicate, and solemn, and rapturous must have been the interviews with his chief disciples, in those days on the mountain and on the plain, when thousands swarmed forth from city and village, and spreading themselves on the green grass were fed by his wonder-working bounty, and his yet more marvellous words; those voyages on the little lake; those mighty gatherings on Sabbath evenings, when the synagogue was out and the sun was going down, and they came flocking, with wives and children, to the house where he was guest, and spread their sick and dying on the earth at his feet; those evenings during the high festivals, when, as we know, he did not tarry in the great city, but pursued his quiet path among olives, across the ravine of Kedron, and up the ascent of

Olivet, to Bethany, and probably to the house of Lazarus; those walks through the length and breadth of the land, in which, accompanied by eager groups, he discoursed of divine counsels and things of the kingdom. In all these conjunctures we behold him the FRIEND, in every lofty and every tender acceptation of that pregnant word. All who accepted him were his friends. He admitted them to the title; he treated them as such. And now that, in his human nature, he is no more on earth, he just as really sustains the same relation to all who truly believe on him and partake of his Spirit. It is this sacred alliance which is brought prominently forward in these discourses of the first Communion season.

The highest proof of friendship is, when friend, as in this case, dies for friend. We do not pause for proof of this proposition. Children understand it; it sinks into the deep conviction of the heart. Death is so dread an evil, that all a man hath will he give for his life. A man will give many things for his friend, vast labours, vast possessions, yea, all things, before he will give his own life. Sometimes we find one willing to give the hazard, to run the chance, that is, to risk life for a friend; but absolutely and without reprieve to give the life, is a different matter. We do not think so meanly of sanctified human nature as to disbelieve it possible. Scripture does not allege that it never happened; Christ does not allege it. We believe there has been many a parent, who, on fit occasion, would die for a child, many a wife for a husband, nay, many a loyal soldier for his prince. But what we affirm is, that when this occurs, it is the indubitable testimonial of the highest love. Other marks may deceive, but this is infallible. If a human friend had died for us, we should cherish his memory with a sentiment little short of idolatry; for we cling with passion and reverence to one who has even jeoparded life for our sakes. This, then, is the acknowledged principle, on which the Lord Jesus founds that which he has to say respecting the love he bears to his disciples. It is a matter not for proof but meditation.

The amazing truth which we have to contemplate is, that this conclusive proof of attachment Christ actually gave. The church is founded on the fact, that Christ died for his friends; he made them friends by dying for them; for they were once foes. "For when we were yet without strength, in due time Christ died for the ungodly. For scarcely for a righteous man (or a man barely just and upright) will one die; yet peradventure for a good man (a man attaching himself to us by affectionate kindness) some would even dare to die;" unusual as is the spectacle, a rare and singular instance might be found in the lapse of ages; "but God commendeth his love toward us, in that, while we were yet sinners, Christ died for us!" It is the great lesson of scripture and sacrament. Has it become a weariness to you? Then your hearts have never been touched by renewing grace; you have never sickened at the evil of sin, you have never rejoiced with the transport of faith. There is a power in genuine experience, which freshens the oldest doctrine to the heart of the believer, and makes him come back to these truths as to breasts of consolation, ever new with the sincere milk of the word. For which cause, the sacrament that sets it forth, so far from losing value and attraction by repetition, is sweetest to the old disciple and the pilgrim near his journey's end.

The death of the Lord Jesus Christ for his people is pronounced by divine authority to be the grand argument of his love; and they feel it to be so. Hence they love to celebrate it. He uttered these touching words to the wondering and sorrowing group, just before the great event. His eyes saw what was hidden from them. He was already, in purpose and dedication, a sacrifice. It was anticipated as a glory: "Father, the hour is come; glorify thy Son!" Already, as the Lamb of God, was he bound with cords and palpitating upon the altar; already his soul was troubled, preparing for "the strong crying and tears" of the awful night. He had a baptism to be baptized with, and was straitened till it should be accomplished. The cup which his Father was giving him was already in his hands. When he spoke of dying for his friends, he had a perfect foresight of the scenes which were to mark the next few eventful hours. It was not the simple article of death, the bare separation of soul and body which he contemplated. He saw the mysterious shadow of Gethsemane, the agony and bloody sweat. He saw the midnight assault, the arrest, the hurrying by torchlight from tribunal to tribunal, the cords, the scourging, the robes of scorn, the insults of the populace, the languor, the exposure, the ignominy, the blasphemy, the crown of thorns. He saw the accursed tree, the nails, the spear, the desertion, the blood and anguish, the complicated dying. He saw this to be a substitution, a suffering for others, for friends, for those who should forsake and deny him, for millions who were as yet his enemies. And seeing all this, he said, with an emphasis which we can now better understand, "Greater love hath no man than this, that a man lay down his life for his friends."

Let our powers task themselves to devise a testimonial of love which shall be equivalent to this. Reason and imagination are at once baffled. And yet we do not begin to apprehend the magnitude of the Divine affection, until we take into view the nature of Him who evinces it. Man, simple man, might testify great love, and testify it by voluntary death, by death unmerited, by death surrounded with every aggravation of torment and shame, by death for the unworthy. This would be affecting and sublime, yet only finite and comprehensible. But, as we love to sing, and to sing without emendation: "God the mighty Maker dies, for man the creature's sin!" The person who sustains this suffering is a Divine Person. It is the infinite Jehovah descending to take the place of the rebel, and to subject himself to penal humiliation and agony.

This is the great fact of Christianity, the capital demonstration of the Godhead. Here we behold more of the heart of God than in all his works and Word beside. Into these things the angels desire to look; and the cherubic emblems hover and stoop over the ark, bending to inspect the mystery of the law covered by the golden propitiatory and the mercy-seat sprinkled with divine blood. For this there had been a preparation in all the foregoing economy of the Old Testament, from the sacrifice of Abel to the Passover they had just been celebrating. All altars and priesthood, all unblemished victims and sprinkling of blood, every sin-offering, scape-goat, basin and hyssop-branch, whispered of the dying love that was to come. All types and emblems foreshadowed this testimony of divine friendship. There has been a reverberation of holy echoes in the arches of all temples, betokening the descent of divine compassion. The fires of all combined sacrifices have been going up, to presignify the whole burnt-offering of this great Day of Atonement, in which the sword of God is to awake against the man that is his fellow, and the perfect and final victim go up in the flame of unutterable and infinite consecration. Christ dying for the ungodly is the central radiant point, at once of divine dispensations, of the world's history, of gospel theology, and of sound experience. Who, by searching, can find it out! Herein is love, not that we loved God, but that God loved us! And it is all that we "may be able to comprehend with all saints what is the breadth and length, and depth and height, and to know the love of Christ, which passeth knowledge, that we may be filled with all the fulness of God." The demonstration is complete, but its measures are unfathomable. When we would know how much Christ loves his friends, our only reply is by looking to the Cross; but we must look forever. Though we come again and again, with the concentrated powers of all human minds, we cannot reach the mystery, "the breadth, the length, the height." "Angels that hymn the Great I Am, fall down and vail before the Lamb." It is reserved for the heavenly state to launch out more fully into the ocean of inquiry, and to survey the unattainable dimensions of such a friendship from God to man.

The love of Christ in dying for sinners, is the ground of their friendship towards him. "We love him because he first loved us." And this in two senses; for first, if he had not loved us beforehand, there would be no grace dispensed to work these affections in our hearts; and secondly, it is the consideration of this sovereign and abounding love which awakens these affections. We are fully aware that a different teaching, from a school of metaphysical theology now near extinction, has been heard in our churches; but among other blessed characteristics of the late Revival of Religion, we note a return to the catholic experience of all Christian ages, in regard to the power of God's love in Christ as recognized by the repentant sinner. "The love of Christ constraineth us." Here is the springhead of all true religious feeling. Mistake on this point may be disastrous. General views of the divine character and excellencies may produce awe, dread, adoration, and approval, but will never enkindle love. The friends of Christ are made such by contemplating his love, and especially by acts of faith directed toward his Cross. O that I knew how to treat this subject aright! Perhaps it will be safest to turn aside from the beaten track of a merely doctrinal theology, and make an immediate appeal to the experience of the new creature.

Take a view, then, first, of the soul unrenewed by grace. And let us not choose for one instance any extreme case of wickedness or unbelief, but one of those gospel hearers who fill our assemblies and are somewhat instructed in the elements of religion. Let it even be one who is not totally indifferent to the things of another world. But he is, nevertheless, as yet unreconciled. Often does he endeavour, in thought, to present to his view the sublime idea of the Great Supreme. Yet, if he makes frank confession, the thought is not pleasing. He is overshadowed and weighed down by the conception of one so high, inflexible, and distant. The spirituality of God overwhelms him; holiness dazzles and humbles; inexorable justice terrifies. The startling truth perpetually reappears, that this pure and mighty Jehovah is his enemy. The distance seems a gulf which cannot be transcended. Efforts at obedience and reform recoil in a sense of incapacity and guilt. There is no inward view of the way in which

God can be just, and yet justify the ungodly. These are among the most wretched moments of life. Often does he turn away from the subject because it increases pain, reveals sin, and awakens enmity. As often is he reluctantly drawn back by the unwelcome fascination of the awful verities. Thus it is with many during the tedious night of legal conviction. They seem to grow worse rather than better. They are under the Law, and the law worketh wrath. Condemnation increases; for, "by the Law is the knowledge of sin." It is far more distressing than the former state of carelessness; into which, indeed, the sinner vainly and madly tries to return. No ray of benign compassion breaks through the cloud of justice which envelopes the throne of the Infinite Majesty. No tender melting views of sin dissolve the heart, which seems harder than before, and sullen in its unloving discontent. No approaches to God as a Father sweeten the acts of a constrained devotion.

But after a while a signal change is experienced. This same soul, disheartened at the sight of its own turpitude and illdesert, and appalled by the view of divine perfections, is led by grace to contemplate a new object, and to turn its regards to the person and work of the Lord Jesus Christ. The sinner forgets himself for a little, while he gazes on this unparalleled exhibition of divine love. He beholds God descending in human nature, to become the sacrifice and the priest. He sees the immaculate Redeemer dying on the cross for the sin of man. He recognizes an atonement and satisfaction to justice, sufficient to obliterate the guilt of all mankind. He opens his heart to the Friend of sinners. He perceives that the whole work of redemption is out of himself, and independent not only of his obedience but of all his feelings and exercises; and that the salvation thus complete is offered and made over to sinners and to him, just as he is, without any preliminary qualification. Now, for the first time, he is struck with the sovereignty of uncaused love. It is nothing in him, or his state of mind, but all in this act and demonstration of heavenly friendship. He owns with wonder the freeness of the salvation. He can no longer deny that it is for him, now, this moment, on his acquiescence and acceptance. The chief of sinners may come. God loves the chief of sinners; the proof is in the Cross; the proffer is in the Gospel; his bonds are loosed; his self-righteousness is left behind; and before he is aware his sinking soul is lifted in the arms of the Son of God, and his tears are wiped away by the pierced hands. Now, now, he exclaims, I perceive the truth which I have heard and repeated a thousand times. God is love! and love to me! God forbid that I should glory, save in the Cross of our Lord Jesus Christ! He is a believer, and while he believes he loves. He sees the things that are freely given him of God. He understands what is meant by salvation without money and without price. God is no longer a taskmaster and a judge, but a merciful and reconciled

Father, through Christ Jesus. He is astonished to observe, that all along, during his whole protracted struggle, this infinite love has been equally free and equally offered; that God was willing, but he was unwilling; and he adores the grace which waited for his delay. Unutterable is his grateful attachment to Jesus his Saviour, who is now the chiefest among ten thousands. He is the friend of Christ; no longer a servant but a son; and from this moment onward he lives a new life, by faith in the Son of God, who loved him and gave himself for him. Thus the love of Christ, as dying for sinners, is the ground of their friendship toward the Redeemer.

There remains an important truth to be considered: the true and certain test of being the friends of Christ, is obedience to his precepts. " Ye are my friends, if ye do whatsoever I command you." It is not profession, my brethren, which makes the Christian. When Naomi had her affecting interview with her two daughters, " Orpah kissed her mother-in-law, but Ruth clave unto her." On this very paschal evening Simon Peter was louder in profession than John; and if Peter's character had been always no other than during the denial, he would have been only a hypocrite. You cannot quarrel with this test. It is reasonable, it is incontestible. The proof of Love afforded by obedience is triumphant. Good works are not our passport to heaven in the way of merit, but they are the infallible fruits of faith, and so the best criterion of attachment to the Lord.

The operation of this principle is not abstruse or recondite. We recognize its influence in the little child who does what is bidden out of love to the parent; in every act of compliance or service that proceeds from common friendship. But it rises to its highest achievements in the grateful affection of the believer to the crucified Redeemer. That dying love works wonders and constrains obedience. Recur to the tender instance, when John and Mary stood at the foot of the accursed tree, gazing intently on the Son of God in his last pangs. "When Jesus, therefore, saw his mother, and the disciple standing by whom he loved, he saith unto his mother, Woman, behold thy Son! Then saith he to the disciple, Behold thy mother!" Can we doubt the result? Love wrought obedience. "From that hour," that hour of love and death, "that disciple took her unto his own home." And when the sacred body, devoid of life, was lifted from the cross and made ready for burial, and when the holy women and such friends as had not fled looked on the heavenly countenance of One who had loved them unto the end, charging upon their own sins the awful event and expiation, do you need argument to convince you that they felt bound forever to obey his highest wish? All the way down through the ages of faith, this love has acted itself out in obedience. Every believer owns in his inmost heart, that he lies under an obligation to surrender all to Him who died for him; as one redeemed not with corruptible things, such as silver and gold, but with the blood of Christ as of a lamb without spot or blemish. Ye are not your own; ye are bought with a price. "Henceforth," says Paul, "let no man trouble me, for I bear in my body the marks of the Lord Jesus."

More need not be said as to the certain efficacy of the principle; but a word is necessary as to the extent of the obedience. It is universal. "Whatsoever I command you;" that is, all my commands. In this life, the obedience, indeed, is never perfect as to its acts and the details of duty, " for in many things we offend all." Yet it is universal in its purpose or intention. True love, taking its origin from the Cross, does not discriminate and select, does not prepare for some duties and refuse others, but girds itself for all. And this tendency of the will is a better evidence of grace than any or all particularities of performance. Friendship to Christ perpetually utters this language: I will hear what God the Lord will speak. Lord, what wilt thou have me to do? I will perform whatsoever my dying Saviour has commanded. I have sworn and I will perform it, that I will keep all thy commandments. He therefore who speaks thus, I will obey up to a certain point and there I will stop short, is not the friend of Christ. He who says, I will keep the commandments at large, but this or that commandment I will not keep, is not the friend of Christ. He who whispers to himself, I will be pure in all things else, but this one secret, cherished, easily-besetting, darling sin, I will not relinquish, is not the friend of Christ. The true disciple abandons in purpose and endeavour all known transgression. And if we turn our thoughts inward to find one particular exercise in which more of true religion is concentrated than in all others, we shall discover none more certain than this, the absolute unselfish oblation of the whole man—mind, heart, and will—as a sacrifice to Christ, out of thankful regard to his dying love. And when, as is sometimes our privilege, we stretch forth our hands to the bread and the wine at the Lord's Table, and rely on that broken body and shed blood for our justification, the faith thus exercised is inseparably connected with a solemn act of self-renouncing and unreserved dedication to the holy will of our redeeming God. This is the living sacrifice, the reasonable service, with which God is well pleased. To keep back any thing is to deny our Lord. He asks only the heart; but he asks it all. And in gracious souls he has it. It is his. He has bought it with his Cross and Passion, and carries it away in triumph; embracing in almighty arms the ransomed one, who desires no other Master, and is happy to be borne away captive by Him, whose commandments are not grievous, whose yoke is light, and whose service is freedom.

IX.

THE BLOOD OF SPRINKLING.

THE BLOOD OF SPRINKLING.*

HEBREWS xii. 24.

—— "The blood of sprinkling, that speaketh better things than that of Abel."

THE Old Testament is to some Christians almost a sealed book, especially in those parts which treat of the rites and ordinances pertaining to the tabernacle and temple. But this is an inferior stage in religious knowledge and experience, and should not be willingly rested in. After having obtained a just view of Christ as Mediator, from the clear representations of the New Testament, we go back to the system of Levitical types, and find it all there. It would be but an imperfect, undeveloped scheme of salvation, which should be derived from the New Testament without the Old. Indeed, the New constantly assumes and paraphrases the

* New York, January 15, 1857.

Old; and many of the most precious Gospel declarations of Christ and the Apostles would be unintelligible hieroglyphics, without the key of Moses. It is the manner of these great teachers to express spiritual, gracious and eternal things in terms of the temple and the altar; and this in conformity with a system, planned from the beginning, in which all the type and symbol of the Mosaic economy is a preparation for the clear light of the latter day. Those, therefore, are the most deeply taught and richly experienced believers, who, after having learnt the simple principles of evangelical truth in the New Testament, go back with them to the Old Testament, and behold a hundredfold more beauty and majesty in the same truths as arrayed in the forms and laws of the Jewish service. In our endeavour, then, to find the Cross in the Holy of Holies, and the Gospel in those smoking altars, we have our best aid in the Epistle to the Hebrews, which might be named a Key to the Tabernacle, or the Old Testament explained by the New. The theology which results from such studies is diametrically opposed to that of the metaphysical and sentimental school, who cite little scripture, and almost ignore the gorgeous pageantry of the old priestly service. Though a distempered fancy may here, as elsewhere, work mischief, these rites, which fill so much space in the Pentateuch, admit of an application much more detailed than is commonly enjoyed; and under Apostolic guidance we shall do well to make ourselves largely acquainted with this neglected mine of truth.

Even cursory readers perceive the striking parallel between the bloody offerings of the temple and the oblation of our Lord and Saviour Jesus Christ; but few have taken pains to trace out the analogies, latent in the particular parts of sacrificial work, every one of which casts light upon the doctrine of redemption. At such a season as this, when every eye ought to be bent towards the atoning Lamb, we shall do well to enter somewhat into the more concealed significancy of this ceremonial, for the wine of sacred truth does not yield itself without pressure, and the honeycomb of grace requires its laden cells to be broken.

Consider with me, for a very few moments, the several steps which belonged to a regular and complete sacrifice, under the Aaronic liturgy.* FIRST, there was the selection of a suitable, unblemished animal, as the victim; let us say a lamb from the flock. This reminds us at once of the Divine election of the Only-Begotten Son, as the Lamb of God which taketh away the sins of the world. SECONDLY, the innocent creature was solemnly presented, for this peculiar purpose, near the door of the tabernacle. Answerable to this is the actual appearance of the Incarnate Son, in human nature, and especially his solemn separation and oblation of himself, the priest and victim being in this case one and the same. THIRDLY, we behold a most imposing ceremony: the sinner who offers sacrifice lays his hands

* Λειτουργία. Heb. ix. 21 et al. locis.

upon the head of the animal, confessing his sins. In the parallel instance of the scapegoat, the high priest is said to "put the sins of the congregation on the head of the goat." Jewish writers record the words with which this imposition of hands was sometimes accompanied: "I beseech thee, O Lord, I have sinned, I have done perversely, I have rebelled, I have done so and so (mentioning the transgression); but now I repent, and let this victim be my expiation!" Who does not recognize in this the sinner under the Gospel, who, with clearer views, comes not to the visible but the invisible altar; not to the son of Aaron, but the son of David and Son of God; laying his hands not on the lamb of the perishable flock, but on the head of the divine sacrifice, and saying, "I have sinned, I have done perversely, I have rebelled; let this victim be my expiation!" So closely did the Hebrew connect this ceremony with the acknowledgment of guilt, that it grew into a maxim, "Where there is no imposition of hands, there is no confession." They were equally accustomed to regard this laying on of hands as symbolically removing the guilt of sins from the sinner to the sacrifice. That which the Israelitish worshipper did, long before the Great Sacrifice on Calvary, and even before the slaying of his own typical offering, the Christian penitent now does by an act of faith, looking back to the oblation made once for all by the Lord Jesus. And every time he casts the eye of believing towards his humbled, scourged, buffeted, bleeding, crucified Saviour, he lays his hands anew upon the sacred Lamb, saying, Let this victim be my expiation! FOURTHLY, the sacrifice was slain, and consumed (sometimes wholly), upon the altar. This was the great atoning act. Here is blood for blood, and life for life. The basis of all its significancy is laid down, Lev. xvii. 11 : "For the life of the flesh is in the blood; and I have given it to you upon the altar, to make an atonement for your souls: for it is the blood that maketh an atonement for the soul;" or as some render it, "for the blood atoned through the soul." It is not the matter of the blood which atones, but the soul or life which resides in it; so that the soul of the offered victim atones for the soul of the offering penitent. In the imperfect but most speaking representation of type, the sacrifice of the innocent symbolic substitute goes up to God in the smoke of the burnt-offering, a sweet-smelling savour— if we may borrow another phrase from the vocabulary of Moses—a token and a pledge that the satisfaction is not only offered but accepted. It is by that which is here represented, to wit, by the self-oblation of the Lord Jesus Christ, that the breach between heaven and earth is made up; and so far as the efficacy of the atonement is concerned, the work is complete and can never be repeated. All other pretended sacrifices, bloody or unbloody, are profane mockeries and insulting disparagements of that sacrifice of Himself, "once for all," which terminated when Jesus cried, "It is finished!" FIFTHLY, and last in the order of sacrificial action, was the SPRINKLING OF BLOOD, to which your attention is more particularly called, as involved in the text, and as full of meaning appropriate to this ordinance. Aspersion or sprinkling is a symbolical act employed with both water and blood. The sprinkling of water is a token of symbolical cleansing, and is just as valid for this purpose, as if the whole body were washed by plentiful affusion or immersion, otherwise it would not have been so largely employed in the ritual language of the Old Testament. To sprinkle is to cleanse. Mark, therefore, Lev. xiv. 7, when a leper was to be purified: "And he shall sprinkle upon him that is to be cleansed from the leprosy seven times, and shall *pronounce him clean.*" As soon as he was thus bedewed, his consciousness responded, "Now I am ceremonially clean." It was to carry home this consciousness that the act was ordained. Among the "divers washings," (baptisms,*) we may confidently enumerate what took place in the consecration of the Levites, Numb. viii. Observe how they were cleansed: "Take the Levites from among the children of Israel, and *cleanse them.* And thus shalt thou do unto them to cleanse them, *Sprinkle* water of purifying upon them," etc. In another instance, where ceremonial defilement was contracted, a clean person was to take hyssop and dip it in water, and sprinkle it upon the tent and inmates; all which prepared the Hebrew

* Διαφόροις βαπτισμοῖς. Heb. ix. 10.

people for comprehending such language as that of God by the prophet: "Then will I sprinkle clean water upon you and ye shall be clean; from all your filthiness and from all your idols will I cleanse you," Ezek. xxxvi. 25. In all these cases, whether in symbol or reality, there was conveyed to the soul a divine purification and a sense of it.

Now, if we turn from the application of baptismal water to the application of sacrificial blood, we shall observe the analogy hold good, and shall see the rite conveying to the sinner a consciousness of acceptance with God. In regard to God, the slaying and oblation was enough: in regard to man, the blood must be sprinkled. God might be appeased, and yet the sinner might be destitute of any pledge that it was so. Hence the importance of the seal; just as in our day the importance of sacramental sealings, in regard to acts long since consummated. "This sprinkling of blood was by much the most sacred part of the entire service, since it was that by which the life and soul of the victim were considered to be given to God as supreme Lord of life and death; for what was placed upon the altar of God was supposed, according to the religion of the Jews, to be rendered to him." * But the same typical sprinkling reaches the offerer and sometimes the whole congregation, in token of their participation in the finished work. Those who honour God's Old

* Outram on Sacrifice.

Testament lessons will not turn away from a short examination of several cases as prescribed in the Law.

In the cleansing of one who had been afflicted with leprosy, after the slaying of one of the two sacrificial birds, the priest was to dip hyssop (among other things) in the blood, and sprinkle upon the leper seven times. Lev. xiv. This is a very simple and very striking service, in which the sprinkling of blood is used for purification.

But greatly more solemn is the next case, Lev. xvi., in which the method is detailed in which the high priest, once in the year, on the great day of Atonement, shall enter into the Holy of holies. A bullock, as one of the nobler animals, is slain and laid on the altar. Then, verse 14, "he shall take of the blood of the bullock and sprinkle it with his finger upon the mercy-seat eastward, and before the mercy-seat shall he sprinkle of the blood with his finger seven times." The mercy-seat, or, far more properly, the PROPITIATORY, was the awful centre of the shrine, displaying its golden effulgence above the ark of the covenant, and just beneath the covering wings of the overshadowing cherubim. To sprinkle the blood here, was to bring it to the throne of Jehovah, amidst the blaze of the Shekinah, unapproachable save by the typical Mediator. It was to declare before Infinite Justice, that the satisfaction was complete, by venturing even there with that which was the life and soul of the sacrifice. This is blood which "speaks." The apostle Paul refers to this, Heb. ix. 18,

"For when Moses had spoken every precept to the people according to the law, he took the blood of calves and of goats, with water and scarlet wool, and hyssop, and sprinkled both the book and all the people, saying, This is the blood of the testament which God hath enjoined unto you:* moreover, he sprinkled with blood both the tabernacle and all the vessels of the ministry. And almost all things are by the law purged with blood, and without shedding of blood is no remission." And after these striking words, the apostle goes on to show, that all this was done in antitype and reality, when our glorious High Priest entered into the heavenly places, to present the merit of his own most precious blood-shedding. As the whole virtue of the sacrifice resided in the life, which, as we have above cited, was in the blood, the solemn presentation of the blood was a sign that the oblation was complete; and the sprinkling of it on sinners was a token to them that the guilt of their sins was remitted. We have dwelt thus long upon an external rite, which many pass over as insignificant, because this is God's own method of conveying to us, in the most lively and impressive manner, the cardinal truth of propitiation and pardon. This, then, is that "blood of sprinkling," spoken of in the text.

The way is now open to us to inquire, How THE BLOOD OF CHRIST, THE GREAT ANTITYPE, "SPEAKETH

---

* Compare Luke xii. 20.

BETTER THINGS THAN THAT OF ABEL." Words need not be multiplied in exposition of the clause. The blood of Abel spake dreadful things, when God said to Cain, " The voice of thy brother's blood crieth unto me from the ground." It was vocal with wrath. It uttered the echo of God's vindicatory indignation against fratricide. It was the first human bloodshed, and an event fitted to strike by comparison and contrast. Now, in this view, 1. The blood of Jesus speaks atonement, satisfaction, and access to God's favour. And this it specially does as sprinkled or exhibited in the sight of the Supreme Majesty. It must have been an hour of breathless interest and expectation, when the hundreds of thousands of Israel, gathered on that high day in the tabernacle court, followed with their eyes the high priest in his pontifical array, with the graven jewels and names on his breast, as with stately mien and profound awe he passed towards the sacred tent, bearing in his hands the blood of the altar, and then, lost within the curtains, advanced to the invisible recess of hidden glory. But the gospel shows us something more august than this shadow. " For Christ is not entered into the holy places made with hands, which are the figures of the true, but into heaven itself, now to appear in the presence of God for us. Nor yet that he should offer himself often, as the high priest entereth into the holy place every year with blood of others; but now once in the end of the world hath he appeared, to put away sin, by the sacrifice of himself." The sprinkling of typical blood, in regard to God, declared that sin was atoned for, and that a way was opened for sinners into the Holiest of all. This sprinkling was accomplished when the Lord Jesus, by the blood of the everlasting covenant, made solemn entrance into heaven, in the name of his people, and when—if I may use Levitical expressions, familiar to the Gospel, and provided for this very end—he drew near to the primeval and real mercy-seat in heaven, and there left traces of his own divine blood, as though he said, "I have finished the work which thou gavest me to do; here am I, and the children whom thou hast given me. Spare them, for I have borne their sins in my own body on the tree; of which the pledge and testimonial is this blood, expressed from my human veins in Gethsemane, at the place of scourging, and on the Cross." And so everlasting is the remembrance of this in heaven, that John the Apostle says, in his Apocalypse, "And I beheld, and lo, in the midst of the throne and of the four beasts, and in the midst of the elders, stood a Lamb, as it had been slain." Still does the blood of Christ speak better things than that of Abel, by causing the merit of the Atonement to resound in heaven.

2. The blood of Jesus speaks peace to the believing sinner's conscience. One may be interested in the great salvation, and yet be destitute of certainty. We are constrained to judge thus concerning some of the best of God's people, in their moments of darkness and depression. The same blood which removes guilt by

being shed at the altar, removes fear by being sprinkled on the believing offerer. This is the great meaning of the sealing type. It was so applied to the people with some profusion, for the blood being put into basins, and having water mingled to keep it fluid, was conveyed on a bunch or bundle of hyssop bound up with scarlet wool, till it was all spent in the service. This rite of sprinkling was chosen of God as an expressive sign of the effectual communication of the benefits of the covenant to the persons so bedewed. The blood of Christ was not divided, as was that of the Levitical sacrifice, part being sprinkled on the altar and part on the sinner; but the efficacy of his one oblation produced both consequences. Yet we need both. Even though offered to God, it must be applied to us. The High Priest sprinkles our heart and conscience, as with the hyssop-branch; which explains the lamenting prayer of David, "Purge me with hyssop and I shall be clean." This application is wrought by the Holy Spirit; and how gracious is this effusion! We stand at a great distance, unable to serve God with any liberty, till he thus speaks peace to our troubled souls. This filial serving of the living God is expressly noted as the end for which the application is made, Heb. ix. 13; and let us here learn to rise from the type to the antitype: "For if the blood of bulls and goats, and the ashes of an heifer sprinkling the unclean, sanctifieth to the purifying of the flesh, how much more shall the blood of Christ, who through the Eternal Spirit offered himself without spot to God, purge your conscience from dead works, to serve the living God." Then we can serve with well-grounded cheerfulness, when the warm effusion of Christ's blood is felt upon our hearts, which so lately were sinking with dread.

Let us go back to the Law, which is our school-master to bring us to Christ. Here is an offender, standing pensive and awe-struck before the altar of burnt-offering. He has presented his victim; he has laid on it the hand of confession and imputation; he has seen it deprived of life and laid upon the blazing altar; he has gazed upon the series of symbolical actions expressive of the atoning work and satisfaction to God. But one thing is yet wanting, to assure him of his individual participation in this justifying righteousness; he receives from the hyssop-branch the sacred drops upon his vestment and his person. His pardon is sealed. He says, with a new consciousness, "I am free! This oblation avails for me! God remits my guilt for the sake of sacrifice!" Now all this takes place in a New Testament sense. The convinced sinner has a clear view of the plan of remedy provided in the Gospel, and of Jesus Christ as the one atoning sacrifice. At the feet of this Cross he confesses his sins. He beholds there a propitiation amply adequate for the pardon of a world. He approves the method, and honours its wisdom and love. He perceives the law exalted and God's anger turned away. This, so far as it goes, is faith; but peace is in abeyance. He knows Christ to be a Saviour, but he falters in claiming Christ a Saviour for him, until, O blessed moment! the veil is rent, the priest returns from the most holy place, and sprinkles him with the peace-speaking blood. Now he can cry, "I know whom I have believed;" "Christ Jesus came into the world to save sinners, of whom I am chief;" "My beloved is mine, and I am his;" "My Lord and my God!" Thus the blood of the covenant speaketh to the conscience better things than that of Abel.

3. As a case under the preceding, the blood of sprinkling speaks peace to the soul in regard to daily sins. Oh, shameful, dreadful word! Yet none more true. No dream is more directly opposed to the Scriptures than the pretence to sinless perfection. "If we say that we have no sin we deceive ourselves, and the truth is not in us." Every instructed Christian knows that he sins, by commission or by omission, every hour; and that he requires not only a primary reconciliation to God, on the ground of Christ's one sacrifice, but a constant renewal of the same grace, to keep him in favour, and particularly to persuade him of his acceptance, which is not always easy, in the face of those corruptions which break out even into act. A fair and most important distinction must be taken between JUSTIFICATION, which is a single act, accomplished instantaneously, once for all, at the sinner's first believing, and PARDON, which must be renewed day by day, though its efficacy depends upon the one original sacri-

fice. Such was the glory of that oblation, that it needed not to be repeated, in this differing from the typical sacrifices, which were reiterated as fresh sins arose. Heb. x. 1. "For the law having a shadow of good things to come, and not the very image of the things, can never with those sacrifices which they offered year by year continually, make the comers thereunto perfect. For then would they not have ceased to be offered? because that the worshippers, once purged, should have had no more *conscience of sins.*" But when Messiah comes, v. 10, we are saved "by the offering of the body of Jesus Christ once for all." Nevertheless, that which is ever-enduring in its value and prevalency needs to be applied to us frequently, to take away "conscience of sins;" that is, while there is but one SACRIFICE, there are many SPRINKLINGS. As long as we live, and every day that we live, our rising evils of heart and life are such as would destroy all peace, if it were not for the hyssop-branch in the hand of the Spirit. There is a two-fold application to the soul of Christ's atoning righteousness by the Holy Spirit; one, which is single, and never repeated, the effect of which is *to interest such soul in the redemptive acts;* the other, which is perpetually renewed, the effect of which is *to give peace* to the soul under a sense of pardon. That experience may justly be distrusted in which there is no going again and again to the blood of Jesus for new applications. Thousands have used the words of the great penitential Psalm, with a feeling of their necessity. The royal sinner knew that he had received the Holy Spirit, for he prays that he may not lose the gift. He knew that he had possessed the joy of God's salvation, for he implores that it may be restored. But at the same time he sues for fresh pardons: "Blot out my transgressions;" "Purge me with hyssop;" and for new peace of conscience, "Make me to hear joy and gladness, that the bones which thou hast broken may rejoice." The divine affusion of the sacred blood upon the heart and conscience, tends, as the Christian life goes on, to make the subject a more obedient and a happier Christian; which seems to be contemplated by the Apostle Peter, when he designates believers as "elect according to the foreknowledge of God the Father, through sanctification of the Spirit, unto obedience, and sprinkling of the blood of Jesus Christ." The same ideas of obedience and renewed pardon are presented in connexion by the Apostle John: "My little children, these things write I unto you, that ye sin not. And if any man sin, we have an Advocate with the Father, Jesus Christ, [who never sinned,] and he is the propitiation for our sins." The true oblation reaches that which Aaronic oblations could not reach, namely, the conscience; for Paul says, that those were gifts and sacrifices, that could not make him that did the service perfect *as pertaining to the conscience*." Grace and mercy result in peace, named in its higher measures the "peace of God which passeth all understanding." Love hath for its nature to make itself known and to have itself believed. The infinite love of God to the soul is not satisfied until it pours itself into the consciousness, saying, " I have loved thee with an everlasting love, therefore with loving kindness have I drawn thee." God might have postponed the disclosure of the soul's safety until the day of judgment; the blood might have been carried within the veil of the visible heavens, and offered at the cherubic throne, without ever being applied to our souls in this earthly state. But far different has been the gracious purpose of our High Priest, who condescends to assure us of our redemption, and to sprinkle us with his blood. The word of the Gospel, in the written revelation, precious as it is, and fundamental as it is to all edification within, utters assurances only of general favour. There must be a distinct act of the Spirit to carry this home to the individual consciousness. And so many are the doubts and misgivings, engendered by indwelling sin, that we need our beloved Saviour to tell us again and again that he is at peace with us and loves us still. The words which he employs for this purpose are the very words which stand recorded in his written testament; but they are uttered with a new tone of personal love and a voice trembling with individual compassion. And sometimes he vouchsafes to employ the idiom of signs and pledges, more penetrating than that of speech, and to address us thus: "Take, eat, this is my body: This cup is the new covenant in my blood, shed for many, for the remission of sins." But the retrospective sacrament would be as inoperative as the prospective sacrifice, unless there were superadded the gracious work of the Spirit within, applying the blood of Jesus Christ to the heart, and witnessing with our spirits that we are the children of God. More simply, the Divine influence increases faith, renders its object more clear, precise, complete and free from error, and makes its acting more constant and intense. In this the Word is greatly aided by the sign and seal. And when the word of promise, set forth in this two-fold way, is made good to the soul at the communion, the effect is the same as if the bridegroom's own lips audibly should say to the particular participants: "I am come into my garden, my sister, my spouse; I have gathered my myrrh with my spice; I have eaten my honeycomb with my honey; I have drunk my wine with my milk; eat, O friends; drink, yea, drink abundantly, O beloved!" Such invitations will be peculiarly welcome to those who halt with the wounds of recent sins, and who seem to hear the challenge, "Simon, son of Jonas, lovest thou me?" But as surely as the bread and the wine shall presently be offered to your taste, so surely Christ offers to you, sinful though you be, all the advantages of the blood of sprinkling.

X.

THE THIRSTY INVITED.

THE THIRSTY INVITED.*

Isaiah lv. 1.

"Ho, every one that thirsteth, come ye to the waters."

Who is there among us, that remembers near the home of his infancy or the play-ground of his youth, some cool and crystal spring, that burst forth from its covert of rock, or its margin of grass, and freshened all the scene around? Such an object of natural scenery lives long in the memory. To such a source of innocent delight we resort again and again, without weariness and without satiety. That which attracted us first, charms us still, and the reason is, that it is living, perennial and inexhaustible, yielding supplies to wants which are perpetually returning. As long as men thirst, they will value the clear cold fountain. But if,

* New York, July 9, 1854.

even in this temperate clime, we are often made to comprehend the invaluable excellency of this great and lavish gift to our craving humanity, how much livelier must be the feeling, in those torrid regions, where most of the scriptural scenes are laid! A spring of water is always a desirable object; but how surpassing its fascination amidst tropical heats, or in the scorching wastes of the desert, where the panting caravan looks out for hours to catch the first signs of verdure! Consider this, and you will no longer marvel at the large place which is occupied by wells and fountains, in the beautiful pastoral and nomadic pictures of the Old Testament. The literature of the patriarchs is eminently an out-door and a summer literature, which we best understand when we leave the luxuries and constraint of cities, and dwell abroad, under the fair heavens, and amidst the bright and picturesque surroundings of an oriental life. The imagination and memory of the Bible-reader are familiar with such objects in the ancient landscape; the wells of Abram, Isaac and Jacob; the fountain opened to despairing Hagar; the well of Rebekah, and the not less lovely well of Rachel; the well of Jethro and Moses; the palm-tree wells of Elam; and that fount of which thirsting David cried, "O that one would give me drink of the water of the well of Bethlehem, which is by the gate!" Bearing these associations in our minds, we can the better catch the meaning of promises which declare that the thirsty land shall become springs of water, and that God will lead his people to fountains of living water. But why seek remote illustrations of that which finds its prompt response in the bosom of all who ever were athirst? It is to such, in a spiritual sense, that the invitation of the text is addressed, "Ho, every one that thirsteth, come ye to the waters!" And we may, without laboured investigation, consider it as offering the benefits of the gospel to those who are perishing. I ask you on this holy day, to examine with me the fulness, the freeness, and the universality of the offered gift.

I. The fulness of the offered gift. It is water; it is abundance of water. There must be something in this natural object, which is suited to symbolize the provision made in the gospel for the salvation of mankind. Man is so constituted that he must have water, or perish. Give him all things else, but deny him every liquid refreshment, and you destroy his life. Nothing more forcibly shows this, than the familiar fact, that even on the vast ocean, the mariner, surrounded by a world of waters, must nevertheless carry with him the fresh products of the living fountain. The appetite for this supply is so strong, that when long ungratified, it becomes a frenzy. And how bountiful is the supply! In hill and valley the springs of water bubble up, with a sweet caprice and delightful irregularity, or the hand of labour penetrates deeply to the cooling vein, in both cases with a liberality like that which pours a vital atmosphere around our planet. The evaporation from earth and ocean, and the descent of copious showers maintain in plenitude this great reservoir for the cleansing and cheering of mankind. It is indispensable to the natural life of the race. And so is the gospel to the spiritual life. Men must partake of it, or perish. When duly enlightened, they feel this to be their condition, and thirst for righteousness. Such an invitation as that of the text implies that the supply is large; or it could not suffice for all. The provision of grace leaves nothing wanting, for the worst conceivable individual case, or for the utmost number of persons to be saved. We must be careful not to undervalue the remedial methods and so to limit the Holy One of Israel. In this case God has acted like himself, with a large and sublime munificence; more striking even than in the wonderful arrangements of original creation and providence, because these do not contemplate a creature malignant and self-destroyed. If any one thing, even the slightest, had been left undone, which was necessary to the salvation of the sinner, the work would not have had this completeness. But all is furnished.

It need not be here made an affair of argument, that the great demand is for a righteousness for those who who have none; that mysterious and potent something, which shall heal the difference between heaven and earth, answer the claim of law, turn away the wrath of Jehovah, cleanse the guilt of sin, give a title to life, and afford a pledge of continuance in a holy state and of everlasting blessedness and perfection beyond the grave. The all-comprehending gift is the gift of God's own Son. "God hath given unto us eternal life, and this life is in his Son." The Incarnation, the obedience and the vicarious suffering of the Lord Jesus Christ, are the source of all the streams which here issue in such fulness. But the point where above all others the waters gush forth from the smitten rock is the Cross of our Redeemer. There, when his last cry of pain is over, and out of his side issue water and blood, we have the consummation of a gift to man, which is full beyond expression. Sinners by myriads may come in, and yet there is room. The invitation may be large, for the provision is vast. Not only is the springhead of these mercies great, but it cannot be greater. The consideration of this is very necessary for the steady confidence of our faith; and this is felt most deeply in hours when conviction of sin is peculiarly pungent. The righteousness of Christ is infinite. We are made just by this, and by nothing else. Now that which gives to this righteousness any merit, gives it all merit. The divinity of him who obeys and suffers, exalts the meritorious obedience and suffering to a maximum. Were all the sons and daughters of Adam, who have been, are, and shall be, to gather in one numberless mass, with the Cross for its centre and object of desire, there were enough for all. When Jesus bowed his head and gave up the ghost, he completed a sacrifice which is absolutely illimitable. Yea, though all worlds were peopled with sinners, here were enough for all; we say not in God's purpose, nor in his covenant growing out of purpose, nor in the actual application of redemption according to covenant, but in the value of the Atonement. If more were to be saved, it would need no more righteousness, and no more effusion of the sacred vital flood, although the contrary has been alleged as our belief. If this is not fulness of redemption, we must despair of communicating this idea by language. And yet we must proceed to add to this statement in a particular respect. The atonement might be complete, and yet not be effectual. In God's holy purpose, it needs to be applied. Some have represented the covenant of grace as simply placing man in "a salvable state." We go further than this. Man may be in a salvable state, yet never reach a state of salvation. The plan of God proposes to bring men actually into the kingdom. The invitation is to come to a provided fulness of effectual grace; to faith and its consequences; to perseverance in holiness and everlasting life. These waters break over the verge of their receptacle, and seem to fall like the inviting spray of a great fountain, holding out promise of infinite capacity beyond all that is seen. Till we can conceive of something greater than God, we need have no fear of trusting the whole weight of our salvation on the method which he has revealed; for he has made it, so to speak, commensurate with himself; by laying his very divinity in pledge, and causing the value of the salvation to repose on the eternal glories of his own nature.

II. The freeness of the offered gift awaits our notice.

This is implied by the strong terms of invitation, Ho, EVERY ONE, COME YE! It is still more clearly signified by the words immediately following, where the figure is slightly modified, though the general idea of THIRST remains prominent; "yea come, buy wine and milk, without money and without price." It is not to a purchase, but a gift. The gratuitousness of the communication could not be more strongly expressed. It is here held forth and proclaimed with divine earnestness, that he who comes to the salvation of the gospel, receives it without any offer of recompense or any worthiness on his own part. The fountain of life has indeed its price, a price which has been paid. It cost the agonies and death of the Son of God. To secure our salvation it was necessary that a struggle and a humiliation hitherto unknown in the universe should take place. The price has been laid down, for us, but not by us. Eternal justice has been satisfied on our behalf; but to us the invitation is without money and without price.

The reiteration of this truth may strike some as needless. They are ready to exclaim, "Who doubts that the gospel is free?" In reply we must observe, that while no truth is more affirmed in our creeds, none is more denied in our practice. It is hard to make men believe, that they may come to the Lord Jesus Christ gratuitously, that is without any previous condition. There are few believers who do not remember the moment when this unconditional freeness of the gospel broke upon their minds as a great revelation. They had been lying long beside the pool of healing, waiting for some one to put them in. They thought there was a long and difficult preparation before they could venture to come to Christ. They interpreted the invitation as made to such and such persons, having particular qualities, and they were not sure that these qualities were in themselves. They could not approach the fountain because they did not feel enough; they dared not believe, because they did not grieve enough. Or, in some of the endlessly shifting varieties of delusive experience, they were setting a price on pardon, and seeking to make up the amount; they were working on their own hearts, to make them more fit for Christ; they were essaying a half-way work, which, without erasing the word "grace" from the record, should leave to self some of the glory of preparation. And the moment when all this was swept away, is memorable in the believer's history. It is the moment which immediately precedes FAITH. Up to this instant, he has been trying earnestly to do something, which shall make him more fit to receive Christ. Now, he sees that the whole deed of righteousness is done already, that its full value is offered to him in the gospel, and that he is authorized to accept it.

But so subtle and protean is self-righteousness, that even the free words of the invitation may be distorted into a legal condition. "Every one that thirsteth." The busy demon at the ear, who dreads nothing so much as that the sinner should believe, here whispers, 'But perhaps you do not thirst, or you do not thirst enough, or you do not thirst aright.' Such queries might indeed be urged forever, and run to an infinite series, if any sort or kind of preparatory condition were required. The question might still be, Do I possess this condition? And it is a question which can never be answered. We have known persons who were engaged during the entire course of their lives, in agitating the inquiry, whether they feel enough; whether they feel their need of Christ; whether they are not too unfeeling; whether they hate sin enough; whether they are sufficiently in earnest. All these are proper questions, *in relation to another matter;* but here they are out of place, and serve only to keep the sick away from the physician. These lingerings and scruples arise from a source, to which I beg your profoundest attention. They arise from founding hope on feelings of our own, instead of founding it on God's veracity. The truth of God's promise is the everlasting rock. Here build and be safe. All else, especially all within us, is a quicksand. The word of the Lord endureth forever. True faith utterly forgets itself, and credits the assurance of God's free pardon. It looks away from its own worthiness and its own unworthiness, and hears God saying "Ho!" "Come ye!" Come without money and without price! And it comes : without turning to the right hand or to the left. The question no longer is, What am I? but what is God? Is he true? Has he spoken? It sets to its seal, that God is true. It acquiesces in a righteousness already finished. So it saves.

The doctrinal truth which lies at the basis of all these exercises is, that the procuring cause of our acceptance with God, is not any thing done by us, or in us, not any work, preparation, frame or feeling, but only the perfect righteousness of the Lord Jesus Christ. The trumpet sounds thus, from over the fresh fountain, "Whosoever will, let him take of the water of life, FREELY." And the persuaded soul, now taught the great lesson of self-renunciation and self-forgetfulness, and swallowed up in admiration of the stupendous gift, falls into the open arms of dying Love.

When a wretch, just at the point of expiring with thirst, opens his lips to receive the cool reviving draught, does he think of this act of his, though voluntary, as constituting any previous claim? As little does the believer ascribe any meritorious virtue to his sinful believing, which is no more than his acquiescence in the method which God has provided. Thus unbounded is the freeness of the offer which is made of all evangelical blessings, including pardon, peace, and eternal life.

III. The universality of the offer is here: "Ho, every one that thirsteth." Salvation, or in other words, Christ the author of salvation, is offered to all nations of mankind. The topic is so large and inviting, that I must admonish myself to dispatch it in few words. Nothing is more familiar to us, nothing was more strange to the ancients, than that the favour of God should be made coextensive with the world; and while it was a stumbling-block to Judaism, it was the theme which, of all others, lifted Paul to the highest rapture, as apostle of the Gentiles. The middle wall of partition was broken down. The vail of the temple was rent. The waters of life, seen in vision by Ezekiel, broke over the Eastern threshold of the temple, and flowed in a mighty stream. Jesus offered himself a sacrifice not for Israel only, but for all nations. "He is the propitiation for our sins," said John, "and not for ours only, but for the sins of the whole world." And coincident with this purpose was the great commission, "Go ye into all the world and preach the gospel to every creature." It was foreseen by Isaiah, the evangelical prophet. In God's wonderful providence, grace had been limited to a chosen nation, but now the system was enlarged, so as to be a universal religion, and henceforth "God commandeth all men, everywhere, to repent." This blessed gospel is now on its triumphant progress through the earth, and the day is fixed in the counsels of heaven, when it shall be "made known to all nations for the obedience of faith." The gracious summons is to all realms and peoples.

The blessings of religion are hereby offered to men of every state, class and character. To be a human creature, and to hear the gospel, is to come within the comprehension of this grace. It proclaims its fulness and freeness to young and old, rich and poor, learned and simple, high and low. It does not single out certain classes as those who may be saved, but declares that all may be saved, even as all who are athirst may drink. It does not indeed promise that men shall be saved in their sins, for the very salvation delivers from sin, and this water is in each who tastes it a well of water springing up to everlasting life, and manifesting its virtue by holiness of thought, affection, speech and work. But as to the prerequisite for accepting the offer, the Gospel does not demand holiness; this does not yet exist; it is to be produced; it is part of the benefit to be sought. No one should suppose himself excluded from the promise of free pardon and life, because of any thing in his condition or character. Provided he come as a sinner all athirst for pardon, and believes in Him who justifieth the ungodly, he is sure of welcome. And, as no man's proper name is in the grant, the only warrant which *any* has, is the promise which is made to *all*. The general invitation becomes particular, when it is appropriated by faith. In a mutinous army, if the commander or prince publishes an act of forgiveness and amnesty to all who are willing to receive it, the rebel who hears, believes and submits himself, makes the gratuity his own. Thousands hear the terms of the gospel, but do not accept them. But the reason why any one accepts and is saved, is not that the provision was not sufficient for all, or the proffer of life equally made to all, but simply that he, an undeserving wretch, yields to the moving of the gracious

Spirit, takes God at his word, and makes the universal offer his own particular salvation. To the very end of the present dispensation, the preaching of the gospel authorizes all sinners of mankind to come and be freed from sin.

More particularly, the salvation is free to the chief of sinners. This is necessary to its universality. If there were one degree of turpitude which was excepted from the general pardon, what sinful heart is there, which would not sometimes be tempted to think that degree its own? But there is none such. The infinite merit of Christ, which is the sole basis of the offer, proves that there is none such. The blood of Jesus Christ cleanseth from all sin. He is able to save to the uttermost, all that come unto God by him. There is no dye of guilt, which these waters do not cleanse. Considered in itself, there is no amount of iniquity which transcends the virtue of Christ's atoning sacrifice, or is beyond the reach of God's gracious invitation. The very murderous treachery of Judas might have been pardoned, nay would have been pardoned, on his faith and repentance. If there is a sin in our day which is unpardonable, it is such, not because the blood of Christ lacks efficacy, or because the promise of the gospel excludes it, but because such sin, by its very nature, rejects and despises the sacred blood and the gracious promise. Every one that thirsteth, though all crimes were accumulated and concentred on his head, may approach and be made whole. There are moments of conviction, in which you might attempt to convince the sufferer of any thing rather than that such sins as his can be forgiven. He admits that others may be saved; but not himself. The Spirit of God, in foresight of such cases, converted Saul of Tarsus, and has left on record that golden passage, for all ages, which ends thus, "I am chief." It is a doctrine most important to be preached, and to be often reiterated, in the spirit of the text, lest any rebel, however atrocious, should fail to admit the glorious universality of the offer. Some of the most signal trophies of grace, in which sovereign power and love have shone in the brightest colours, have been men whose crimes seemed to outrage heaven; but each of whom has learnt to cry with David, "Pardon mine iniquity, because it is great!"

The offer of life ought therefore to be considered by each individual hearer as addressed personally to himself. It is a counsel which applies to all divine communications made in the house of God; but pre-eminently to this, which offers eternal good to all without exception who will receive it to their bosoms. The day and hour have come, in which, after such long delays, you may find in Jesus a merciful Saviour. The providence which has brought you hither, and the influence which has opened your ear to hearken, make the message as truly your own, as if the voice of God in distinct articulation uttered your individual name from heaven. Christ, with all his benefits, is yours, if, forsaking all things else, you accept him as offered in this gospel. O be persuaded to bow the stubborn neck, and bring the long reluctant lips to these celestial waters!

And let me add a word to Christian believers, whether newly converted or far advanced in pilgrimage. To you also is the invitation given. This is not a well in the desert, of which you may only once taste and must then leave forever, but a river of life, at which you may perpetually slake your thirst. The Israelites all drank of that Spiritual Rock which followed them; and that Rock was Christ. The current from the smitten rock pursued the journeyings of the camp. The unchanging Redeemer in his fulness is always beside you and within your reach. As ye have received the Lord Jesus, so walk ye in him. Come buy wine and milk, without money and without price. You may be already justified indeed; but are there not a thousand wants within you which crave supply? Has not your path been through a wearisome land, and are you not sensible of an inward thirst, which nothing but spiritual refreshment can assuage? You need daily purifying; you need daily increase of knowledge; you need strength for the remaining journey, and healing for the fevered wounds of your conflict. Behold the boundless provision, and hearken to the liberal summons. Approach anew to Him who is the source of all your life, and who cries anew, "If any man thirst, let him come unto me and drink."

Blessed be God—the source to which we are invited is a familiar fountain. In regard at least to our knowledge of it, it was the household-spring of our childhood; and it has been our cool resort from the arid journeys of our mature years. And though we have, days without number, forsaken the fountain of living water, and hewed us out cisterns, which can hold no water, yet are we not deeply convinced, beloved, that there is none so full, none so heavenly, none so free! Many a time have we gone to it, all parched with the ardours of our wearisome path, and found the Diffuser of gracious refreshment ready to take us back and satisfy us with his love. Again the sound of falling waters is in our ears. From the clefts of the saving Rock, the holy stream breaks forth in profusion. "The Spirit and the Bride say, Come. And let him that heareth say, Come. And whosoever will, let him take the water of life freely."

XI.

THE INWARDNESS OF TRUE RELIGION.

THE INWARDNESS OF TRUE RELIGION.*

Luke xi. 40.

"Did not he that made that which is without, make that which is within also?"

THESE words draw our attention to religion as something inward and spiritual. In this they resemble the rest of Christ's instructions, which were intended to bring men to a service of mind and heart, rather than of outward observance. The piety of the Pharisees was altogether external. Hence they were shocked when this new teacher disregarded all their forms. One of their sect, who on this occasion was the host of Jesus, wondered at his approaching the repast without the prescribed rite of baptism. "And the Lord said unto him, Now do ye Pharisees make clean the outside of the cup and the platter; but your inward part is full

* New York, April 9, 1854.

of ravening and wickedness. Ye fools, did not he that made that which is without, make that which is within also?" That is, You forget that it is God with whom you have to do; God, who sees the heart; God, who created the spiritual part; God, who is a Spirit, and demands a spiritual worship. My single theme is, RELIGION AS AN INWARD WORK.

In attempting to exhibit the greatness of the work within, I shall observe the following order: 1. The value of single holy sentiments and emotions, especially in their bearing on the eternal state. 2. The consequent importance of the hidden life, made up of such thoughts and exercises, and the greatness of the Spirit's work in sustaining such life under the Gospel. 3. The unspeakable grandeur of the regenerating act, as the source of this life, and these emotions.

I. God's scale of measurement is very different from ours. He accounts that small which seems gigantic to us; and often esteems that great which we despise. Instances might be brought from things tangible and visible, though these are not to detain us. For example, the structure of a violet or the wing of a fly is more complex and wonderful than the steam-engine or the telegraph. When we seek for grandeur, we generally think of size or of multitude; being governed very much by our own organs, or the petty objects around us. Especially are we prone to err, when we compare things material with things moral. The two belong not so much to different classes as to different worlds. We cannot measure a good man against a mountain or a planet. We cannot adjust our balance and put a generous thought into one scale, and a thousand talents into the other. I may add, we are perpetually making this absurd attempt, and weighing spiritual realities in our earthly balance. The evil cleaves to us, even when we deliberately pass over into the domain of moral and religious truth. In estimating the results of pious endeavour, for instance, we are governed in a great degree by the eclat of the triumph, the publicity of the benefit, and the tabular show of statistical enumeration. The day of final revelation may bring into focal light and glory some objects which the world has not paused to look at. A poor widow cast into the treasury-box two mites, which make a farthing. The coin was base and trifling, and the act apparently insignificant. But the deed attracted the eye of infinite Wisdom, which penetrated beyond the ring of the paltry pieces, beyond the trembling wrinkled hand which timidly let them drop, behind the care-worn face of poverty and devotion, to the inward sentiment in that widow's heart. This it was which gave value to the donation. This it was which God regarded; setting on it a value above all the costly munificence of the opulent, above all the splendours of architecture in the temple, above all the glories of Moriah and the holy city, nay—for all that we know —above all the material excellencies of this great globe itself. Yet this inward sentiment was invisible, imponderable, inappreciable. When visitors were once admiring the library of a great prelate, he said, "One thought of devotion outweighs them all." It was well said, and in a spirit belonging to our subject; but who can bring forth the scales to verify the conclusion? The holy thought is too ethereal to await our tests. It may be evanescent, lasting but a moment; yet there it is; it is known of God; it is the product of his Spirit; it stands forever recorded with his approval. Let us freely confess, that in our common estimates we misjudge with regard to the greatness of that which is mental and moral, especially where it is accompanied with no extension in time and space. "Perform the duty of this single moment," said the eccentric but pious Lavater, "and thou hast done a good deed for all eternity." One holy act, one heavenly thought, one upward wish of an infant soul, may be precious in the view of God. Our notion of greatness is different; we should say to a man, Go raise an army, subdue a kingdom, build a pyramid. There is a sublimity in moral rectitude, or conformity to the will of God, which we are ill qualified to measure, in our present state, where every thing is referred to physical laws. These laws, in their grandest manifestations, as those of orbs moving in harmonious silence through the astronomic spaces, are only as lasting as perishable matter. The hour may come when the attraction of gravitation shall no longer be as the squares of the distances; but the hour shall never come, when faith, and love, and the image of God shall not be infinitely excellent.

Does it not follow from this, that we are in danger every moment of underrating those operations and exercises which take place in the secrecy of the human bosom? Even when we make them objects of attention, which is seldom, we rate them by the visible results of the acts which they produce. But their moral quality has a value, independent of all overt effects, a quality which confers on these effects all their excellence. It is a solemn consideration, that the very emotion which this moment is bubbling to the surface of our internal fountain, may have a world of importance, may be intensely sinful or intensely holy. And on this estimate, so much beyond our reach, may be founded some of God's awful determinations respecting the acts of creatures in this state of trial. Of one thing we may be certain; the infinitely holy and omniscient Judge takes cognizance of what passes in human minds. He cannot look with indifference on the thoughts, imaginations, wishes, purposes, choices and habits of our souls. Slightly as we regard them, each has its moral estimate in God's account. And this gives a serious importance to inward things, which, if duly pondered, might modify our whole view of life. Now it should be observed, that all these rapid transactions of the immaterial nature within us are absolutely hidden from the gaze of others. Man looketh at the outward appearance. The subject of these sentiments or emotions may be a recluse, the tenant of a deserted isle. Nevertheless he is a soul, spiritual and immortal, and there is that going on within him which may outstretch in its greatness the boundaries of the vastest monarchies. Your lines of measurement by inches, leagues, or semidiameters of orbits, cannot be applied to spirit. That soul, on God's scale, may be longer and wider and higher and deeper than the whole material universe. Its acts and fluctuations have a relation to God's law, to God's image, and to immortality. Hence the great work of God is expended, not on the mundane fabric, which is to perish, but on the soul, which is to last eternally.

To approach a juster valuing of inward things, pause with me a moment or two on this last thought. Man looks forward to an interminable existence. The continuity of his being is unbroken. His conscious identity is to suffer no rupture or suspension. We naturally suppose that his knowledge will increase, and with it his capacity of emotion. Now the grand truth of our system is, that our immortal condition is to be fixed here. Happy or miserable are we to be, according to what we are in this world; and happy or miserable in degrees apportioned to our soul's state here. The character, though not the amount of holiness, is settled before death. The entire series of our experience below is a preparation for what awaits us above. There is not a purpose, a desire, or a state of mind, in this our pilgrimage, which has not its bearing on the eternal career. What importance does this confer on even the most transient exercises of the soul! Each is the seed which embosoms in itself a fruitfulness of immortal joy or woe. Let no man, then, think lightly of what is passing in those darkened chambers. Angels—if angels see aught of human hearts—hang with unutterable interest over the struggles of the spirit, as now it wrestles with a strong temptation, and now emerges into light and love. Man beholds it not, save by some faint infrequent indications; but all these workings are naked to the eye of God.

II. The importance of the inward life, made up of such thoughts and exercises, is obvious. Reflection on so much as has been offered, will lead us to reconsider some of our hasty judgments as to the importance of that invisible work which is going on behind the curtains of every undying soul. To the gifted eye there is revealed a battlefield, over which principalities and powers hover, with a wistful interest, and in comparison with which the conflicts of a Pharsalia or a Waterloo— if we leave out the consideration that each combatant is, after all, an immortal creature—must dwindle to a mere contest of insects. In a sense higher than they ever dreamed themselves, is the saying of the ancients true, that the soul is a microcosm, a little world. It has its periods, its convulsions, its wars, its deluges, its revolutions and its conflagrations. To each of us, individually, it is more than the universe itself, being his all; and this it is, silently, secretly, and without respect to other creatures. Each soul has that to transact, in God's sight and with God, which throws into the rank of things indifferent the shock of nature and the crash of worlds. The eternity beyond is made to depend on the character this side of death, as holy, or the reverse. Who can refrain from reiterating the exclamation of our Lord, "What shall it profit a man if he gain the whole world and lose his own soul?"

A reigning error among all those who profess Christianity, is, that we care more for that which is without, than that which is within. And even when we seem to seek inward reformation, we begin too frequently with the stream instead of the fountain, the external rather than the internal. It is a great moment in any Christian's life, when he awakes to the conviction, that of all the works he has to perform, the greatest is within his own breast. Even if it had no fruit outwardly, this culture would be momentous in regard to eternity; but indeed it is the very germ of all fruitfulness. "Keep thy heart with all dilligence," etc. Ministers and people may give themselves too exclusively to visible activity, and then the lamentation is in place, "They made me keeper of the vineyards, but mine own vineyard have I not kept." This arises from low thoughts of the work of God within the soul. "Did not he that made that which is without, make that which is within also?" Nay, did he not rather make that which is within? Is it not this, on which his eye is chiefly fixed? The humblest thoughts of ourselves are consistent with a profound reverence for the spiritual influence in our bosoms. It is a great and awful fact, that the Holy Spirit inhabits the believer. "What? know ye not that your body is the temple of the Holy Ghost?" If this internal work be neglected, poverty will come upon all our Christian life. The noise and bustling vanity of the age tend directly toward such disregard. It must be opposed by renewed diligence in cultivating deep, inward, spiritual religion. We must not measure our attainments in piety, by palpable usefulness, or the stir of beneficent action, however much this is our duty. The grand affair of life is the building up of the spiritual temple. We may disparage the power that is operating within. It is the common mistake of retired and suffering Christians. Because they are not called to public manifestations, they think there is no advancement. But knowledge may be rising in a compact and solid structure. Faith may be diffusing its mighty influence on every side. Holy devotion may be sending up clouds of incense, acceptable to God. Intercessory prayer may be stretching its arms of love, to take in all the brotherhood of Christ and all the family of man. Appetite and passion may be dying, by repeated blows. Purity, like that of Jesus, may be arising as a picture on the soul's tablet, dim perhaps, but brightening. Patience may be approaching to its perfect work. Submission to God's chastising hand may be gaining strength in the furnace. The world may be waning, and the attraction of heaven waxing more luminous. Joy in the Lord may be like the fragrance of a field which God hath blessed. And gentle humility, the ornament and preservative of all graces, may be growing more constant. Is all this nothing? Is it not the very process to which our Master calls us? It is he that maketh that which is within. Such reflections are needful for many a solitary believer, who sighs to think that no opportunity is given for great deeds in God's behalf. "They also serve, who only stand and wait." There is growth in the world of vegetable nature, not only during sunshine, but in the night. There may be progress, even where there is no joy. The roots may be striking downwards into the soil, and the vital juices of the stock may be maturing, while the late coloured flowers are folded in pensive weakness and weeping with night-dews. Inward, inward must we go, for the true elaboration of gracious virtues. Let this be strongly impressed on those whose circle is bounded by the walls of a narrow home. Let the poor mother, whose dependant charge binds her all day long to the humblest domestic service; let the widow, who cherishes her faith amidst complete insulation; let the bereaved lonely one, whom the world has dropped from its catalogue; let the invalid, who is cut off from all social labour; let the aged, who wonders why a useless life is lengthened out, know and believe, that to them also it is granted to glorify God as truly as to the king or the apostle. Let them cease to measure the work of grace by the external standards of a human activity. Did not he that made that which is without make that which is within also?

The same reasoning may be applied to another class

of instances, about which there is frequent misapprehension in the churches and even in the minds of the ministry. We too much measure the work of God among men by the single criterion of the number of souls converted. This, it need scarcely be said, is a glorious work. But the Spirit of God has other operations besides the conversion of sinners. It is not for us to bring the two into comparison. Of the influences of the Spirit mentioned in Scripture, the great majority concern the inward work on souls already renewed. The apostolical writings are almost exclusively addressed to those who are called saints. Sheep must not only be gathered into the fold, but led to pasture. We might, by carrying out the false view now censured, lay thousands of foundations, without rearing any edifice. Or rather, we might seek to lay them; for it is ordinarily found, that where gracious experience in believers becomes shallow, there are few conversions. Now the truth to be considered is, that in every renewed soul, God is carrying forward an invisible work, more important than the administration of a kingdom. How the apostle Paul yearned for the advancement of this, in churches and individuals! How he laboured and prayed for it! I find nothing similar, in the experience of brethren, or my own. "I would," says he to the Colossians, "that ye knew what great conflict I have for you, and for them at Laodicea, and for as many as have not seen my face in the flesh; that their hearts might be comforted, being knit together in love, and unto the full assurance of understanding, to the acknowledgment of the mystery of God, and of the Father, and of Christ."

A wise Christian will watch for the blooming of a single grace in the garden of the Lord, with as real an expectation, (but O how much loftier!) as that with which the tasteful maiden looks for the opening of some cherished flower in her conservatory. A single grace, that buds and blows, comes from God, and is a thing of beauty in the esteem of Christ, purchased by his sorrows, and part of his immortal wreath. With what intense anxiety will the devoted florist attend the opening of some rare and extraordinary flower, as of the Victoria Regina, or the Night-blooming Cereus! Let us not be less awakened when a Christian soul bursts forth into the manifestation of faith, hope or charity. A believer, we will suppose, long infected by an unrelenting malice, at length comes to the point of exercising a free and full forgiveness of the offender, even as God for Christ's sake forgave him. It is an inward work; but how lovely in the sight of heaven! What an epoch does it mark in the soul's history! Call not those labours unfruitful, which are blessed to one such result. Or a formal, worldly, lingering disciple, is brought at length to an entire and absolute dedication to God of all the heart so long withheld. Or, some mountain of avarice is heaved off; and the believer henceforth holds his possessions as a steward for Christ. Or, a sufferer is made to give up his own will, and bow with loving resignation to the will of God. Or, hope suddenly becomes assurance, and the fear of death is taken away. These are God's daily works in the church, and we offend against Sovereign grace if we despise them. Because they are inward, they can be detailed in no report of successes; but they are not the less to the praise of almighty love. When such flowers are blooming in the garden of the Lord, we must not complain that all is winter, or speak as we hastily do, of the absence of the Spirit.

III. But lest any should misunderstand me, I now acknowledge, that the greatest of God's inward works is the work of Regeneration. It is this which is the root of all subsequent growth. To this our Lord remands the Pharisees instead of all cleansing of the "outside of the cup and the platter," saying, "Make the tree good." No change from better to better can be compared with the change from darkness to light. No point in the history of a soul has such importance as its new birth. At this moment only it begins to live, in a spiritual sense. The very transition into heaven is not so critical; for this is but the continuance of a life already begun. There is joy in the presence of the angels of God, at every such transformation. We may talk of great junctures in human life; but it were trifling to compare any of them with the translation from being an heir of wrath to being a member of Christ. All distinctions of rank disappear when such a boon as this is conferred. It is to be feared that few kings are made children of God; but suppose such a case. Let him be the greatest monarch on earth, and at the most high and palmy state of dominion and glory. Yet the day and the hour in which he is called to newness of life, he is exalted beyond all the pomp of earth. Or take the case of some Lazarus of the street, ulcerous and forlorn. The Spirit of God touches him, and straightway he is richer than all the thousands in purple and fine linen. God has wrought on him the great inward work. When some infant soul is savingly affected by regenerating grace, it is more glorious than the creation of a new world. The same is true of the veriest slave, the Hottentot, Caffre or Cannibal, who is made a new creature. Is it so then, that we are living in a world (the only one) where such wonders of regenerating power are transacted every day? Have we on every hand those who are still ignorant of this mighty operation? Is there in our possession the instrumentality by which God is pleased to bring the dead to life? And is our period for applying it, and seeking the salvation of men, exceedingly short? Then, brethren, it is high time for us to start from our stupor, and begin to long and labour for the renewal of the sinner. I have not undervalued other modes of usefulness; but unless this is gained, all is lost! To be the means in God's hand of converting a sinner from the error of his way, is the greatest honour of which we have any knowledge. Most of us would rejoice to save the life of a fellow-

THE INWARDNESS OF TRUE RELIGION. 259

creature; what ought we not readily do or sacrifice to rescue an immortal soul!

How far have we advanced in our proposed inquiry? We have seen, first, the value of single graces, in an immortal soul; next, the value of an inward life, comprehensive of these graces; and lastly, the momentous greatness of regeneration, which confers and establishes this life. Such is Religion, as an inward work.

The whole current of reflections tends naturally towards an application to ourselves. The Lord our Sovereign is the creator of the inner as well as the outer man. He demands the homage and service of the spiritual part. On this his glance of scrutiny is unchangeably fixed. In this he finds the subject of his greatest transformations and triumphs. There must be change here, within, or all is ruin for eternity. How vain the attempt to satisfy his righteous claim, by the tender of an external compliance! Yet this is the attempt which besotted men are perpetually repeating. The particular mode of observance may vary with age and country, but the reliance is still on something which is not the heart. It may be the cleansing the outside of the cup and the platter; or the paying of tithes, ablutions, ceremonial sanctity. It may be alms, the repetition of prayers, the attendance on rites and forms. It may go further, and be the profession of the true religion, and the rendering of an unblemished outward morality. Yet in all this the principal thing is unprovided. Nothing has yet reached "the hidden man of the heart." There has been no work of God upon the secret motive principle. The nature is unchanged. All is unregenerate. How can we speak and hear these things, without sending forth the anxious inquiry, "Have we experienced this transformation?" What avails our external activity or our high profession, if the heart remains untouched? One may be pure before men, and yet may hear Christ saying to him, "Your inward part is full of ravening and wickedness." Outward obedience is invaluable, when it is the fruit of a holy heart; but all the teaching of our Lord shows that the work must begin within. Obedience is the child of Love. Prophecy, alms and martyrdom are nothing without this inward principle. "Though I bestow all my goods to feed the poor, and though I give my body to be burned, and have not charity, it profiteth me nothing." Has there been a change within? Does it reveal itself by new views, tempers, desires, joys and acts? Ah, beloved brethren, how much better are most of us outwardly than inwardly! How much higher is the esteem of others for us, than our judgment of ourselves! And yet we know ourselves but in part. If all those points of our external behaviour could be abstracted, which are produced by a reference to human opinion; by a fear of losing reputation as Christians; by regard for consistency of character; by vanity; by custom; by fear; by shame; how much would remain of genuine vitality, of regard for God's law, of holy operative love? If nothing, then are we but as whited sepulchres; and the great hidden work has yet to be begun. No perfection of exterior service can make up for a want of the life of God in the soul. The reformation of things outward, and the performance of good acts, unless from a principle of regard to God, are only like hanging fruits on the branches of a sapless tree, dead to the very root. So Christ taught. So the gospel everywhere affirms. Except a man be born again, he cannot see the Kingdom of God. If those who hear me, in conscious impenitence, would but lay this to their hearts, it would have an awakening power. The medicine is very bitter; but it is for your lives. The process of return to God is humbling and painful, and involves many despairing thoughts of your own condition. For this reason, multitudes are deterred. But is it not better to come to this reckoning in time, than in eternity? A great step is taken, when the soul is convinced that there really is such a thing as inward renovation, and that this has yet to be experienced. Shrink not from the revelation of yourself to yourself. Use no profane forces, to drive away the impression which half awakens you to say, " I will arise and go to my Father!" That whispered suggestion is from above. Such stirrings are sometimes the heavings of lungs to receive the first vital breath. God grant you this inward work of almighty power!

XII.

NEW DISCIPLES ADMONISHED.

NEW DISCIPLES ADMONISHED.*

Acts xi. 23.

And exhorted them all, that with purpose of heart they would cleave unto the Lord."

AFTER the addition of new converts to the Church, the matter of next importance is that they should abide steadfast and go on improving. It is not enough that they should sit down at the Lord's Table, nor even that they should be truly renewed. Christian love will further desire that they should adorn their profession, and go on to form a character of Christian strength and lustre. The New Testament abounds in proofs that this was the wish and aim of early teachers and brethren. As apostles and evangelists went from land to land, it was unavoidable that they should often leave groups of inexperienced believers, perhaps reeking with

* New York, May 16, 1858.

the associations of Gentilism. To prevent the perversion or vexation of such, was a principal intention of apostolic epistles and visitations. For example, at Antioch, one of the earliest centres of missionary diffusion, where the disciples were first called CHRISTIANS, some of the brethren, scattered by the persecution in Judea, had been very successful in preaching the Lord Jesus. v. 20: "The hand of the Lord was with them, and a great number believed, and turned unto the Lord." These are the ancient and authorized terms; of which we need not be shy; they 'believed,' they 'turned unto the Lord;' that is, to the Lord Jesus. Tidings of such conversions are always welcome to the Saints. News came to the Church which was in Jerusalem, who deputed Barnabas, often named afterwards, in connexion with Paul, to visit the new believers of Antioch. "Who, when he came, and had seen the grace of God, was glad, and exhorted them all, that with purpose of heart they would cleave unto the Lord." Such then is the primitive strain of advice to new converts; and it is as pregnant and pertinent now as it was then. But it contains some peculiarities of expression, upon which much depends. Who is meant by the Lord, to whom the numerous converts were exhorted to cleave? For those who have carefully studied New Testament usage, the question can have but one answer. The Lord Jesus Christ, mentioned just before, v. 20, as having been preached to them, and to whom they "turned," v. 21, is undoubtedly he to whom they were to cleave. Such is the force of the name Lord, when used absolutely. Here there is the additional reason, that the Redeemer, as Jesus, is expressly named in the context. So, v. 24, when "much people was added unto the Lord," we readily understand, that as converts they gave themselves to Jesus Christ, and enlisted under his banner. And there is special tenderness in this view, which regards entrance on a religious life as coming into immediate connexion with the beloved Son of God and Saviour of sinners.

But what is meant, when converts are exhorted to *cleave unto* the Lord Jesus? The word is significant; to *cleave* is to *cling*, to *adhere*, to *stick fast;* and where the blessed Redeemer is the object, it is to remain in close and permanent connexion with him, so as not only to be constant and persevering, but in perpetual fruit-bearing progress. The unfolding of this, however, is now to be our topic, in a series of brief particulars.

The grand affair of life, to be held before new converts, is that they cleave unto the Lord. This is so to be pressed upon their minds, as that they shall set about it with what the text calls "purpose of heart." It is something that asks the will. The duty enjoined is the result of foresight and deliberate purpose; not one of those things which we fall into, or are overtaken by; not a matter of indolent acquiescence or passive resignation; but what we arrive at by bent of soul, plenary choice, and a decision which disregards all risks. The one thing which the right-minded convert lays before him as indispensable, and seeks to compass by every effort, is to cling fast to Jesus. This the term imports. And, unquestionably, the direction implies that the persons thus exhorted are already near to Christ, nay, joined to him. How absurd were it, to ask one to abide where he is not. These people of Antioch were already "turned," and "added" to the Lord. There they were; and there—so Barnabas desired and pleaded—they were to abide. By which we are reminded of our Lord's so frequent use of a term, radically the same in Greek, though different in English; as when he says, "Abide in me, and I in you"—"if ye abide in me, and my words abide in you"—"if a man abide not in me, he is cast forth," a withered vinebranch. These are suggestive of many useful thoughts to newly awakened persons, for whose sake we must now notice several senses in which they must abide in Jesus, or cleave and cling to him. The attention of those who lately, or within a few months, have acknowledged Christ before men, is particularly invited to these expositions of the duty, which above all others now concerns them. What is included then in their cleaving unto the Lord?

I. To cleave or cling fast unto the Lord Jesus, is TO ADHERE TO THE CHRISTIAN RELIGION. The evil to which this stands opposed is apostasy, or drawing back unto perdition. The guilt and ruin of this were incurred by many even during our Lord's personal ministry. They turned back and walked no more with him. Of many the apostles had to say, "They went out from us, but they were not of us." Salutary fear of so tremendous a folly, sin and destruction, is often a means of preventing it. To cleave to the Lord is the purpose, and should be the endeavour, of every Christian disciple, however tempted to go back. The pilgrim meets many on their return. Even if these deserters never abandon the communion, they turn back in their hearts unto Egypt. After the solemnities accompanying their confession of Christ, they give up all signs of evangelical piety, and live just as they did before; usually to go greater lengths still, from having done so horrid a violence to their moral sense. But it is the full purpose of a sincere believer, however weak, that he will never abandon his Lord. All unite in Peter's cry, "Lord, to whom shall we go? thou hast the words of eternal life."

II. To cleave unto the Lord, is TO ADHERE TO HIM AS THE REVEALER OF TRUTH. This stands opposed to all departures into heresy and error. To abide in Christ, is to abide in his words. The danger of the contrary is great, and is increased when the endangered person is wise in his own conceit, and thinks his own powers sufficient for his protection. Early times saw such, predicted of old as "heady, highminded," "men of corrupt minds, reprobate concerning the faith." 2 Tim. iii. Some, in Paul's day, "having swerved," had "turned aside unto vain jangling; desiring to be teachers of the law; understanding neither what they say, nor whereof they affirm." 1 Tim. i. 6. And the same apostle foretells a day, when men "will not endure sound doctrine—shall turn away their ears from the truth, and shall be turned unto fables." 2 Tim. iv. 3. These are sufficient warnings to make us cleave unto the Lord, as the fountain of the truth which we have believed. Let the young professor beware of that which is mentioned as characteristically the sin of the *novice;* viz., the being puffed up with pride, the condemnation of the devil. 1 Tim. iii. 6. Let him suspect the zealous vender of a religious nostrum, which shall give him in some compendious way a peace not warranted by common Christian experience. Let him remember, that the new convert, whose appetite often surpasses his power of discernment, is singularly liable to be duped by error. Let him humbly decline the office of teaching that which he has scarcely learnt. Let him be "swift to hear, slow to speak." Thus, as new-born babes desiring "the sincere milk of the Word," that they may grow thereby, young Christians shall acquire solid strength and confirmation. In order to all this, the only security is to abide in Christ, as the Prophet of his people, clinging to him for instruction, and waiting at the posts of his doors, as the primeval Wisdom; the Way, the Truth, and the Life; the Sun of righteousness; the true Light, which lighteth every man that cometh into the world. Thus, with fatherly affection, speaks the apostle John: "And now, little children, abide in him; that when ye shall appear, we may have confidence, and not be ashamed before him at his coming."

III. To cleave unto the Lord Jesus is TO MAKE HIM THE OBJECT OF OUR CONSTANT FAITH. This is the opposite of a most easy and dangerous habit, namely, unbelief. Such clinging of the soul to Christ regards him as our Atoning Priest. If we ever came to him, we came thus reposing on him for righteousness and salvation; if we cleave to him, stay by him, embrace him, hang upon him, and never let him go, it will be by constantly reiterated acts of the same faith. All strength and joy rest upon this foundation; all fruit of praise and love grows out of this root. "As ye have therefore received Christ Jesus the Lord, so walk ye in him, rooted and built up in him, and stablished in the faith, as ye have been taught, abounding therein with thanksgiving." As preventive of the evils already mentioned, there is no such power in anything as in faith. As it apprehended Christ first, so it holds him fast. Not more fitly does the babe lie in the mother's arms, than the young believer is recumbent amidst the pardoning mercies and loving kindnesses of the atoning Lord. Though aged in the world's computation, he may be only a child in experience. Therefore he clings to his strength. If accepted, it is in the Beloved; if pardoned, it is as ungodly. Could his soul by possibility be for one instant severed from his Surety, he would be as unprotected as ever; hot thunderbolts of justice would find him out. His only safety is in being covered and shielded by the blood of expiation; and this is over him just so long as he is "in Christ." The emphatic preposition IN imports not merely adherence, but union; and this union is set forth by diversities in language, for human speech labours with the unaccustomed thought. Turn again to John xv. 4, "Abide *in me*, and I *in you*." "He that abideth *in me*, and I *in him*, the same bringeth forth much fruit; for *without me* ye can do nothing."

All other advices to new converts are less important than this, of looking constantly to the Cross of Jesus Christ. When you cease to do this, it will be a breach of continuity between the vine and the branch; the vital sap will flow interruptedly; and the vivid green will give place to dryness and decay. So long as you hate the remains of sin, and truly repent of them; so long as you feel shame and grief for the transgressions of former days; so long as you are disheartened with daily failures; so long as conscience challenges you for corruptions, you will be constrained to cleave unto the Lord, and to live under the baptism of his cross; that, with Paul, you "may be found in Him," "not having your own righteousness, which is of the law, but that which is through the faith of Jesus Christ, even the righteousness which is of God by faith."

IV. To cleave unto the Lord, no man can deny, is TO ABIDE BY HIS COMMANDMENTS, owning him as our Ruler. Messiah is a King. This he avowed to Pilate. In this character he is received by every repentant soul.

Every rebel who lays down his arms, approaches the throne of Jesus and does him homage. New converts to any religion follow a leader, and are named after a head. To cling to him and yield to his will, follows as a matter of course. Entering on a Christian career is not a mere change of opinion, school or party, but the beginning of a new life. Every one understands it to imply a new path of conduct. What Christ our Lord demands, comes before us sometimes in the shape of positive act, and sometimes in the shape of forbearance or abstinence. Either way, we own his government, obey his will, and receive law at his hands. Either way, we adhere to him as our Lord. The life indicated by these demands includes the highest morality; so that it is a solecism to speak of an immoral Christian. Why should we cite chapter and verse? The entire New Testament, from the Sermon on the Mount to the denunciations at the close of the Apocalypse, bears on its face the prohibition of every sin, in Christ's follower. Inward, secret, spiritual sins are probed for and extracted to the light by the ethics of the Gospel. The conversion which does not, in some good degree, convert a man from his sins, is spurious. Abiding in Christ is abiding in his service, walking in his will, doing that which shall please him, and living to his glory. And this derives new force from the consideration, that holiness, whether of heart or conduct—in other words, cleaving to the Lord in duty—can by no means be secured, except by cleaving to him in acts of personal faith and affection. But this leads us to another point, which may indeed be considered the very same under a new aspect.

V. To cleave and cling to the Lord Jesus, is TO FOLLOW HIS EXAMPLE. To every convert he says, as to those beside the lake of Gennesaret, "Follow me!" This is more than obedience; it is imitation; it is doing not only what the Master commanded, but what he did himself. We walk in his very footsteps, as closely as we know; that is, we cleave to him. It is as though we took hold of his skirts, amidst the crowd of conflicting tempters; determined not to lose sight of him, but to keep him always in our presence. The instances are too numerous for detail; let us attend to two leading cases. 1. The Lord went about doing good. Sincere disciples follow him in this. Remembering what he said about the twelve hours of the day, and the night which cometh, they are on the alert. "I must work the work of him that sent me, while it is day," is both his language and theirs. Active beginnings are useful, and none can begin too soon. Of most it may be said, what they are during their first months of profession, they will be through life. Selfish pleasure, in the comforts of experience and ordinances, may fix the soul in a habit of religious inactivity. Duties which do not terminate on ourselves, are not easily remembered by the narrow-minded. Hence the adage should make our ears tingle: "To do good and to communicate, forget not, for with such sacrifices God is well pleased."

There is no stimulus to labour, like the example of Christ. 2. The Lord bore his Cross. Sincere converts come near him, and cleave to him in suffering. " And whosoever," said his own blessed lips, " doth not bear his cross and come after me, cannot be my disciple." We are not to make our own cross; that were superstition or presumption; but we are to bear Christ's cross. Learn to expect it. Try your shoulders beforehand. Count the cost. Ask yourself concerning the cup which he drank, and the baptism which he was baptized with. Many a convert runs well, for a while; but the cross affrights him. He that receives the word into stony places " heareth it, and anon with joy receiveth it." You expect great perseverance from such warmth. Yet what follows? " He hath not root in himself, but dureth for a while; for when tribulation or persecution ariseth, because of the Word, 'ah!' by and by he is offended," he stumbles, he falls, he is left behind. Many a summer-bird which kept on the wing and carolled gaily during the May season of revival and sacraments, flees away at the first approach of storms. We must make up our account to cleave to Jesus, through good report and evil report. And in every other duty we are to walk as he also walked.

VI. To cleave to Christ is to abide by him, AS THE FOUNTAIN OF GRACE AND GIVER OF THE SPIRIT. At regeneration the once alienated, severed, depraved soul is touched by the Holy Spirit, who employs truth or light as his instrument. At this instant of illumination, the rescued being is brought into connexion with Christ as the Head. At this engrafting into Christ, the vitality of the Head becomes the vitality of the member. Or, better to preserve the harmony of our figure, the life of the vine is the life of the branch; all from spiritual union. To maintain this union, is to cleave unto the Lord. As the convert has been brought to Christ Jesus, so he is to cling to him. The analogy of the VINE, John xv., is explanatory of this: "As the branch," says our Lord, "cannot bear fruit of itself, except it abide in the vine, no more can ye except ye abide in me." "As the Father hath loved me, so have I loved you; abide [continue] in my love," that is, 'cleave to me; cling to me; hold fast to my love.'

A consciousness of weakness belongs to the most thorough converts. Humility is a sign of conversion. Not a desponding, but a trustful humility; because the child of God rests in Jesus, as his strength; and hears the whisper, "My grace is sufficient for thee."

Prayer in secret is the chief means of clinging to Christ in this sense. In closet devotion, unless it be formal, scanty, or hurried, the young Christian comes to the feet of the Lord, touches the hem of his garment, and gazes into the eyes which beam with love, even if he does not lean upon his bosom. Cleaving to Jesus, he has communion with him, in regard to all his offices, excellencies, and divine graces. Using the word prayer to comprise all devotional contemplations and ascriptions as well as beseechings, it is the very cleaving of the loving soul to our Saviour; and is the capital means of growth in grace. "Praying will make us leave off sinning, or sinning will make us leave off praying." Such converse with God, especially over the inspired volume, secures against defection and error, procures pardons, sprinkling of the expiatory blood, and the Spirit of adoption; mortifies secret, lurking, insidious sins, quickens the pulse of zeal and the pace of service; arms for battle, lifts the courage, and sweetens the cross. Thus may the new disciple advance day by day, looking unto Jesus, the Author and Finisher of his faith; cleaving unto Jesus, the vital heart, from whom all the circulation of holy thought, feeling, choice and act derives its impulse.

VII. Finally—To cleave unto the Lord, is to cling to him AS OUR PORTION AND HAPPINESS. No one is converted to a naked sense of duty, allowance of obligation, willingness to suffer, or purpose to do right. All these grow out of discipleship, but they are its acid fruits; riper, mellower experiences load the branches on the sunny side. Faith looks to Jesus, recognises his divine triumphant loveliness, yields to his invincible charms, and sinks with delight into the arms of his infinite affection. Abide there, O young disciple, O recent believer; cleave to that bosom; hang upon that arm. Let Jesus be not only thy Saviour, but thy bliss. Let thy soul's utterance be: "I charge you, O ye daughters of Jerusalem, by the roes and by the hinds of the field, that ye stir not up nor awake my love till He please!" That so high an enjoyment of Christ's presence should be uninterrupted, or even very frequent, is perhaps more than we ought to expect in the present mingled state, where shower and sunshine checker our April-day. But if you have not attained to knowledge of any such preciousness in Christ, ah! there are yet before you chambers opening into your porch of early profession, all replete with joys. If you mean to persevere in a cold, staid routine, of heartless, joyless, tearless religion, it is not hard to predict that you will swell the ranks of those professors who speak loudly and give largely, while they betray the absence of all genuine joy in the Lord, by rushing with avidity into the covetousness, the ostentation, or the frivolous amusements of the world. Christ and his joy need no eking out by the pleasures of sin and folly. God grant that those who have lately sat down at the Lord's table, may be from the beginning accustomed to hang upon the Master for their soul's gratification. It is when they go away from him that Satan seizes them and wins them to his snare. "If any man love the world, the love of the Father is not in him." Cleaving to Christ is renouncing the world, as our happiness. "These things," said our Lord, about to die, "have I spoken unto you, that my joy might *remain* in you, and that your joy might be full," xv. 11. Remark how fulness of joy is found in union with Christ.

This bliss of cleaving to the Lord, in a believing connexion, may be shared by many; and the disciple cannot but feel the warm contact of a loving throng pressing with him, shoulder to shoulder, towards the heart of Jesus. Such was the tenor of his prayer, xvii. 22 : " And the glory which thou gavest me have I given them: that they may be one, even as we are one, *I in them and thou in me*, that they may be made perfect in one." Look around, then, upon those who are with you in Christ, and resolve to know and to receive one another in the Lord.

What has the text yielded us ? What have we learned to be meant by cleaving unto Jesus ? That we hold fast to his religion, abhorring the thought of apostasy—that we adhere to him as the Revealer of truth, avoiding every heresy and error—that we rest upon him by faith as our atoning Priest—that we kneel to him as our King—that we cling to his example—that we keep near him as the source of all spiritual, sanctifying influence—and that we abide in him as our everlasting portion and ultimate good.

Beloved friends, who have so recently plighted your faith to Christ, can any laboured application be necessary ? You know this Jesus. You have found him, or rather he has found you, afar out of the path, perishing on the wild mountains. He has borne you back to the fold, having laid you upon his shoulder. He has clasped you in his arms. You are on his bosom, encircled in his righteousness, held and comforted by his Spirit. Can you harbour a thought of escape from cords of love ? " Will ye also go away ? " God forbid !

Be exhorted, " with purpose of heart to cleave unto the Lord." It includes your whole duty at the present juncture. But for performing it you need that purpose of heart, that immovable determination, which can be neither turned aside nor rent away. The more you ponder on the Christ of the Scriptures, the deeper will be your admiration and love, the firmer your resolve to be inseparable from your Guide. Yet I behold you in weakness and dangers, which, alas, you cannot apprehend aright. Ten thousand skeletons along your way, whitening your path through the desert, should remind you that professing Christians may fall. Your only safety is in being always near to Christ. The only power which can keep you there is the Holy Spirit of God, who at first opened your eyes and conducted you to the Redeemer. Pray that he would take the things of Christ and show them unto you. Cry daily to him, that he would maintain your union with the living head. " Ye are complete in him." Every thing depends on your having right views of Jesus; believing on his name and clinging to him for justification; resorting to him for perpetually renewed pardons; and communing with him, as the Head of influence and the soul's portion. Christless conversions will come to nought. Look to it, brethren, that the Lord Jesus holds the royal, supreme place in your system and your experience. Account the day lost, in which there is no sense of commerce with the skies, and tender intercourse with the heavenly Bridegroom. He stands at the door and knocks; he is ready to come in and sup with you. Open the door. Yield to the divine wooing. Let Christ be all in all. Beginning thus, you will assuredly go aright. Lowly adherence to the Lord is the very secret of peace, power and progress. Never give up your hold; grasp him, keep him, cling to him, abide in him, live and die for him. "For ye are the temple of the living God; as God hath said, I will dwell in them, and walk in them, and I will be their God and they shall be my people."

XIII.

LOVE CASTING OUT FEAR.

LOVE CASTING OUT FEAR.*

1 John iv. 18.

"There is no fear in love; but perfect love casteth out fear: because fear hath torment."

"The fear of the Lord is clean," says David, "*enduring forever;*" yet here we learn that fear is cast out. Again it is said, "The fear of the Lord is strong confidence;" "be thou in the fear of the Lord all the day long;" and "Happy is the man that feareth alway." Surely, we may conclude, this is not the kind of fear which is to be cast out; but some other, which is neither profitable to us nor pleasing to God. And such a fear there undoubtedly is, as we shall presently see, when we turn our attention to the point more closely. All these commendatory expressions bestowed on Fear, relate to godly fear, which is only another name for

* New York, June, 1848.

true religion. In the Old Testament, particularly, as you must have observed, piety is frequently named the Fear of the Lord; perhaps as frequently as in the New Testament it is named Love. Not that either is peculiar to these parts of Scripture respectively; but beyond a question, good men are oftenest spoken of in the Old Testament as fearing, and in the New Testament as loving. Indeed our blessed Creator chose to reveal himself in that earlier day amidst more clouds, more through the smoke of altars, more in judgments, more from Sinai, more as the God of holiness and wrath; and to delay that more inviting radiance of his compassion, in which we are privileged to rejoice. Good men loved him then, and good men fear him now; but Old Testament love was much like fear, and New Testament fear is much like love. Abraham and Moses tremble while they draw near in filial belief; but John, while he reverences, rests upon the very bosom of his God. We may be assured, however, I repeat it, that the aweful reverence which was felt by patriarchs and prophets, and even by the seraphim who veil their faces, shall never be cast out, even by the perfect love of heaven. In this sense we cannot fear too much, and perfect fear of this kind does not cast out love, nor in the slightest degree impair it. We have therefore still to inquire what this fear is, which is mentioned in the text.

Looking attentively at the passage, in its connexion, the best key to sound exposition, you will perceive that this fear stands opposed to terror in the last day: v. 16, "herein is our love made perfect, that we may have boldness in the day of judgment." Fear in the day of judgment, my unpardoned friend and brother, is a dreadful fear; a fear which you ought to consider; a fear which you ought to cast out; a fear which you are beginning to experience at times, and which may come upon you amidst your dying agonies. God deliver you and me from the fear of the Day of Judgment! You will further perceive that this fear stands opposed to peace of mind and all pleasure : "because fear hath torment." The original word is used in only one other place of the New Testament, and means punishment. There may be some allusion to future woe, or retributive pain; but we need not alter our text: the fear we are inquiring about *hath torment*. It is not a sluggish or a trifling, but a tormenting fear, which is to be cast out. This great and distressing apprehension therefore, which true love expels, is what we must for a little while submit to a thoughtful examination.

I. Fear, my brethren, even about minor things, is not a pleasing emotion. In all its forms and in every degree, it belongs to those states of soul which we would gladly avoid. Yet to be altogether without it is to be either far more, or far less than man. In our present condition it is necessary to fear. The passion would indeed be unreasonable, useless and absurd, if we were in no danger. But the truth is, we are in perpetual danger. From the moment that the babe asserts its vitality by a first exclamation, till the closing gasp, we are in peril. The apprehension of evils is an instinct or constitutional propensity which we have in common with the lower tribes. By this we are enabled to shun a thousand evils into which we should otherwise fall to our destruction. It is temerity or foolhardiness not to fear. It is neither unreasonable nor unmanly to fear real danger. The child, the drunkard, the madman or the idiot, is exempt from apprehension, in circumstances where an Achilles or a Wellington would feel the wholesome alarm. The pilot who should laugh at the dangers of a passage and go on rocks; the householder who should lie still in a conflagration; or the traveller who should descend into an active volcano, might purchase the fame of fearlessness, but would die as the fool dieth. The unmanly dread is that which unfits for action, and which increases the danger. Still, the fears to which man is perpetually subject show that he is no longer in a perfect state. Fear, look at it as we may, is a shadow cast over the human path by sin. It tells of danger; and danger whispers of penalty. "Fear hath torment."

Other emotions or passions carry some degree of pleasure: fear carries none. No man elects it. Every man would gladly be rid of it. To escape it is to avoid an enemy. Whatever may be the object dreaded, the emotion, even when salutary, is distressing. So far however from being salutary, in most instances, it is enfeebling and disastrous. We fear a thousand enemies that never come in sight, and ten thousand that never had a being. We are ingeniously inventive in our fears; conjuring up phantoms, and adding to the apprehensions of to-day the wilder apprehensions of to-morrow; alarmed for ourselves, and alarmed for others; trembling while it is well with us, lest it should not abide so; and while it is ill with us, lest it should grow worse. Single instances of fear, constantly repeated, produce a fearing habit, till sometimes the wretched soul can do little else than fear. Such is the case of many, whose natural disposition this way is increased by misfortune, by disease, by age, by melancholy, by superstition, and by a sore and evil conscience. For this is the true ghost, that haunts the chamber and draws the curtain of the timorous.

Thus far we have viewed fear, as respecting the ordinary evils and threatenings of common life; its pains, losses, and disgraces. You, my hearers, best know, whether you have ever feared; what it was that you were afraid of; and what it was that gave pungency to the trial.

II. But there is one object which is more particularly formidable, and the very naming of which causes a chill of dread to run down your body; it also never fails to bring up some thought of sin and penalty. It is so terrible, that I seem to behold the entire human race, for six thousand years, at their utmost stretch of exertion flying from it; yet so certain, that of all these unnumbered tremblers only two are known to have escaped. DEATH is the king of terrors. Hence when

Jesus, death's conqueror, subjects himself to the great enemy, this is one of the reasons given for that unparalleled submission, "that through death he might destroy him that had the power of death, that is, the devil, and deliver them who, *through fear of death*, were all their lifetime subject to bondage." This is deliverance indeed; and from bondage. All other fears, short of eternity, are nothing to this. It has prompted men, in instances innumerable, to exertions which had been otherwise impossible. It is true of natural men, whoever said it, that "skin for skin, all that a man hath will he give for his life." Hence the power of religion shines resplendent, when men " hate their own lives ;" " love not their lives unto the death ;" and choose martyrdom for Christ's sake. Even for worldly objects, however, men have been found willing to sacrifice life; but no motives have so remarkably taken away this dread of death, as Christian faith. The dread may be detected by you, in your own hearts, on a little inspection.

III. All this, however, Christian brethren, fails to conduct us to the full meaning of our text. This is not all the fear that is to be cast out; even including death, as we have just done; unless—O mark the words—we further include that for which death is feared. Could we die as infants die: with no forebodings; with no accompanying tempter down the valley to the irrevocable gate; with no subsequent anguish; death would be reduced to the bare endurance of a bodily pang; often greater in appearance than reality, and not more than you or I perhaps have suffered already. You do not need me to inform you what "makes cowards of us all." There is a reckoning after death. Were you ensured, in regard to that, your chief terrors would be quieted; and though for many lesser reasons you might indeed desire to live, yet, heaven being certain, you would feel instantly relieved from that mountain fear under which you are now crushed. Witness, O conscience, that our master-dread is of eternal retribution! What else is the meaning of our apostle, when he says, "Herein is our love made perfect, that we may have boldness *in the day of judgment!*" Do not our fears run on before as if hastening to that day? and will they not in that day, from such as know not this boldness, extort cries, vain cries, for the protection of rocks and mountains? How vain a covert "from the face of Him that sitteth on the throne, and from the wrath of the Lamb!"

It is remarkable how extensive has been the prevalence of such terrors among mankind. Account for it as we may, a large part of the human race have had them. Christianity does not cause them. They prevail where the name of Christ was never heard. They are cries from the deep, dark recesses of human nature, shuddering before the divine retributions. They come to us from the shades of ancient mythology, echoing the names of Rhadamanthus, Tartarus, and Phlegethon. They are repeated in the burnings, mutilations, self-tortures, and human sacrifices of all generations. Fear of the wrath to come has reared its myriads of altars. Explain it as we may, the fact is undeniable. There is a profound sensibility on this subject, natural to mankind. We doubt not it is a principle left standing, even among heathen, as a stock on which to engraft the true religion. Could we know the whole reality, we should be amazed to learn how universal such apprehensions have been, even among the most barbarous nations.

Under the fuller light of revelation, we find great fears among men, in regard to their condition in the other world. So widely are these anxieties scattered, that a principal employment of false teachers is to do them away. Once convince a man that you possess a secret means of removing his fear of eternity, and you make him your friend. You have touched the point of exquisite sensibility. Only relieve him there, and you have destroyed his chief enemy. Hence, just as men are daily the prey of empirics and charlatans in physic, from their thirst for dainty methods of cure, so they fall readily into the snares of deceivers in religion, from their anxiety to be secure in conscience. Otherwise, how could we account for the large reception, by whole nations, of that stupendous imposture of sacerdotal absolution, the unction and the viaticum? as though any ceremonial whatever could reach the spirit or prepare it for judgment. Or how account for that other delusion, whereby people, with the very words of Christ in their hands, set up so-called churches, to persuade men that God means to break his word, and that the wicked shall escape all punishment. These and the like errors invite the souls of men, eager to escape from a dreadful horror of judgment. You may readily convince yourself how much this has to do with your anxieties, if you will only imagine your hour of dying to have come; if you will only present to your view the bar of Christ; and if you will only calculate the amount of relief, which would be afforded by the certainty of acceptance at his hands.

IV. These are indeed the chief manifestations of that which alarms us; but Fear has a wider domain and a more magnificent object. Even Death and Judgment, awful as they are, derive all their terrors from a greater fear: they are only expressions of the WRATH OF GOD. This wrath it is which is enkindled by our sin, and which like an infinite fire inflames the rage of Tophet. When we trace up our fears to their principle, we find them fixing on one august but dread object,—the Lord God Almighty, considered as a God of infinite holiness and infinite justice. "God is angry with the wicked, every day." It is not more clearly revealed that there is a God, or that there is a Christ, than that the Justice of Jehovah goes forth toward the destruction of the guilty. Is it not so? Does not the voice within you, my hearers, testify to the justice of such fears? "If all in this assembly were to rise, one after another, in answer to the question, Art thou prepared to die? it is not likely that the majority would reply with that firmness which marks a thorough assurance. Vague hopes; inconsiderate confidence; at best unfounded reasons; these are what we should find in most. Over us all there hangs, from time to time, a heavy cloud, betokening the anger of God, and his infinite opposition to sin. We may not always have the object precisely before our thoughts, as a definite point in theology; but we are not at ease; we lack something to constitute peace; we feel that God is offended; we dare not meet him. And what is this, dear brethren, but the inward witness of conscience? For what purpose has God placed this detective spy within us, but to give warning of this very thing? These apprehensions may vary, but they are in kind the same. What is all this but fear of God's justice? Not, I beseech you to observe, that holy fear of God, with which we began, and which will abide in heaven; but the distress of a consciously sinful soul in God's presence. Ah! it is the rankling of this arrow, barbed and poisoned, deep and inextricable. Many a one there is, in Christian assemblies, who goes and comes for years, carrying this hidden wound in the bosom. More suffer thus than the world suspects. On this trouble, neighbour does not talk with neighbour. Often it is hidden from wife and children. Yet there it is, a wounded spirit; a conscience unreconciled with God. Under this head therefore we must include, in their infinite diversity, all the painful apprehensions which men have, through all their lives, in regard to their failures to please God, and their sense of his displeasure. These fears lie in ambush to come upon us in chosen moments. They "bide their time." Just as a malignant and perfidious enemy will sometimes wait till his victim is feeble, or solitary, or in darkness, and then waylay him, dart upon him, and inflict the fatal blow; so these fears (which are in abeyance, and let a man alone in times of health and wealth, of youth and prosperity) gather around him when he is in illness, in despondency, in bereavement, in poverty, and in declining years. When you shall be in your chief worldly troubles, then I forewarn you, expect your chief spiritual troubles. If you have neglected God in your summer-days, look for assaults of your adversary when trials begin to thicken. Would to God, I could duly impress on men of business and of health, the ruinous game they are playing with their immortal souls, by procrastinating this grand settlement to days of debility, pain and despondence; to days, alas! that may bring no opportunity of thought.

V. A clearer view of this fear would be obtained, if we could see it in one of its great critical moments, such as the time of conviction of sin. This is a crisis in the disease of fear. It is not different from all the rest; but now the apprehension has risen high, and receives that last drop which makes it run over the brim. God is the same; the danger is the same; it is the soul that is different. Its gaze is fixed inward on itself.

David's word comes true, *My sin is ever before me.* All other thoughts are absorbed. Instead of this or that blemish, like a single drop of blood, behold! all has become one gory vision of crimson and scarlet! There is neither sleep nor nourishment. No sorrow is like this sorrow, where deep. You know not what you are preparing for yourself, by neglecting repentance. This is a condensation of many fears into one, before which the stoutest minds have been appalled. Now, the apprehension of God's judgment rises to an acme, and the soul is in a paroxysm which it cannot long endure. If it continued, it might unsettle reason. But no authentic case is on record, or known to us, of any instance in which simple sorrow for sin, however poignant, has resulted in alienation of mind.

VI. By which we may be led to turn aside for a few moments to consider an injurious objection. We often hear it said that persons are driven to madness by thinking of their sins; or that religion has crazed them; and even in some instances that they have been urged to suicide. Now I dare not undertake to say how far a man who has obstinately rejected the offer of salvation may be left of God, even in this world: but after many opportunities of intimate acquaintance with cases of what is called *religious melancholy*, I can solemnly declare my absolute conviction, that the phrase, in its common acceptation, is used in misapprehension. Such melancholy is not religious, in any such sense as that it is caused by religion. It is undoubtedly true, that persons are found in a state of deep melancholy and even insanity, whose thoughts run perpetually on religion. It would be wonderful if it were otherwise. All unsound minds seize on topics of high interest. Religion affords such topics. Just as the disturbed mind fixes on property, family connexions or ambition, so on religion. And this without its being true that religion, or even its abuses, caused the alienation. We have therefore known the same individual agonized to-day about the salvation of his soul, and to-morrow about remedies for his body; insanely in both cases. Yet neither religion nor medicine was chargeable with his aberration. The case of COWPER, the poet, has often been cited against us; but truly stated, it is wholly and powerfully on our side. There never was, indeed, a case more striking of what is called religious melancholy. The gloom was black; the fear was desperate. Yet, to charge this to religion, is grossly unphilosophical as well as unjust. Long before COWPER's religious experience began, he evinced so marked a tendency to madness, that, as is well known, he made an attempt on his own life. When afterwards he attained to evangelical views of truth, he received from them his first balm and consolation. From religion he received nothing but good. If, afterwards, he relapsed into a sullen, impenetrable gloom, it is no more than is usual in such cases. To all sympathizing friends, instances of this kind are most trying; but they belong more to the physician than the pastor. Reasoning and instruction are for the most part thrown away on them. We must commit them to God, in the use of those physical and moral means which experience has shown to minister to a mind diseased. My apology for this digression must be the importance of right ideas on this grave subject, and the fact that its distresses usually take the form of exaggerated fear.*

VII. Let it never be forgotten, that much as we may boast of our reason, our mental discipline, and our self-control, there is nothing at times more beyond our command, than our own thoughts and passions. How much are we at the mercy of God, herein! Who has not known the time when he would have given half his worldly goods to be exempt from one importunate suggestion or harrowing image? Dreadful apprehensions of God's anger, whether well or ill founded, are among the most intolerable of all our states of mind. The citadel itself is assaulted. The supporting power itself cries for support. "The spirit of a man will sustain his infirmity; but a wounded spirit who can bear!" It affords a powerful argument against a life of sin, that the habits of mind engendered and fostered by such a life, are opposed to self-control, and promotive of self-afflicting cares and misgivings.

VIII. Taking the highest and most general view of our subject, the person supposed lives in SLAVISH FEAR

---

* Upon this greatly abused topic, and on kindred distresses, I recommend a small but valuable treatise of my esteemed friend, the Rev. JOSEPH H. JONES, D. D.

of God. Now what condition of a human soul can be thought of, more unnatural or more destructive than to live perpetually in panic with respect to its Creator, its Portion, its Saviour, than to hate the thought of the Greatest, Best, and Loveliest! What more hopeless, than to shrink with horror from the countenance that is always turned on us, and be impatient of the searching eye which we can never escape! This is what impenitent men are preparing for themselves in greater measure than they have yet experienced. Even now they sometimes shake with terror, or avoid it only by a violent force put upon the thoughts; but the great mystery of fear is yet to be revealed to them.

IX. Even children of grace, in their less favoured hours, in times of temptation, and sometimes at intervals, all their lives long, are troubled with doubts and terrors. They fear to die. They still more fear the Judgment. If on certain rare occasions, the darkness is broken, and the believer, trembling, says, "Lord, thou knowest all things, thou knowest that I love thee!" this twinkling star, just above the horizon, soon sets, and all is obscurity. Far be it from us to measure grace by sensible joys, or to say that doubting Christians have no faith. Much more true is it, that presumptuous, undoubting vaunters of their own cloudless skies and Pharisaic assurance are in danger of surprise and overthrow. We believe holy souls may be in fear; but we also believe that their fears have no part in their holiness. "There is no fear in love;" as our text declares. There is no happiness in fear, "because fear hath torment." We should all endeavour to rise as speedily as possible out of this region of mists and clouds. A life which has to be largely spent in discussions of the question whether we are in the path or not, is every way inferior to a life of going forward in the way. The degrees of fear vary; but all "fear hath torment." The head cannot be erect, as should be that of a king's son. There cannot be the higher attainments in piety. The more generous and stimulating motives are absent. "The joy of the Lord is your strength." Perpetual fearfulness is as bad in religion as in the world. It writes a signature of gloom on the countenance, which discredits religion and deters companions. Heroic Christianity, noble daring, championship for truth and humanity, call for livelier hopes and unwavering confidence. Hence all who profess to follow Christ, should listen with a wistful expectation to every proposal of means for casting out this fear.

X. Before leaving this branch of the subject, let your minds dwell a little on the condition of those who are justly exposed to the perpetuity of these fears. Their conscience, if not seared, is a daily suggester of evil forebodings. They are wrong, and they know it. The thought of guilt is the thought of punishment. This servile dread, though well-founded, has no virtue in it. Were it increased ever so much, it would only be more like the state of evil angels, who "believe and tremble." Their anguish at God's justice is mingled with no evangelical sorrow for sin: it does not make them love God any more. Nay, it is generally mixed with some repining and rebellion. It prompts the question, "Why hast thou made me thus?" It drives away from God, and thoughts of God. Let this continue, and it frequently issues in the most vehement opposition to divine things.

If, my dear hearer, you are conscious of no filial attachment to God; if the thought of God gives you trouble, or exasperates the pang of conscience; if the law is terrible, and the Gospel a dead letter; if you still labour for the meat that perisheth, and still forsake your own mercies; then, of a truth, you need no preacher to tell you that "fear hath torment." But this is a state which admits of degrees. You suffer more, it may be, than you once did. Who knows but you may go on to greater suffering? It will, indeed, be your own choosing of death rather than life; but the thing is possible. I have no promise from this book, to assure you that you shall not reap as you have sowed. There is nothing in philosophy or scripture to demonstrate that the fear of to-day may not ripen into the greater fear of to-morrow; or that the passions and torment of an evil nature here may not be carried forward and developed in another state. If death were the certain antidote of pain and fear, why then, my brethren, the suicide would be the wise man, and the Iscariot who went to his own place, only leaped more boldly and rapidly to that heaven, for which his brother apostles toiled through sorrows and blood. But no! you will be the same persons beyond death. What solemn object is that, which yonder rises out of the ocean, among mists, on the further side of dissolution! What throne and tribunal emerges from that expanse of indistinct futurity! "It is appointed unto men once to die . . . but after this . . . the Judgment." Are you athirst for salvation? Behold, it is ready for you, and you may drink "of the fountain of the water of life freely." But take care how you flatter yourself, that as a matter of course all fear shall be left behind you when you die. "The fearful," I say, "the *fearful*," are specially noted, Rev. xxi. 8, with the unbelieving and the abominable, as having "their part in the lake of fire." Fear is an ingredient in their cup. "Fear hath torment."

All which is presented to you, not to sink you in despair, but, on the contrary, to show you the gulf from which true religion stands ready to deliver you. If "fear hath torment," which cannot be denied, yet "perfect love casteth out fear;" which is the second topic awaiting your consideration.

XI. That the Love here spoken of is *love towards God*, admits of no reasonable doubt. The whole context shows it. Immediately before, he has been mentioning fear—fear of God. Immediately after, he gives this ground of the love intended: "We love him, because he first loved us." It is true, v. 20, in a following verse he speaks of love toward brethren; but he speaks of this as a consequence and evidence of love to God.

The Love of God in a large sense, is the whole of religion and the fulfilling of the law. All the second table results from the first. "Every one that loveth him that begat, loveth him that is begotten of him." Love is a familiar passion. It is no part of our plan to treat of its varieties. No agent is more mighty. Among all nations, in all ages, it is an element of incalculable moment in the problems of history. It is the moral cement of the universe. Just so much order, harmony, and union are there in the world, as there is love. It is a self-manifesting principle. We *know* when we love. It is a lively, operative principle, breaking forth into acts, services, and sacrifices. This is true even of that common terrestrial love which exists between parents and children, friend and friend. It is the same affection in kind, when we rise towards God. The subject is the same; it is the same human spirit which loves. The object is varied; for it is God who is loved; and the degree admits of indefinite enlargement.

Yet, when we come to consider this holy passion of the soul, we must not fail to take into view one important trait of it, which is, that it is *love toward a perfect and infinite Being*. I fear this is not enough considered. There are peculiarities of all love towards a superior. The mother loves her babe; the good master his servant; the teacher his scholar; the guardian his ward;

the commander his soldier. Brother and sister, husband and wife, companion and companion, between these there are strong affections; but they flow towards inferiors or equals. The regard for a *superior* is something different. Consider the love of one whose life has been saved by his Sovereign. Ascend a little towards the love of a disciple for his master; you are here only beginning, at an infinite remove, to tread the path upward to the love of GOD. Love toward one far above us is a love tempered with veneration and awe; and, as was said before, this kind of fear is not to be cast out. The soul bows and sinks, as wondering how it dares to love. The supreme excellence, which fixes the eye and fills the circuit of vision, and is known to fill the universal sphere of all vision of all united intelligences, the Lord Almighty, fountain and sum of all glories and all beauties, is a sun too dazzling to be gazed on with careless eye. Of all human affections, there is none more solemn. Words fail; often external acts of worship fail. When the prayer of God's house is most lifted up, and the spirit of worshippers most attuned; when the chorus of the great congregation is fullest, and the swell of a multitude of voices most emulates the choir of heaven; even these expressions fail, and the loving heart is conscious of an emotion which rises and soars beyond them all, till it despairs of utterance, and sits down to say, "Come then, expressive silence, muse his praise!" The fearfulness of a soul flying to God in praise, is the trembling of a dove that closes its pinions to sink into the nest. "Return unto thy rest O my soul." It is an awful sweetness; the cloud of frankincense amidst which the worshipper lifts the vail and enters into the holy-of-holies. There is a perfect consistency between the reverence and the love. The greater the awe, the greater the happiness. Beyond a doubt, the hallowed stillness and adoring fear of heaven is more deep and awful than even the joy of death.

What on earth is more solemn than a believer's death? Yet what is more joyful? The love, then, of a soul toward God, is a love of what is superior, yea, supreme. It finds its object at the utmost reach of its ascending faculties; it descries that object as infinite, and beholds it evermore transcending all limits of comprehension, and evermore flying from the approach of finite powers. The soul despairs of perfectly embracing; and yet it loves! Not one pang of this exquisite delight, this dread enjoyment, would it give away; though it knows that if God should withhold his sustaining hand, or open more fully the tide of influence into the frail vessel, the soul would fain die under it. It may be that some of those deep sleeps, mentioned in the Scriptures, were compassionately afforded as refuges for sinking nature, under the excess of divine manifestations. Such was the slumber on the mount of transfiguration. The love of God, as our infinite superior, has therefore a sacredness and a sublimity which fully redeem it from all the trivial belongings of natural affection. It is a love to all God's perfections, so far as revealed; for, doubtless, God has unrevealed perfections, and fields of glory in the immensity of his nature, which no faculties of ours can comprehend; hues of beauty to which our sense is blind, and harmonies of wisdom and holiness to which our ear is deaf. But what is revealed is all the object of our love, and this love is the principal thing in religion. He that truly loves God is a redeemed soul and true Christian; he who loves him not, is yet in his sins.

XII. Some sincere persons have been much troubled because the text speaks of perfect love. They know that if they have any love whatever, it is far from being perfect; and that they have never seen evidence of sinless perfection in any; least of all, in those who claim it for themselves. How then can our fears, say they, ever be cast out? If we wait for sinless love, we must wait for heaven. Our love is so faint, so far from what it ought to be and from what our God deserves; so blemished by selfishness, pride, and passion; so interrupted by rival affections; so pulled down earthward by sloth and carnality; so overhung by unbelief; that never, never, even for a single hour, could we pretend to plead such affection as perfect love. Let me reply, for this is a hinderance which must be removed out of the way. The apostle does not say that every measure of sincere Christian love casts out every measure of fear. This were to condemn and strike from the list all doubting disciples; a proposal sometimes made by zealots and fanatics, but which we have repudiated under a former head. There is not a man that liveth and sinneth not; there is not a loving soul that does not sometimes fear. And "he that feareth is not made perfect in love." It is perfect love that casteth out all fear; every the least degree of it. Even then on the extreme supposition that the apostle means by this word a love that is uninterrupted and sinless, he asserts this, and this only, to wit, that love and fear are so opposed, that the perfect and absolute prevalence of one excludes the other; and further, that where the reign of love is complete, as we know, for example, it is in heaven, there is no fear; and still further, that in proportion to the increase of love will be the decrease of fear. The nearer you approach to perfect love, the nearer to perfect fearlessness, that is to heaven. This, I say, is the apostle's meaning, even on the supposition, that by the word "perfect" he intends uninterrupted and absolute sinlessness.

But there is no need of understanding him to mean this. The word "perfect," as none are so fully convinced as the most diligent and learned students of the original, has several significations. It is applied to Job, who sinned egregiously; and to any thorough Christian, as, 1 Cor. ii. 6; Phil. iii. 15; Col. iv. 12. It is applied to that which is symmetrical, not wanting its essential parts, sincere and genuine, even though not sinless, and though not consummate in its degree. It unquestionably here points to a high attainment in religion; no common reach of experience; one of the summits in our pilgrimage. And it is no ordinary fruit which is here propounded, the casting out of fear —of that fear which occupied our painful attention just now. If, brethren, you would be delivered from such an enemy, know ye, that it is by no every-day attainment in grace. It is a measure of attainable love which is held out to us as a sweet resting-place in the journey up these mountains; but we are not to be deterred from seeking it, by the assurance that angelic, heavenly, sinless perfection, is impracticable on earth. So much it seemed necessary to say, concerning this love as perfect. It is then the holy, sincere affection of a renewed soul towards God, so exalted by divine grace enlarging the experience, as to remove servile and tormenting dread.

XIII. Having now considered what this love is (the subject of the apostle's proposition), let us consider its operation, i. e. how it casts out fear. 1. Perfect love casts out fear, because it is founded on just views of God. No unconverted person has just views of God. If he knew God, he would be saved. "This is eternal life, to know Thee, the only true God, and Jesus Christ, whom thou hast sent." No person, under the anguish of an alienated mind, under pangs of conscience and dead works, under legal horrors, under self-condemning lashes of remorse, has just views of God. All slavish fear regards God in a distorted manner. It may not overrate his Justice or his Wrath, but it amazingly underrates his Mercy and his grace. "God is love;" and the sight of this is connected with all true believing. To see God, is to see his love. To see the Gospel, is to see its grace. It is believing. Faith is a reception of God's character, as a God of infinite grace and mercy. Even true Christians, in those hours when they have servile fears and are tormented about their future destiny, are guilty of lapses in their faith; they cease to believe in some respects; they lose their hold in part on some divine truth; they look at their Redeemer under false lights; in a word, they have not just views of God.

Do not misunderstand me, as if I made love the source of faith. Some have so taught; but in so doing, have made a preposterous derangement of cause and effect. We freely own, that between the affections and the understanding, as also between love and faith, there is a reciprocity of action. He who loves most, will be most able and ready to believe. If any man do Christ's will, he shall know of the doctrine. Right affections tend to clear vision. "The pure in heart shall see God." This is undeniable; but this is not what we mean at present. Faith precedes love. We must perceive the amiable qualities of divinity before we love them. It is the order of nature and the order of grace. But when that regenerating word is spoken, whereby the dead soul awakes, and the blind soul is enlightened, the same fiat that results in just views of God, results in love for those august glories which begin to expand before the enraptured vision.

Now, the very views of God's character which produce eminent love, do at the same time remove fear. You once thought of God as a hard master, an austere judge, if not a tyrant. You trembled as the slave at the lash. You dared not come to God with any intimacy of approach, not even with filial beseeching. You regarded religion as a hard service, however necessary for escaping from hell; and conversion as a repulsive humbling process, which you would gladly put off as far as possible. You often tried to disabuse yourself of your early impressions respecting God, and to make him out such a one as yourself: as tolerant of sin and as regardless of his word. And, failing of this, you earnestly sought to flee from his presence. If sudden danger, or violent illness and possible death, came on you, how terrific and black were all your thoughts of God! You beheld in him every thing rather than the Friend and Father; and you were ready to quarrel with the system of doctrine which exalts his immaculate purity and inflexible justice; as if by your prejudices you could undo the reality of God's attributes. Was not this the view you habitually took of God? It was totally false, grossly unjust to your Maker and Redeemer, perverse, absurd, and ungrateful. O, the blessed change, when grace opened your eyes! How you looked on God, as on a new discovery. How the familiar words, which tell of him in hymns and catechisms, seemed a fresh revelation. Now you wondered how you could ever have had doubts and misgivings about him who is the most Blessed and the most Loving. You charged your souls with the sin of having lived with your chief friend so long, as though he had been your chief enemy. New light has broken in on your cell. You contemplate Jehovah as the infinitude of moral perfection; you are absorbed in the contemplation; and own that you were made capable of love in order that you might love such a being.

Now, my brethren, these are just views of God; though infinitely below the truth. And so beholding Jehovah, as containing in himself all that is entrancingly excellent, and all that is boundlessly benevolent, ineffably pure and great, and immeasurably communicative of happiness to his creatures, you found your love on a view, which at the very same time forbids you to fear. What place is left for servile fear? If any, it must be in some disbelief of such a character in God. Admitting this, you cannot but draw nigh. These aspects of the divine nature are attractive. They draw the soul in confidence. They command the affections in filial repose. Nothing conceivable can so expel doubts and terrors as the true beholding of God as he is; and love and confidence are twin streams which perpetually mingle their waters.

2. Perfect love casts out fear, because it is founded on a belief of God's love to us. Consider what is the reason of all our religious fears. Is it not that we ap-

prehend that God does not love us? For if he really loves us, and intends our salvation, fear on this point is shut out; it were insane to fear. Only acquire the unwavering conviction that God regards you with compassionate kindness, and your dread of all consequences vanishes. Just in proportion as you credit this concerning God, just in proportion as you know him to be on your side, will you be raised above fear. Now, my brethren, I pray you to perceive, for it is the main discovery of the New Testament, that the revelation which you need to banish your fear, is the very revelation which the Gospel was sent to make. The Gospel is none other than a declaration of God's stupendous method of saving sinners. The belief of the Gospel is belief of this; it is belief that God is your friend. It is a looking out of the soul upon God as a God of love, giving himself to us as a Saviour. And it is this view of God and this belief of the Gospel which is the cause of that love which casteth out fear. Do you doubt this? Just call to mind those portions of your experience which coincide with the matter in hand. Recollect what change of views made a change of affections; what it was that melted you into love. Was it not your sudden apprehension of the truth that, notwithstanding all your sins, God loved you? Was it not your coming all at once to recognise the neglected truth, that even your greatest transgressions could not keep you from the enjoyment of God's compassion, if you would but accept it in the Gospel? And is not this just what the apostle says? v. 14: "And we have seen and do testify, that the Father sent the Son to be the Saviour of the world." v. 16: "And we have known and believed *the love that God hath to us.*" Mark, my brethren, what it is that we have known and believed. "GOD IS LOVE: and he that dwelleth in love dwelleth in God, and God in him." There is no fear in love. "We love him because he first loved us." Here we have arrived at the sacred fount of love to God. It flows from a belief of God's love to us. "We love him because he first loved us." Some interpreters, I know, in order to hold up a metaphysical scheme of disinterested benevolence as the sole essence of virtue, would explain this verse to mean only that unless God had loved us first, we never should have loved him: they deny that our view of his love to us is a source of our love to him; they exclude all love of gratitude, as selfish. They might as well exclude all human nature, or all the gush of blood from these hearts. Every true convert, unspoiled by inventions of sophistry, feels the warm current of his soul going forth in love to God, for this very reason, and under this very motive, that *God has loved him.* It is true, we love God for what he is in himself. But the greatest, most intelligible, and most affecting view of *what God is in himself*, is the view of *what he is to us,* of his unspeakable love in redemption. And no man ever so loves as when he beholds this love of God to himself most clearly.

Brethren, it would be unpardonable in me not to

say, that the highest demonstration of this divine pity is in the incarnation and death of Jesus Christ. "The Father sent the Son to be the Saviour of the world." It is therefore at the foot of the cross that our love is most awakened, and that our hearts are melted by the blood of Jesus. For the same reason, it is at this cross that our fears are most removed. Faith, hope and love mingle their tribute just here. Terror cannot abide where the Son of the Highest is seen dying for our sins. All the unworthy fears of awakened sinners arise from their keeping away from the Cross. Bring your hearts hither, and your apprehensions will depart, like birds of night at the dawning.

3. Perfect love casts out fear, because it is of the very nature of love to promote confidence. The principle is familiar. Select your instances where you please, and you shall find this gentle, generous passion always trustful. I have heard of jealousy as the offspring of love; I never believed it. This foul spirit comes of pride, selfishness and envy. True love rests on the object beloved, with all the repose of certainty; even in human attachments. But when the soul flows forth towards infinite perfection and eternal love, it can no more suspect than it can hate. The same state of mind which looks to God with admiration and gratitude, looks to him with hope. Those fears, which we must entertain towards an enemy, or an untried friend, would be treacherous towards one who commands our supreme attachment. The more childlike your affection,

the fuller your confidence. The child in the mother's arms has its little heart poisoned by no misgivings as to the power or will of that mother to do it good. As little can the renewed soul, while in the exercise of love to God, harbour any slavish terrors. Let it ascend higher in its contemplations of divine excellence, and in the flight of its adventurous admiration; let it expatiate upon this ocean of magnificent beauty and awful grace; let it become so lost in the abundance of these attributes as to forget self altogether; let it surrender itself a captive, smitten by the celestial fascinations of immutable and endless Wisdom, Might, Purity, Rectitude, Truth and Grace; let it enter into the bleeding chamber where these are all blended in the dying Immanuel; and here, where love is reigning, it will feel that Fear is cast out. Hope meanwhile spreads the untiring wing, and sets forth upon the eternal flight.

In these three ways, then, we observe love casting out fear; as founded on just views of God; as caused by belief of God's love to us; and as, of its very nature, leading to confidence.

XIV. Now let us hasten towards our close by pressing this, as the grand import of the text: that the more love the less fear. If there is no love, then fear is dominant. If there is little love, there is great fear. If love is flickering and inconstant, there is perpetual interruption from doubt and terror. If love to God is gaining the upper hand, and even by many blows and hard conflicts coming to abide in love, then the habit of misgiving and apprehension is broken, and, as we often observe, even in chambers of illness and old age, the expectation of heaven becomes in a measure constant. Does not all this reveal a certain line of direction, a tendency, a rising towards perfection? If the love could at any moment become sinless, and drop its last weight, how joyfully would the soul rise from the realm of doubt, and leave all fears forever behind it! Brethren, it shall so rise! Presently this mortal shall put on immortality, and death be swallowed up in victory. Our imperfect views of God, even here, are the chief corrective of fears; but "when that which is perfect is come, then that which is in part shall be done away." Then will be brought to pass the saying, that "perfect love casteth out fear."

There is a practical direction of great importance to be derived from the doctrine which has occupied so unusual a portion of our thoughts this day. If you desire to be rid of those fears which vex and disturb you, seek to abound in the love of God. Give over those fruitless endeavours to calm your mind by perpetual probing of its wounds, and brooding over its corruptions. You knock at the wrong door, if you seek the cure of fears from law. The Law has no such office. The Law threatens wrath. The Law condemns and slays. The shortest and surest way to be bold even "in the day of judgment," is to "dwell in love." And where did the beloved disciple learn this love, but on the bosom of Jesus Christ? One irradiation of love, like the roseate tints of evening sky, suffuses this whole epistle. These swan-like notes befit the serene old age of such an apostle. His great argument even against the world is love. "If any man love the world, the love of the Father is not in him." "He that loveth not, knoweth not God, for God is love." "In this was manifested the love of God toward us, because that God sent his Only-Begotten Son into the world, that we might live through him." iv. 9. The lesson is learnt of Christ; and Christ is apprehended by faith. All your doubtings will give way before just apprehensions of gospel grace. If you are still harassed, still in occasional darkness and tremor, it shows that you still entertain some erroneous views of Christ and his work. Purge out this leaven of the Pharisees. Come to the Redeemer for a whole salvation. Add no jot or tittle of your own. See the things that are freely given you of God. Love him that first loved you, and while you sink into his arms, and surrender all to him, with a joyful, absolute self-renunciation, let this confiding love swell and abound, till every figment of distrust shall be swept away. For, against every challenge, in time or eternity, this may be your rejoinder: "He that spared not his own Son, but delivered him up for us all; how shall he not, with him, also freely give us all things!"

XIV.

THE YOUNG AMERICAN CHRISTIAN

THE YOUNG AMERICAN CHRISTIAN *

1 CORINTHIANS xvi. 13.

" Watch ye, stand fast in the faith, quit you like men, be strong."

WE live at a time when our ears have again become familiar with reports of warfare. It is easy therefore for us to imagine a general surveying his forces as they disembark from their transports upon a foreign shore. If now we should suppose him, as commanders are wont to do, about to harangue his troops, what would suggest itself as his most welcome mode of address? Shall he say to them, " Soldiers, I rejoice to inform you that you are about to experience no struggles nor bloodshed; no battle awaits you; all enemies have vanished from the land." Assuredly not, you reply. This were to insult their valour and mock their expectations. It is

* New York, January 28, 1855.

for conflict that the soldier girds himself; and especially to youthful enterprise and courage there is invitation in the sound of the trumpet, and incitement in the call to arms. Nor can the Christian combatant go through his campaign without hardship and blows. The Apostle Paul therefore addresses youthful Timothy thus: "Thou therefore endure hardness, as a good soldier of Jesus Christ;" or thus: "Fight the good fight of faith, lay hold on eternal life, whereunto thou art called, and last witnessed a good profession before many witnesses;" or thus: "Thou therefore, my son, be strong in the grace that is in Christ Jesus." All these are warnings of that opposition, contest, and difficult struggle which fall to the lot of the believer, and for which much force of resistance and assault is required. In the text this idea is manifestly present, and the Christian warrior is addressed in terms which sound of the camp and the army: "Watch ye," be awake, on your guard; vigilantly looking out for the enemy, armed at every point, prepared against every surprise, sensible of your danger and your weakness, and forewarned against your malignant and insidious enemy. "Stand fast in the faith;" know the truth, believe it, believe it strongly; cling to it, against all ridicule, loss, and persecution; be firm and constant in adherence to Christ, the great object of faith, and source of power. "Quit you like men;" the result of vigilance and assured faith; act the manly part. Thus Joab said to his party on a noted occasion: "Be of good courage, and let us play the men for our people, and for the cities of our God," 2 Sam. x. 12. Exhibit the high intrepid bearing which becomes Christians, acting in the name and for the honour of their Redeemer and King. " Be strong ; " go out to this warfare with full confidence in divine aid ; be strong in the Lord and in the power of his might; be stout-hearted and valiant, and by this be successful and victorious.

The topic seems peculiarly suitable to young Christians ; and for their sakes I would deduce from these words the value of AN EARNEST, MANLY AND COURAGEOUS CHRISTIANITY.

As in Christ Jesus there is neither male nor female, the subject belongs not only to Christian men but to Christian women; yet as I appear before a society of young men, and as in all aggressive movements it is they who must take the lead, the remarks which follow shall be directed towards the consideration of this vigorous religion as existing in young men. Reasons will appear in the sequel, why we may lawfully single out such a portion of the race as that which, speaking in general terms, is destined to survive ; and why we are justified in still further narrowing the field, by addressing our admonitions primarily to those who profess the faith of Christ, as the class contemplated by the text, and as that which must be the source of influence to its coevals.

If we might have all wishes in one, we could wish nothing better, nothing greater, than that the youth now growing up should be cast into the right mould. A present generation, duly trained in boyhood and adolescence, will make a coming generation of men, (I wish our otherwise rich English had two words, as most other languages have, to express the thought,) of MEN, who shall stand in the battle. Of poor sauntering triflers, in human shape and men's apparel, we have enough; of literary Sybarites, bred on stories, fugitive poetry and monthly magazines; of minute scholars, glorying in the niceties of metre and accent, college honours, and other tongues; of dressed creatures that sweeten soirées and playhouses with their odours; of things that flutter and die in the light of fashion, as moths about a lamp; of religious professors that almost ask leave to serve Christ of the sons of Belial who surround them; more than enough have we of such young Americans, aping every effete custom and appropriating every fungous abuse of the old countries, and spoiled tenfold worse by every voyage and travel abroad, so that they blush at the marks of an American as much as their fathers would have gloried in the same; more than enough of young men whose everlasting discourse is of the last amusement or the last scandal. But of MEN, spirits in earnest, souls that have an aim, bent towards some object, and that a great one; bearing and doing, training themselves by toil, by temperance, by self-denial, by prayer, for the benefit of the greatest number, it must be confessed with lamentation that we nave but few. And if, as we suppose, the times which are coming on the earth will demand such men, strong to do and strong to suffer, our only mode of providing them is to deal with the young, and to pour the plastic masses into the shaping mould.

Our Saviour long since taught us that the children of this world are wiser in their generation than the children of light. Worldly governments, cabinets and and war-bureaus are wiser and more provident than the church. The great contemporary drama in the Crimea teaches us a hundred mighty lessons; and I marvel, that at such a time there should be people empty and heartless enough to crave, in vulgar playhouses, the excitement or diversion of stale mimicry, mouthed by despicable players whom they would refuse admittance at their doors, or the provocative displays of semi-nude dances, at which a Roman matron would have blushed 'celestial rosy red;' at such a time, I say, when great tragic actions of real life and real death are held forth to view in that more than Trojan peril and endurance under the walls of Sebastopol. Go thither, ye poor effeminate drawing-room Christians, ye carpet-knights of a chivalry whose sword is lath and whose shield is pasteboard; go and learn what *men* can do and dare, when they are warmed by a grand motive. Behold them bleeding in the charge, behold them, harder yet, languishing to death in the wet and fatal trenches. On either side, see the fruits of true manly valour. What assault will they not venture, what privation will they not endure? "Now they do it to obtain a corruptible crown, but we an incorruptible." Our own American youth, we know, would do the like in any cause which interested them, that is, in any earthly cause. In a single hour, if our city were invaded, thousands of such as hear me would rally to any call of the country; and however unprepared by training, abstinence, and discipline, would do their best and die in doing it. But still the inquiry returns, why these and similar displays of manly virtue and self-sacrifice are so much limited to earthly hazards and conflicts? Why should the children of this world still put to shame the children of light? Why do we seldom behold a phalanx of trained Christians going forth, stately and irresistible, to the help of the Lord against the mighty? Are there no great interests at stake? Have we nothing as potent to stir the blood as the taking of a redoubt or the silencing of a battery? Can the great passions be moved only by revenge, bloodshed, crime? Ah, no, my hearers, History can show, even though experience should be dumb; history can show that there have been days when the Christian host was animated by a fire such as never had its equal in conquering armies. The principles of the faith have a stimulating and emboldening power, which, as you well know, was in past ages irresistible in the view of Gentile and afterwards of Antichristian foes. Just recall, for a moment, the earliest progress of Christianity, and consider what sort of men were engaged in that army. Only close students of church history do justice to the rapidity of this conquest. From Jerusalem, Antioch, Corinth, Alexandria, and Rome, as bases of operation, the hosts went forth almost simultaneously to the frontiers of the known world. The celerity of Alexander's famous marches was outstripped by Apostles of whom no record exists, who carried the cross into realms of whose myriad converts no registers remain. There is this in which the sacramental host differs from other armies; every soldier feels the genuine impulse. The Russian, French, or British private, though drilled to a mechanical exactness of evolution and practice, and hardened to a bulldog ferocity, may partake little individually of those patriotic, ambitious or dutiful sentiments which glow in the soul of great leaders. But in the church militant every missionary and every confessor and every martyr was individually able to give a reason of the hope that was in him; and when the Greek slave or the Roman boy or the Hebrew maid was brought before proconsuls and princes, they were as clear in their testimony of what they suffered for, even if not so able to argue on it, as a Paul or an Apollos. It will never do to ascribe the unmanly supineness and apathy of many Christian young men of our times, to any want of animating sentiment in Christianity.

If the Reformation did no more, it taught us, that among the cinders of that old altar there lay coals of fire which needed but the stirring and the heavenly breath, to make them flame up to heaven. All the stories of romance wither and seem insipid when compared with Reformation history. You cannot read an hour about Luther, Calvin, Zwingle, Melancthon, Knox, or Melvill, without feeling that you are communing with men. They had something to live for. They had some principles to die for. There were doctrines at stake. It is a symptom of the wretched, flaccid, pulseless condition of sundry in our day, that they never speak of theology, of catechisms, of doctrinal sermons, but with a sneer. The religion which they would like, if indeed they have thought enough to know their own mind, would be all sentimentality and all softness. Their weakened mental organs reject the strong meat. Know ye, O my beloved young friends, that manly bone, sinew and muscle, do not form themselves on the emollient regimen of a Christianity without doctrine. The men who of old went to the stake, went for doctrines; these doctrines they had learnt in the Scriptures, elaborated in meditation, methodized in system, preached to listening thousands, digested in the succinct formulas of definition, and left for us, their children, in those permanent crystals of the Reformed Catechisms, which are scoffed at by amiable wits and religious *petit maîtres*. Men, MEN, who can stand fast in the faith, who can stand alone, who have vertebral columns, who can bear, who can forbear, who can advance, who on due summons can strike, men armed with the armour of righteousness on the right hand and on the left, that is, with sword and shield, are bred in great study of God's Word, and great familiarity with those high evangelic truths which are the motive powers of the spiritual universe. And this partly answers the question we have raised about the paucity of Christian soldiers, who seem to be in earnest, as earthly soldiers are in earnest. So that the way is prepared for stating two great means of promoting Christian courage and strength.

I. The source of manly earnestness is *truth believed*. It is so in trade, agriculture, mechanics, and warfare; why should it be less so in religion? The crying sin of our young men in the church is voluntary ignorance; ignorance of theological truth in its definite expression and just connexion. How can they hope the fire to burn, when they will not take the time or trouble to lay on fuel? The most intense heat, and consequently the most powerful action, proceed from deep inward conviction of religious truth, derived from laborious study of the Scripture.

I foresee your reply: you have no time. The age is so active, city engagements are so numerous, in a word, you are so busy, that you cannot improve your minds. Now, if this were a sound answer, we might dismiss you at once as hopeless, and say, we expect from you nothing great, nothing steadfast, since all that is elevated and memorable results from improvement of the mind. But this is altogether an evasion. No man who is not a slave is too busy to make himself a thorough religious scholar, that is, to lay up within him the formative elements of manly power. Your engagements, we will suppose, are very great; but are you more busy than DAVID, who had a kingdom on his hands, which he successfully guided in war and peace, and yet found time to meditate on Scripture, and contribute some noble parts towards its completion? Are you more busy than PAUL, a traveller by land and sea, a preacher, author and apostle, whose entire life was a series of lofty deeds and heroic sufferings; and who yet was deeply conversant with the Bible? Are you more busy than MARTIN LUTHER, who preached almost daily, whose correspondence equalled that of a minister of state, and whose published books almost make a library of themselves; yet who daily and profoundly pondered on the Word of Inspiration? Nay, there have been men in every calling and profession, including your own, who amidst full and prosperous worldly employment, have redeemed hours to work the mine of Holy Learning. BACON, GROTIUS, Sir ISAAC NEWTON, and Chief Justice HALE, may show what philosophers and statesmen have been able to bestow on the sacred records. The truth, drawn out of the Scriptures and made the matter of lively faith, is that which wakes up and fortifies the character. And the cause of prevailing frivolity, vacillation and inefficiency, among certain well-disposed young persons, is, that there is nothing which they can be said to believe with all the heart. We may smile at the Commonwealth-man and the Scots Covenanter, for the sourness of their visages; but those stern dark faces showed like lanterns from the torch of conviction within; and mighty faith gave them earnestness of heart and strength of arm. One secret of their fortitude and energy and daring is found in the pocket Bible which each of them carried to the field, which he religiously read in camp, and which was often found next the heart when his dead body was carried from the field. The Book of God, when it is the one book, makes strong characters. Read it, study it, ponder over it; be not content, my young friends, to go over so much daily as a task, or to snatch a passage in the hurry of an odd moment; but lay yourself out to accomplish a thorough investigation of its contents, to acquaint yourself with its order, structure and harmony, to grapple with its difficulties, to systematize its truths, and to enrich your memory with its golden sentences. This is possible, seeing it is but one volume. Thousands have done so, and amidst difficulties as numerous and pressing as yours. Hundreds of Scottish peasants and day-labourers are at this very moment well instructed scribes unto the kingdom of God. And it will be a happy day for our American churches, when young persons of both sexes shall place the study of the Bible at the very head of all their intellectual pursuits. Then shall we see a race, able as well as willing to cope with the wily Jesuit and confound the boasting Atheist. Then shall that life and buoyant activity, which the vital current of holy truth keeps up, manifest themselves in the very portion of society where improvement is most hopeful.

II. If we look again for some solution of our mortifying problem, we shall find another cause of the tameness, irresolution and flight of our common religious combatants, in the want of devotional habits. True manly strength in religion is nurtured at the mercy-seat and at the foot of the Cross. The appearance of zeal may be put on for a little while, but permanent vigour must have a perennial source; and the spring-head must be within. No external activity, though pushed to the utmost, can make up for the want of closet devotion. This is just the point, where the electric attachment with heaven is effected. Here the fire comes down from above. If we would learn how Elijah, Daniel, Paul, Augustine, Luther, Whitefield, Martyn, Payson, and Judson, came to quit themselves like men, we must accompany them to their wrestling prayers. Nor are ministers of the Gospel alone to be imitated; scholars, soldiers, merchants, have learnt this secret of strength, and have thus found a treasury of courage, hope, and success, which the world never suspected. My beloved young brethren, the world has already half-destroyed us, when we are too busy to pray. Better forego food or rest, especially better forego any amount of profit, than learn to live without communion with God in devotion. Let the Mohammedan muezzin, from his tower beside the mosque, penetrate our conscience, when he cries aloud, at daybreak, through all the lands of Islam, *Prayer is better than sleep! Prayer is better than sleep!*

But the great matter to be pressed is unconnected with prescribed times or forms; and the great question to be asked is, Do I habitually maintain a confidential intercourse with my Lord and Redeemer in acts of heavenly communion? If yea, then the channel of strengthening influences being open, there will infallibly be boldness and sufficiency for the conflict of life. If nay, weakness, inconsistency, and defeat must ensue.

The reason why the two things just mentioned promote manly strength in the Christian character, is that by the word of God and prayer, more than by all other ordinary means, we maintain conscious union with God, the fountain of all power. Here we perceive the connexion between an inward spiritual piety and an outward aggression and triumph. No longer need we dissever the contemplative and the active, in life; one is the source of the other. When some mighty cataract bursts over its wall of mountain-rock, we are not to forget that the flood has been gathering force and volume in a long preceding flow. So also the visible activity of an enterprising Christian is to be traced to months and years of secret converse with God.

The more the balance is disturbed by worldly excitement and external bustle in the daily calling, the more there is need of this preponderating weight of home-religion and closet-quietude, to regulate the otherwise jarring motions, like the fly-wheel or the governor in an engine. The recluse student and the sedentary woman require this peculiar discipline of silence and shade far less than the man of business, who from morning till night scarcely redeems a moment for stated reflection. He must, by stern resolution and self-denial, gain some hour to hear God speak, and to speak to God, or he will inevitably shrink and wither down into the every-day worldly professor; who is bold at a bargain and cowardly in faith; earnest on week-days and half asleep on the Sabbath; indefatigable in trade-labours and unheard-of in operations for Christ's kingdom or his poor; hot upon 'Change and ice-cold in Church.

But the subject is too awful for satire. We need, in degrees beyond all power of expression we need, men with blood in their hearts, who shall be as courageous, as unflinching, as diligent, and as hopeful in the concerns of God, as hundreds are daily seen to be in the concerns of the world. We need not pause to show how immediate would be the effect on Christians and on society, if a general outburst of such zeal and effort should be witnessed in our day. And therefore we may at once proceed to the important truth, that the only hope of such an event must be founded on the increase of manly piety in the young. Unless those who are now ductile can take the image and superscription of such an earnestness, the next generation will be no stronger or nobler than the present. Mournful as the declaration is, it is not to be disguised, that we who, in our march, have turned the crest of life, and whose journey is westward and down the hill, have already taken our habit and character. We may regret the past, but changes for the better, though possible through grace, are not likely to be numerous or remarkable. And then, our career is chiefly run, and all that remains must take much of its colour from the good or evil of our better days. Strength of manly Christianity for the time that is coming must have its foundations laid in the youth of the present time. In this view of the subject, it is pleasant to consider that we of the more aged party are the minority, and our number is lessening very rapidly; while you, young men, are numerous, a reinforcement fresh and vigorous, ready to step into our places. May God grant you grace to wage this warfare more valiantly and successfully than we have done! Our best hopes for the Church of the future, under God, is in what we descry of promise in young Christians. Unless we depend on miracle and supernatural intervention, the progress of religion for the next twenty or thirty years will be according to the knowledge, piety and ardour of the youthful levies into our grand army. And this ought to be a powerful inducement to every ingenuous and public-spirited young man, whatever may be his vocation, to aim at a higher measure of devotion and love, than he has been accustomed to see in his companions.

Consider what kind of Christian character and conduct must be demanded by the period about to dawn. Deliberately ask yourselves, is not manly earnestness in Christ's cause especially required for the times which are coming upon the earth? "WATCH YE," says the text. It is a word of command, as when a guard is turned out; the military order to keep awake, because dangers are imminent and foes are expected. WATCH YE. It calls the young men of America to mount the walls and reconnoitre the field. And no one who has at all kept abreast of the signs of the times can give a glance toward the future, without starting up aroused and earnest at the probabilities of trying times and new emergencies, which will call for stout hearts and strong hands. The combination of omens during a few years naturally leads reflective patriots and Christians to search afresh into the prophetic oracles; and both Providence and the Word teach us to await a period in which a robust Christianity shall have all its nerve brought to the test. Wo to the young man who goes up to this battle with weak and sickly habit, with slender faith and with waning love! On what side can we look, without recognising the tokens of approaching commotion? We thought, in our simplicity, that wars were almost obsolete; but the gathering tread of the ten thousands in the Tauric peninsula, and the dead by disease and sword, correct our mistake. The tides of our own American politics no longer run smooth; and the controversies are as novel as they are momentous, so that we know not even at home what a day may bring forth. Elements stir in our bosom which may be thrown out with volcanic eruption on any one of several questions, domestic and foreign. Then we are not so far from the old hemisphere as once we were. Directly or indirectly, the present European, or more truly Eastern war, may, as a remote consequence, involve our own national peace. Nay, a revolution in remote Asia may prove very soon to be not merely between Chinese and Mantchou, or between autocracy and revolt, but between error and truth, between Belial and Christ, between persecuting outlawry of missions and the unexampled diffusion of the Gospel in that vast empire. An earnest mind will also pray for triple strength and triple manhood, in considering the fortunes of Rome, and the probable contest between America and the Pope. Wars and rumours of wars will possibly be accompanied or followed, in some lands, by infidel and popish persecutions; and so the sons of those present will need to be strong in the Lord and in the power of his might. Different as our interpretations of prophecy and our prognostications may be, there is, I suppose, no one among us, who looks for a quiet time, halcyon days, an Augustan age of art and letters and gentle luxury, for our immediate descendants. No prophet am I; but when I look intently on my sons, and on you my dear young parishioners, I seem to myself like one who hears and sees tokens of a sifting, and a shaking, and a suffering dispensation. "I am pained," cried Jeremiah to an incredulous people; "I am pained at my very heart: my heart maketh a noise in me; I cannot hold my peace, because thou hast heard, O my soul, the sound of the trumpet, the alarm of war!" And we also, in the midst of subterranean concussions and trumpet calls, think of possible convulsions and trials of fortitude, and desire for those who come after us a Christianity in earnest.

BE MEN, therefore, in knowledge, in faith, in self-denial, in endurance, in effort, in diligence, in perseverance, in love. Or to comprehend it in a word, "Be ye holy." That which contributes to your inward piety will secure your strength. As has been already said, no increase of outward labour, no pragmatical hurrying from toil to toil, no forwardness of mere act, no almsgiving or other beneficence, will certainly make you mighty men of God. All these may exist where grace is low or even absent. But devoted attention to the Word and prayer will do it; faith and vigilance and love will do it; communion with a dying Saviour will do it; the "unction from the Holy One" will do it. Let me vehemently exhort you to seek a Christian experience higher, broader and deeper than we, your predecessors and teachers, have exhibited; or than you observe in the religious world around you. For if Christ intends great blessings for the next age, it is likely that he will pour a three-fold anointing on the young men of this. Happy shall be the Evangelist of that period, a period thus resembling the primitive and apostolical days, who shall feel free to say; "I write unto you, young men, because ye have overcome the wicked one; I have written unto you, young men, because ye are strong, and the Word of God abideth in you, and ye have overcome the wicked one." 1 John ii. 13, 14.

XV.

DAILY SERVICE OF CHRIST.

DAILY SERVICE OF CHRIST.*

Matt. xxv. 37.

Then shall the righteous answer him, saying, Lord, when saw we thee an hungered, and fed thee? or thirsty, and gave thee drink? When saw we thee a stranger, and took thee in? or naked, and clothed thee? Or when saw we thee sick, or in prison, and came unto thee?"

Out of this divine picture of the groups around the last Tribunal, let us take a single point, detaching it from the rest. The modesty, humility, and self-forgetfulness of the righteous, shall introduce what we have to say on a matter of great importance. The good deeds of their life they scarcely recognise as having been such. They seem to forget that which God remembers, even their works of mercy. Certainly these blessed of the Father, brethren of the Son, and heirs of the Kingdom, do not belong to the class who trumpet

* New York, June 13, 1858.

their alms and rear monuments to their own goodness. Having done good by stealth, they blush to find it fame. Christ's applauses surprise them, and at an hour when the faces of millions on the left are gathering blackness, their cheeks are suffused with ingenuous blushing. They stand amazed that the Son of Man, now come in his glory with all the holy angels, should so overwhelm their trifling services with a glorious reward. Nay, they can hardly recollect any service at all. The ministries were so trifling, and were bestowed on objects so inconsiderable, often with such mixture of bad motives, and such deficiency of good, that it amazes them to find every transient item legible in the book of the Judge, now seated upon the throne of his glory. Such is the representation given by our Lord himself, of the feelings with which a righteous man will receive the gracious award.

Now, in parabolic sayings of this kind, no one will expect exactness of recital, as to the very words uttered before the throne. It is enough that we catch the great lessons breathed by the spirit of the passage. Every true servant saved by grace, will discover "at that day," how momentous have been the consequences of acts too small to be remembered. He will see, that a righteous man may have been continually putting forth unconscious influence; may have been ministering to his Master, when his mind was busied chiefly about his brethren; and that, while he sought the gratification of a benevolent heart, he may have rendered a service honourable and grateful to his Lord. Among the numerous teachings, therefore, of this magnificent vision, one may suffice for the present occasion. It is this: NO ONE CAN ESTIMATE THE AMOUNT OF SERVICE RENDERED TO CHRIST IN APPARENTLY LITTLE THINGS.

To trace this current of good deeds to its source, is not difficult. Wherever there is regeneration, there is love to Christ. Wherever love to Christ exists, it presently shows its fruits, in love to the brethren. The connexion is publicly owned by Him, who, pointing to the right, says, "These, my brethren." Benevolence, thus directed, leads to beneficence. True Christians do "not love in word, neither in tongue, but in deed and in truth." "Love unfeigned" is perpetually passing into act, with regard to every member of Christ who can be reached. The Lord Jesus vouchsafes to receive every such benefit rendered to any one of his people as conferred upon himself. And lest there should be a misgiving on this point, as if our Lord took account only of favours bestowed on distinguished disciples, he expressly instances the most inconsiderable. "And the King (the introduction of which title just here, merits our particular notice) shall answer and say unto them, Verily, I say unto you, inasmuch as ye have done it unto one of the least of these my brethren, ye have done it unto me." No act of kindness, even the smallest, is unobserved or disregarded by our King. He says in his heart of every such act: "It is done to ME." Yet the passage before us shows, that he who puts forth this act of bounty or mercy may entirely lose sight of its terminating on any object greater than the sufferer whom he relieves; indeed, even at the moment of relief, he may not explicitly own the reference of the act to Christ. One may therefore really minister to his Redeemer, when his soul is chiefly taken up with some Lazarus at the gate, or some wounded wretch left by robbers on the road to Jericho. The Master, nevertheless, accounts the deed as done to himself.

That we are to do all things "to the glory of God," and "in the name of the Lord Jesus," is fixed in the minds of all believers, by two remarkable maxims. But conscientious inquirers sometimes doubt whether any acts can be justly said to have this quality and intention, unless there be a distinct view of the Lord, as the object to whom the service is rendered. Doubtless, a view thus distinct is good, and much to be desired, since we cannot too much place our blessed Master before the mind, as the end of all our actions. At the same time, the passage which we are considering shows that, provided we be in a state of grace, we may be feeding, refreshing, lodging and visiting the Son of God, when, to our own apprehension, we are only comforting the hungry, thirsty, homeless, or imprisoned brother-man. And this is sustaining, in no common degree, to those who consider the limitations of human thought, and the small scope of many sincere minds, which cannot look far beyond what is nearest to them, especially when they add the cheering truth, that of such acts, which Jesus will thus own, there are thousands in the calendar of any one Christian year. Indeed, in this way, a true follower of Christ fills up his life. The new nature is continually working its way outwards, according to the various objects which invite its flow; and benevolence, inspired of God, seeks new ways of communicating happiness, even in the smallest particulars. Nor are these effluences of the sanctified nature, in the way of kindly acts, the less Christian, even if at the moment of performance the happy spirit does not distinctly think of its being done to Christ himself. The inward spring is perpetually running, marking its track by the green margin which it irrigates. A kind, merciful, unselfish heart is always looking around for some one to be the object of its care; and love is the same in its kind, when it gives a kingdom, and when it gives a flower. The clean raiment, gently laid beside the pauper's bed by the modest hand of a child, is as honourable in God's sight as the thousands builded into marble. This internal principle of goodwill, in a soul created anew after the image of the Divine beneficence, acts itself out to all the human species of whatsoever religion, language, condition, creed, or colour; and even makes itself known towards the lower animals, and all sentient beings. "A righteous man regardeth the life of his beast; but the tender mercies of the wicked are cruel."

We must nevertheless return to the brotherhood, the members of Christ, as the chosen objects of charity, affectionate care, and seasonable help. As we have opportunity, we do good to all men, but specially to those who are of the household of faith. The image of our Lord is in our poor neighbour, and we love it, even when we are not thinking of the reward which He will bestow. The very name of Christ, even where the image is obscured or dim, or not in any way apparent, goes for something in our esteem. Thus we honour the supposed signature of a friend, until we discover it to be forged. In foreign, and especially in unbelieving lands, the heart thrills towards one who is even nominally a Christian. Suppose we are mistaken; suppose we do a kindness to one who is undeserving; what then? Christ is deserving, and we did it in his name. It is marvellous what conscience some people make of never giving an alms amiss; as if it were the greatest of blunders to confer an irregular kindness on some poor suffering creature, not so good as they; as if charity were the only mode of erroneous outlay; as if every superfluity of their wardrobe, every extravagant bauble of their ornament, every costly rarity on their board, did not go to run up an account of perverted stewardship, greater in the aggregate than all they ever bestowed with their own hands upon the poor, right or wrong. If you behold Christ in your supposed brother, you honour Christ by the ministry, even if peradventure you mistake the character of the beneficiary. God only reads the heart. Those whom we doubt, and whose profession we discredit, may have been held down by troubles and temptation, and may, in the sight of the Allseeing, be as worthy as yourselves. If you are "the children of your Father which is in heaven," you will remember that he maketh his sun to rise on the evil and on the good, and sendeth rain on the just and on the unjust.

My hearers, I would not reject from some semblance of this brotherhood the vilest and worst of the sons of Adam. Each is a man and a brother. The nature which the Son of God assumed, in his incarnation, is their nature also. They share in the very humanity which He took. There is a sense in which He "tasted death for every man." There is an applicability of this death and its piacular fruits to every man. There is a commandment that the glad news of this love shall be preached to "all nations" and to "every creature." There is therefore a unity of the whole species, not only as the science of the world has demonstrated, in one parental pair, but in the assumption of their very nature by our Redeemer. And hence a true and scriptural philanthropy seeks the happiness of man, as man, and as claiming a human kindred with Him whom we love and adore. While then we are unquestionably bound to look with peculiar regard on those who are Christ's inwardly and spiritually, by a vital union, we are nowhere urged to any solicitous inquisition, how good a sufferer must be before we shall help him for Christ's sake. And if we should be happy enough to wrest a poor wretch from shipwreck, jail, or starvation, we do not suppose our Lord will any the less remember the tribute, if in the end it should turn out that the person, far from being a decent church member, was no better than she who broke the box of aromatics, or she to whom the Master said, " Go, and sin no more." If we imitate the divine goodness, let us never forget that when God's saving mercy comes to us, it always finds us unworthy. Whenever in the Scriptures we are exhorted to acts of beneficence, we are sent to the miserable as miserable; that is enough. Certification of desert, especially of godliness, is not presupposed. " Blessed is he that considereth the poor; the Lord will deliver him in time of trouble." Ps. xli. 1. And still more parallel: " He that hath pity upon the poor lendeth unto the Lord: and that which he hath given will he pay him again." Prov. xix. 17. Jesus records the loan, and makes remuneration, even to him who cries astonished, "When saw we thee poor and had pity on thee?"

The very striking portion of the language used by the redeemed which now occupies us, tends directly to this point: that a servant of Christ may be performing acts which the Lord accepts as benignantly as if terminating on himself in person, when all the while the humble happy servant, though habitually loving Christ, was unconscious of more than the glow of love and pity towards a fellow-creature. We do not say that reference to Jesus, the Chief-beloved, will not dart in, from time to time, amidst the charities of life, like stray sunbeams through the network of branches in shady places of the grove; such is always the heavenward reference of regenerate souls; but the rapid and almost instinctive impulses of Christian kindness often leave no time to look fully at anything but the famished, weeping, or bleeding sufferer. It will be apparent, upon the least reflection, that difference in degree or amount, the more or less of the benefits conferred, makes no difference in the principle. Do any good, be it great or small, to a brother of Christ, and you do it to Christ. What new rays of encouragement are here shed over the walks of our common life, which is made up of seeming trifles! It is as if the Lord Jesus had come with his hallowing presence, into the scenes of our daily occupation; to sit beside our well, to tread the planks of our fishing-boat, to smile on us with remonstrance when cumbered with much serving. Nothing is small, which the Master accepts as tribute. Little things become great, when done in a great cause, and out of loyalty to a great King. It is not the price, but the homage. Only a sordid, mercenary, venal mind would prefer the value of dollars and cents, accumulate the ciphers as you please, to the value of a ring, a lock of hair, a word of hearty postscript, an old tear-stained Bible, marked all through its tattered pages, a smile of love, a dying kiss. These are life's imponderables, which are also invaluables. The cup of cold water, in the name of a disciple, refreshes the soul of the Master and has his sure reward. The two mites of the widow (less than the cost of three sparrows) go for more than the thousands of the opulent. The heart is all. The giver stamps the gift, and the intention defines the giver. So likewise in regard to the person benefited; little things, we may say again, become great, when done in behalf of Christ's "little ones." And these are continually about us. The poor we have always with us; and God hath chosen the poor rich in faith. Ostentatious charities, of great figures, performed by proxy, should never take the place of personal kindnesses, though known only to God and the recipient.

Life is so ordered in providence, that what we call great deeds occur only now and then. Even princes and conquerors cannot be always magnificent. Especially we, who are not distinguished, must find our occasions of obedience in the shop, the farm, the school, the kitchen, the office, the ship, the family. If we are not doing good here; if a barren sentimentality beguiles us into dreaming of some future, romantic, conspicuous service; if we pass by the sister, the servant, the alms-person that rings timidly at our gate, or the errand-boy who brings supplies, while we plan beautiful schemes of distant and collective good; we are not the persons whom Jesus means. Common life, in its humblest domestic flow, is full of opportunities for honouring our Lord. You can scarcely make a single turn within the circle of home and daily work, without finding occasion to act out some inward principle of divine benevolence. "One of the least of these" Christ's "brethren," may sit beside your hearth, in the person of some parent, grandparent, or widowed relative. Christ may expostulate with you, for your neglect of some kinsman who is "waxen poor," and whom with coldness and pride you abandon to the tender mercies of strangers. "If any provide not for his own, and especially for those of his own house, he hath denied the faith, and is worse than an infidel." Acts of mercy towards those who are daily meeting us in the unromantic paths of ordinary intercourse, fall properly under the head of ministries to the Lord. A true Christian will endeavour to enliven every particular of service to fellow-creatures with this consecrating intention. This spirit of love will give verdure and fragrance to performances otherwise withered and repulsive. Thus, for example, the home duties of Woman, restrained as she is from publicity and the guidance of affairs, may be woven into a blessed tissue of service, often unconscious, to Christ Jesus the Lord. Charity will not house itself, we admit, nor selfishly shut out thoughts of sufferers abroad. But we always discover that those who are permanently and consistently most useful abroad, are those who have first proved themselves most faithful in charities at home. And, whether at home or abroad, the great majority of mankind must expect their usefulness, in other words their work for Christ, to consist in a series of familiar and oft-recurring acts, each apparently inconsiderable by itself.

> " 'Tis a little thing
> To give a cup of water; yet its draught

Of cool refreshment drained by fevered lips
May give a shock of pleasure to the frame,
More exquisite than when nectarean juice
Renews the life of joy in happiest hours.
It is a little thing to speak a phrase
Of common comfort which, by daily use,
Has almost lost its sense; yet on the ear
Of him who thought to die unmourned, 'twill fall
Like choicest music." *

How blessed a service! how munificent a Master! By this ubiquity in his suffering brethren, he is always present wherever a generous office can be performed. And let us not forget the very acts of mercy, the particular charities wrought by the righteous, and remembered by the King, charities confined to no age or nation, but practicable in whatsoever spot we encounter famine, parching thirst, exile, nakedness, disease, or bondage. Let us go in quest of Jesus, among the half-starved occupants of the tall, overcrowded tenant-house, where the restoring beverage, so familiar to our tables, never courts the taste of the scorched and hectic pauper; or sick-beds, where the foreigner and emigrant pants for breath in summer and shivers in winter; or, most neglected of all, in the prison-house, abode at once of shame, vice, ignorance and woe. All these, and such as these, all forms of misery, begotten of sin, and swarming most opprobriously in cities, under the very eaves of Christian wealth and lofty fashion, cry to us in

* Lord Talfourd.

the name not merely of humanity, but of our Lord. Every system of means which offers access to these representatives of our Master, and affords ways of serving him, should be honoured and upheld. But we should not allow individual effort to be swallowed up by great organizations. The machinery which intervenes between us and the Saviour, to whom we would minister in his poor members, is an evil, even if a necessary evil. Association, subscription, collection, stated agency, beneficent proxies, these are indispensable; but observe for what reason. They carry the alms of him who is too weak, too busy, or too old, to go always in person; they divide and methodize the work, so that no part may be overlooked, and no part over-served; and they cause a few, trained and practised, to do the work of many. But, after all, those organizations are best, which, while they secure these objects, assign most of their task of visitation and aid to free-will agents, and so increase rather than lessen the amount of individual charity. The Sunday School is one, and only one, of a class which somewhat realizes these ideas. When converts in large numbers are brought into the church, and with the impulse of new love look around for a way to do good, every one knows that the instrument which first and naturally presents itself is the Sunday School. The day is coming, when we shall have many others, equally aiming at the rescue of fallen humanity. At present, this form of charitable organization carries in its train much more than scriptural instruction on the

Lord's day; for Sunday School teachers are more and more Bible readers and Tract distributors in alleys and attics; Good Samaritans by the way, to pour oil and wine into hearts wounded by intemperance and unbelief; visitors of infirmaries, ships, and prisons; exhorters and reprovers of sin at wharfs and ferries; seekers for the sick poor, up and down the vast dimensions of our metropolitan misery. If you would find the thousands who do this work, while you sit on your luxurious sofas, and criticise the indiscreet outlay of public charities, you must look to the teachers in Sunday Schools. In my judgment the elite of beneficent and therefore happy Christians in America is in the Sunday School ranks. And though after all these weary days and anxious nights, some of them may exclaim, "When, O Master, saw we thee in distress and ministered unto thee," they will not fail of their reward. As a means of bringing out the latent and diversified talent of a congregation, the Sunday School is at present above all others. But the time is not distant when, under the influence of fruitful awakenings and the pressure of increasing love for Christ, the principle now very much confined to Sunday Schools will, by a happy extension, be realized in sister organizations, so diversified as to detect and employ in appropriate ministry every lurking talent of the brotherhood. While, however, we are awaiting a period when the inward energies of the Church shall be called out with more equable and universal effect, let each of us, in his own post, be living for Christ. We have nothing that we have not received; let there be nothing held back from the Lord. We serve a forbearing and munificent King, who, though he needs none of us, vouchsafes to treat our poor doings as if he were the party obliged. What a contemptible tribute is the fullest obedience of our best day, considered in itself! If we had " done *all those things*" which are enjoined, we ought still to say, " We are unprofitable servants; we have done that which was our duty to do." It was " duty," *dues* to be rendered, what we *ought;* we *owed* it; matter of debt. But mark how he receives it, how he gathers up the bruised, withered, scattered flowers which seemed dying in our hands, and makes of them a garland; binds them on his brow as a diadem; points to them before his angels as an honour. The self-condemning disciple sees no beauty or worthiness but in his prince. Conscious of short-coming, he hears the plaudit, and looks around among the right-hand myriads in quest of him whom it may befit. Not *me*, assuredly. " When saw *I* thee, in sorrow, and ministered to thee!" Yes, *thee*, blushing saint—thee; the Master's eye seeketh thee. The moment has arrived for discoveries, and while the wicked is horror-struck with the fiery record of his secret sins, the " Mene, Mene, Tekel, Upharsin," read by the universe in those asbestos leaves, the child of God is amazed to find that every kindness to a little one is tabled, owned and rewarded; " good measure, pressed down and shaken together." The secret charity has become public; according to that word, "there is nothing covered that shall not be revealed, neither hid that shall not be known;" which ought to teach us that every thing in the nature of service to Christ, has a certain greatness. I deplore from the bottom of my soul the disposition of some Protestants to undervalue and carp at acts of mercy to the poor, the sick, or the dying, because Romanists have made much of them. God forbid that neglect of Christ's poor should ever be a characteristic of Reform! God be thanked, that true Protestantism has always walked in the steps of that Catholic charity which is older than popes and monkery. If a Good Samaritan do a deed of mercy, let no meanness or inward sense of delinquency lead you to scowl at it. "Go thou and do likewise;" go and do better. To take a single instance; the great difficulties which private families, however wealthy, sometimes experience, in getting nurses for sudden emergencies of illness, ought to make us all exclaim, "How must it be with the poor!" and to concert measures for training Christian attendants for the sick; a service which has no more necessary connexion with Popery, than has the binding up of a bleeding wayfarer's wounds. For one, I will take the liberty of loving and applauding the act of mercy to a sufferer, by whomsoever performed; and this without groping into those hidden motives which can be read by God only. "THE DAY shall declare it." It shall declare thy feeblest, most faltering deed. O, Christian woman! O, little child! Here is the principle to preserve us from deeming anything little. The kind word, gesture, look, to a mother or a brother—some withhold these who are very public with good deeds to strangers—shall be owned as unto Christ. O, what a Master! Who will not love him and serve him! Let me close with the words of Bishop Andrewes: "There is glory which shall be revealed; for when the Judge cometh, some shall see thy face cheerful, and shall be placed on the right, and shall hear those most welcome words, 'Come ye blessed.' They shall be caught up in clouds to meet the Lord; they shall enter into gladness, they shall enjoy the sight of Him, they shall be ever with Him. These alone, only these, are blessed among the sons of men. O, to me the meanest grant, the meanest place, there under their feet; under the feet of thine elect, the meanest among them!"

XVI.

MIRTH.

MIRTH.*

PROVERBS xvii. 22,

"A merry heart doeth good like a medicine."

IN reading our admirable version of the Holy Scriptures, a little scholarship and a little knowledge of antiquity are useful, in order that we may not put modern and degraded meanings on terms which are grave and venerable. If we consult the Anglo-Saxon roots, or even the father of English poetry, we shall see at once how this applies to the words *mirth* and *merry*. If in modern parlance we distinguish between cheerfulness and mirth, ascribing to the latter a more giddy, unseasonable and vociferous effusion of hilarity, we shall lose the entire force of our text and other passages. *Mirth*, in good old English, included even the graver kinds of cheerfulness. The old Psalter praises God

---
* New York, February 28, 1858.

with "awful mirth;" both words being such as have suffered deflection. And the adage of Solomon is cleared by the exhortation of the Apostle James: "Is any merry, let him sing psalms." A merry heart is therefore precisely a cheerful heart; and that it " doeth good like a medicine," is one of those truths which every one of us, my brethren, has found true, blessed be God, in his own experience. In the course of remark on a somewhat unusual topic, which however is given me by inspiration itself, I shall endeavour to bring forward some truths respecting the nature and results of true cheerfulness, and the best way of seeking this healing influence. If the termination of the discourse should be unlike its beginning, let us pray that it may not leave any the less of salutary impression on the heart. CHEERFULNESS is a symptom of inward health, as truly as bodily alertness is of outward health. In regard, however, to mind as well as body, the symptom may itself become a remedial agent; the effect may in its turn act the part of a cause. For example, a sound appetite, which is a sign of vigour, may itself tend to the production of further vigour. And so, true cheerfulness, springing from mental health, may fall into a chain of causes, promoting yet greater health. You are therefore invited to consider the means of promoting that genuine Cheerfulness, or Mirth in old English, which doeth good like a medicine.

I. The primary truth in this part of the philosophy of life, is that true Cheerfulness is a concern both of body and mind. The junction of the immaterial with the material part in our nature is not like the annexation of two alien substances by a tie. Unlike as are body and soul, they were made for one another, and never in their normal condition to exist apart. If sundered for a little, it is that they may be rejoined. They are united in every part. Body acts on soul, and soul acts on body. This indeed was denied by one of the most ingenious philosophers that ever lived, the great Leibnitz, who taught that mind cannot influence matter nor matter mind; but that the Creator had made the two, like instruments tuned together from eternity, always parallel in action, each responding to the other, yet with no mutual agency. No one now believes in a hypothesis so ingeniously perverse. Sense and consciousness testify to us every moment that body acts on mind and mind on body; and in nothing is this reciprocal agency more undeniable than in health and disease. A sickly body sours, or saddens, or inflames the mind: a mind on the rack attenuates, wrinkles and enfeebles the body. The old theory of animal spirits still colours the language of common life, even when physiology rejects the notion of these subtile substances running up and down the system. But all hypotheses apart, who knows not that what we call good spirits quicken the pulses and clothe the frame with flesh, while fasting, loss of functional power, or injury to the organs, engender melancholy? In the large and proper acceptation of the term, we include the well-being of body and soul together, when we use the word health. He is not healthy, though with a frame of iron, who has moody flights and delirious fancies. How delicate was the adjustment, how perfect the temperament of the parts, when the father of our race was created and placed in Eden! Body and soul were twin portions of a wonderful contexture which worked sweetly and without a jar. Marvellous will be the change in the coming state, when these vile bodies shall be fashioned like "unto Christ's glorious body;" from the resurrection to go on without hinderance, in union with corresponding souls, to a glory never known in Paradise. The nearest approach we can ever have to this state, in the present life, is where the *mens sana in corpore sano* possesses health and strength. Of such a condition true Cheerfulness is the accompaniment and indication. This we may maintain without running into absurdities like those who talk about disease being a crime, and who would send all mental and moral ailments to the shop of the materialist for relief. The attempt to serve God and our neighbour with a broken constitution or a drooping mind, as many here have learnt by experience, is liable to great disappointment. As we would not undertake a friend's business with a beast of burden which was lame, so we should be loath to bring to the work of the Lord a body which drags heavily at every step. Yet sometimes God himself so plainly lays the trial upon us, weakening our strength by the way, as in the case of Hezekiah or Trophimus, that our lesson becomes that of resignation, patience, and quiet hope. Even then, it is our duty to use means for recovery. Even then, one of these means is that cheerfulness of heart which doeth good like a medicine, and without which all the *materia medica* might be exhibited in vain. Let those who enjoy health and hilarity, acknowledge dependance, and consider from whom the blessing comes. As there is a pride of family, of beauty, of riches, so there is a pride of health; and some of the most signal and admonitory reverses we have ever known, have befallen families and individuals whose habit it was to vaunt that they owed nothing to the physician. Every day, if possible, every hour, let us give thanks that our health has had no interruption; or, that it has continued long; or, after illness and decay, that it has been restored. "It is of the Lord's mercy that we are not consumed, and because his compassions fail not." That balance of the faculties, mental and bodily, which causes each and all together to work to the greatest advantage, manifests itself by a natural lightness of temper and clear animation of spirits, which is most remarkable in youth, but which we sometimes observe even in the autumnal days of a beautiful old age. It is the greatest of all blessings to the body; but at the same time it is a blessing which nothing bodily has power to confer. And, therefore, we must look higher.

II. Inasmuch as the soul has the prerogative of governing the body, there are numerous happy cases, in which there is a cheerful heart in a suffering and sickly frame. In every such instance the inward principle doeth good like a medicine. Many a patient had perished years ago, but for the fortifying, sustaining, and even curative power of a happy heart. Conflict there may be—there must be—because the effect of most bodily maladies, pains, and injuries is to subdue the mind; but where the intellectual and moral strength is paramount, we have beheld even tortures made tolerable, and feebleness of lungs or limbs set aside by the internal power. No matter how exceptional such instances are, they are sufficient to prove, how really independent of external circumstances an immortal soul may become; to refute the fallacy, that because the soul acts through organized matter, there is no longer any soul after dissolution; and to induce us all, in times of health and strength, to acquire those habits of mind and heart that may stand us in stead, when we come to the enfeebling trials of age or illness. Where cheerfulness survives, after the departure of health or bodily ease, we shall usually observe one or more of the following causes to be present.

First. Something in the nature of the malady or distress which does not spend its power on the mental part. "The spirit of a man will sustain his infirmity, but a wounded spirit, who can bear?" Some diseases make a speedy and direct assault upon the nervous system, including its great origin, the brain. Some, especially in acute cases, so fill the frame with vexation, annoyance, or even anguish, as to leave no freedom for thought or possibility of peace. But others, and these the most numerous, though often severe and sometimes fatal, make no advance to the mind's citadel, and so leave reason in its supremacy. But this is not enough. Hence,

Secondly. Cheerfulness in suffering may be due to natural elevation of spirits. Constitution, education, companionship, employment, opinions, customs of living, these are mighty confluent streams which go to form a river of habit, good or evil, in respect of cheerfulness; which habit is too powerful to be turned aside by any ordinary contingencies of disappointment, pain, or weakness. Those whose profession leads them to be much in sick rooms are familiar with instances of this, which, to the inexperienced, would seem fabulous.

Thirdly. The only source of genuine cheerfulness on the bed of sickness and death is the grace of God in the soul. But we have tarried long enough beside the chair of the invalid. May God grant to all such the cordial of inward heavenly joy! A third consideration, applicable to every individual in this assembly, and founded on laws of nature, awaits our notice.

III. Since both soul and body are made for exertion, there is nothing more conducive to cheerfulness, the result of their joint health, than fit employment. A house bereft of tenants goes to decay. A vehicle laid up without use rusts and moulders. A fine piece of machinery is never so safe, as when lubricated and moving. Body and soul, made for perpetual activity, must work, and work together, in order to be in good condition. Of all engines, the human body is the most amazing. From the days of Socrates, as reported by Xenophon, philosophy has been studying the mechanics, the chemistry, the vital forces, the adaptations, the final causes of this structure, so fearfully, so wonderfully made. There is no step forward, to new principles in physics, in optics, in the growth of structures, which does not find itself anticipated by some marvellous realization of its idea in the human body. Considered as a working engine, there is none which works so cheaply, with so little waste, and so long, or which contains such provision for its own repair. How every survey of the skilful mechanism shows that it was made to move. Its central, propelling engine never stops, except in cases which cause instant dread of death. Heart, lungs, and brain, play on through all the thousand nights of sleep. An instinct of nature prompts the young to be in almost perpetual motion. Absolute rest there is none. And if, from necessity or choice, any approach to immobility becomes the habitude of body, as is the case in some sluggish and morbid natures, the result is lethargy and endless disturbance of the vital functions. This frame was made for labour.

Equally true is this of the yet more subtle, because spiritual part. The soul is essentially active. Of a mind that does not think, no man can frame a notion. The human mind is made to be active. It is inquiring, and athirst for knowledge. Its active powers irresistibly seek for some object on which to exert themselves. Healthful, moderate repose, chiefly by change of employment, is good; but entire, continual, unbroken quiescence is misery. Never was there a more dire mistake than that of men who abandon the honest and useful business of life, under the pretext of rest. Unless they have singular resources, in science, literature, or philanthropy, they sink into hebetude, weary of the everlasting holiday, let their heart corrode with sullen thoughts, and sometimes fall a prey to evil habits or premature dotage. Philosophy, no less than Religion, enjoins—unless where invincible necessities from infirmity or age clearly speak another language—that we should live working, and die in the harness. Hence the value of a trade or calling, and of working at it. I believe it lengthens life. I believe it staves off tribes of maladies and conceits. I am sure it promotes that spring and elation of soul, without which life is a long disease. If you would find the most wretched man or woman in your neighbourhood, look for the one who has nothing to do. Unless allowed to prescribe employment, even the best physician cannot cure the valetudinary complainer. For after all has been said, employment begets cheerfulness; and " a merry heart doeth good like a medicine."

IV. But man is not merely an intellectual, he is a moral being, and hence healthful cheerfulness requires as its indispensable condition a good conscience. To be truly happy in mind, the soul must be at harmony with itself. I know the objection that you are framing in your thoughts, and I will dispose of it at the outset. You are thinking of numerous persons known to you, who are immoral, and yet intensely and extravagantly mirthful; you have even known flagitious sinners, who were proverbial for laughter and good cheer. You recall to mind the thousands who haunt every place of amusement, and whose habits go to sustain the dens of boisterous wassail. Now, on a calm and serious view of the case, leaving religion out of the question, you will scarcely choose this species of hilarity as that which you would wish for a beloved son. It is scarcely such as will endure for a lifetime, or gild the declining hours. You have probably seen enough of society to know that much of this ostentatious mirth is purely factitious, made up of the sympathies and contagion of good-fellowship and wine. Nay, you must be young as an observer, if you have not found that your merry friend indulges in a certain feigning. He is not so merry as he would have you believe. The wreathed smiles of his artificial visage partake of grimace. He is more smiling when met than when overtaken; more full of jest with strangers than at home; loud in company, stupid by himself; in a word, bidding fair for an old age of stupor, gluttony, or drink. You know perfectly well, that if youth be left out of the account, the people who run after public amusements are precisely those who cannot enjoy solitude, and who have never learned to endure themselves. O, that some of those, who recognise their own face in this likeness, would lay to heart the truth that their conscience is diseased!

1. Conscience of crime is a tormentor. There is scarcely a Gentile sage or poet who has not said so, in description and example, for it needs no inspiration to reveal how this scorpion of the bosom can sting. The cases are so horrible, where habitual and repeated sin has reached the point of silencing and palsying conscience, that it is hard to say what may be the temper of a soul which has passed under this cautery; but who among us would seek such a callous heart as the abode of cheerfulness? Of all passions none breathes more of the atmosphere of hell, than remorse. This ought to gain the attention even of those who have as yet been kept back from presumptuous sins; because no one ever became suddenly vile, and they know not what may be the end of the way upon which they have entered, or whether their closing scene may not be maddened by despair.

2. Far, very far on this side of atrocious crimes, there may be such continuance in transgression, as may embitter the conscience, and make quiet joy impossible. This case may be well studied by the young man or young woman, who, after a religious education, has restrained prayer, neglected the Scriptures, stifled convictions, and gone into the world for happiness. There is a conscious dissatisfaction under all the gayety. The day of pleasure is often followed by a night of disquie-

tude. The intervals between one and another of those nocturnal assemblies which quench forever the religious emotions of many, are dull and pensive. The very face of the maiden, who ought to be rosy, jocund, and alert, is "sicklied o'er with a pale cast of thought." Something is wrong. The pride of the house is wretched. Summer tours and winter dissipations, such as modern piety may approve, fail to restore the elasticity of a once healthful creature. The unwelcome truth is, the immortal spirit will not brook the treatment of such charlatanry. The soul craves its peculiar and appropriate food and refreshment. The immaterial and aspiring nature sighs for God. And how can it be cheerful?

More of the world's sadness and gloom than the world chooses to reveal, is caused by hearts ill at ease, and consciences disquieted with sin. There are persons who for years drag about a body wasted by the restless, consuming mind. While worldlings charge religious people with gloom, they are themselves often kept in misery by their want of Christian peace. It requires no godliness to make one suffer from conscience. Natural principles, among all nations, suffice for this. Conscience utters the voice of law, or expostulation, of remonstrance, sometimes of menace, of retribution, of vengeance. It is for relief from such pangs that the troubled, aching soul goes to the Gospel. But thither the deluded follower of pleasure or gain cannot bring himself to go. And till he goes, all his mirth and gayety are illegitimate and irrational, even if they are not simulated and hollow. Thousands walk our streets and flaunt in our assemblies, wearing the garb and the smirk of an assumed and conventional hilarity, who would sink to the earth, like the child's top, the instant they should cease to whirl. If they durst sit still long enough to feel the pulses, they would know that they are sick at heart. They have forsaken the fountain of living water, and have hewed them out cisterns, broken cisterns, which can hold no water. Amidst much forced merriment, they are utterly void of all that vernal cheerfulness which is as characteristic of a well-regulated sound religion, as sweet flowers are of Spring. And the tendency is from bad to worse.

3. Even in the ordinary narrow acceptation of the term in the world's idiom, a good conscience promotes ease of mind. It smooths the pillow. It removes acerbity from the tone, in hours of business. It reconciles the father to his family group, and the son and daughter to their home. But, in order to clear away clouds, calm the sullen swell of the mysterious ocean within, and throw sunshine over the late darkened countenance, there is need of something more determinately gracious. Simple social morality, honour in trade, truth, candour, hospitality, neighbourly kindness, domestic affection—all beautiful, all good, on a lower scale of value—have no adequacy as answering a holy spiritual law, and therefore no power to pacify an enlightened conscience. Though a sinner may be either

exorbitantly gay or deeply stupid in his sins, he cannot feel these sins and be cheerful. Here I touch the sensitive spot that denotes the disease. No transgressor against an infinitely holy God can have healthful mental enjoyment, such as does good to soul and body, while he is vexed with the conviction of his heinous guilt. And the point to be observed is, that no sinner can infallibly prevent such conviction and such distress. In this respect, as in others, the soul that forsakes God remains still in the hands of God. It is not for him to say when he shall be disquieted for his sins, how long this disquietude shall last, or to what extreme of torment it may rise.

In a Christian land like ours, many a heart, wrung with agonizing reflections, never reveals itself to the ear and heart of human friendship; and ah! cannot, will not, reveal itself to the ear and heart of a compassionate God, in the outpourings of confidential prayer. Nothing is more wide-spread than uncomfortable feelings with regard to religious deficiency, which are strong enough to kill cheerfulness, but not so explicit and developed as to lead to decision. Yet such vague trouble of mind is often the precursor of salvation. False peace, it is true, sometimes comes in; introduced by erroneous doctrine, self-righteous satisfaction, or spurious exercises accepted as graces of the Spirit. But even this fails, either by want of permanency, or by leaving the heart still unblest with the radiance of a serene joy. To walk on earth with the erect countenance of Christian cheerfulness, there must be peace with conscience and peace with God.

4. There is no such thing as a good conscience, except where there is a persuasion of acceptance with God, through the mediation of the Lord Jesus Christ. This persuasion causes the face to shine as did the face of Moses when he came down from converse with God upon the Mount. Here is an irradiation which makes the soul lift itself in holy cheerfulness, just as the sun in May makes the violet and the rose unfold their leaves with freshness of beauty. " Wisdom maketh a man's face to shine." And of this heavenly wisdom or spiritual knowledge and service of God, the wise man says : " So shall they be life unto thy soul, and grace to thy neck; when thou liest down, thou shalt not be afraid, yea, thou shalt lie down and thy sleep shall be sweet." Prov. iii. 22, 24.

It is proper just here to observe, in order to meet a difficulty of candidly inquiring minds, that the earliest exercises of penitent, returning minds are not always joyful. There may be bitterness beneath the soil and in the knotty trunk, when the clusters and fruitage above are dropping with sweetness; or, as convalescence from sore disease is sometimes preceded by a fearful crisis, so the first transition from worldliness to serious thoughts of God and heavenly things is commonly marked by alarm, humiliation, and grief. The anxious seeker's path circles the Old Testament Sinai, often many times, before it strikes off thitherward toward Mount Zion, and opens yonder at the Cross. But when it leads the wayfaring soul to "Jesus the Mediator of the New Covenant, and to the blood of sprinkling, that speaketh better things than that of Abel," it presents to him a region of springtide joyfulness. There may be weeping clouds, there may be alternations like returning winter, but still the Sun of Righteousness is there. It is a Beulah, a land of cheerfulness; such cheerfulness as even does the body good, and drives the crimson tides with new impulses of life to members lately collapsed and chill. Are any notes of gladness more ravishing than those which the convert hears, amidst these green pastures beside these still waters? Listen to what issues from the mouth of a glorious and beloved Friend, till now unknown; hearken! "Rise up, my love, my fair one, and come away. For lo, the winter is past, the rain is over and gone; the flowers appear on the earth; the time of the singing of birds is come, and the voice of the turtle is heard in our land. The fig-tree putteth forth her green figs, and the vines with the tender grape give fragrance. Arise, my love, my fair one, and come away." Song, ii. 10–13. When Jesus speaks pardon and love to the soul, he gives cheerfulness and joy. At no epoch is this so strikingly felt, by reason of contrast, in passing from an anxious into a rejoicing state, as at first believing, the love of espousals. But I am so far from thinking these to be the highest raptures of religion, that my persuasion is firm and daily increasing, of "the marvellous loving-kindness" of God, to his unworthy but redeemed people, in the latter stages of their journey, even to the very last. To every true convert Jesus seems to say "Believest thou? thou shalt see greater things than these!" When, therefore, we invite such as are the prey of unhealthy anxieties to try the effects of the grand restorative, we invite them, not to sighs and tears, not to manifold austerities of service, not to a forsaking of all their present solace without hope of indemnity, but to a peace of God which passeth all understanding, and a reasonable ground of habitual cheerfulness, on which, as on a tried foundation, they may (to say the very least) rest more securely than on any support sought or conceived of by the soul of man. Directly or indirectly, you are constantly seeking some tranquillity of soul, some rest for the immortal spirit, some slaking of the insatiable thirst. You struggle for it, as the tendrils of the vine wring their way in tentative movement towards the light; you turn towards it as the crushed worm under your feet writhes in search of ease. Out of religion, out of propitiation, out of the Lord Jesus Christ, you will never find it. You will, like those fifty fabled daughters of Danaus in the classic story, spend life, pouring water into vessels pierced like sieves; or, more heavily rolling the mighty stone up the arduous mountain, that at each remove it may again turn upon you with thundering bound. And when you have tried all that worldly mirth can do, you will say with the repentant king, "I said in mine heart, Go to now, I will prove thee with mirth, therefore enjoy pleasure; and behold this also is vanity. I said of laughter, it is mad, and of mirth, what doeth it?" Ecc. ii. 1, 2.

XVII.

BELIEVERS ARE WITNESSES.

BELIEVERS ARE WITNESSES.*

Isaiah xliii. 10.

"Ye are my witnesses, saith the Lord."

CHRISTIANITY, as being from God, the sovereign Ruler of the Universe, asks no patronage from the great of this world. Learning, rank, opulence and power, which have weight elsewhere, are as nothing here. As if to show this in the strongest possible manner, God chose to establish his Church of the new dispensation in absolute neglect of all such auxiliaries. He might have gained over the sagest of the Porch, the Academy, or the Lyceum, the professors of Tarsus and Alexandria, or the rabbins of Tiberias. He might have arrayed his evangelists in imperial purple, and heralded his gospel by lictors and sound of trumpet.

* New York, June 20, 1858.

He might have caused princely armies to trample down opposing nations; "But God hath chosen the foolish things of the world to confound the wise, and the weak things of the world to confound the things which are mighty; and base things of the world and things which are despised, hath God chosen, yea, and things which are not, to bring to nought things that are, that no flesh should glory in his presence." And hence, even when, in the progress of ages, the Church has subsidized many of these very influences, she has received them as followers, and never yielded them homage. Christianity has now so entrenched itself within the science, the letters, the public institutions, and the kindly affections of mankind, that it looks with a benignant pity on mistaken creatures, who condescendingly talk as if evangelical truth, by their good leave, was not so bad a thing, and as if, with a liberal construction and some reserves, the Bible might, after all, be received even by liberal thinkers. The decayed Hidalgo, who stalks proudly in rags which his ancestral cloak scarcely hides, is not more ridiculous in his pride. Nay, the king who emerges from the straw of Bedlam, bowing as he yields sufferance and admission to his keepers, is quite as rational in his supercilious complacency. After a thousand battle-fields, amidst innumerable trophies, Revelation sits as a queen. From every nation and in every dialect, the wise and great flock to do her homage. The banks of the Nile and the Tigris, the monuments of Judea and the catacombs of Rome continually augment the glorious accumulation of their evidence. The scholarship and philosophy of the world are on the side of the Cross. And yet, over against our host of confessors, our Bacons, Pascals, Newtons, Henrys and Owens, we descry puny figures coming forward to lend the shelter and countenance of their insignificant pennon! And who, forsooth, are they, that the "Virgin daughter of Zion" should ask, or even brook their aid? By what names are these called, who are thus eager to inform us of their tolerance of Jesus, and their good opinion of the Lord of hosts? Peradventure some sciolist, undisciplined in any one severe science, undrilled in any ancient tongue, unfamiliar even with the books of Scripture, but pert and voluble at counters, tables, clubs and drawing-rooms, and admired in his flippant cavil by groups more ignorant than himself. Or, it may be, some narrow pedant, all behind the age, who has dozed in the cave of the Seven Sleepers, while the world has been rolling on, and who in his simplicity is ignorant that the materialism and philosophism of Voltaire, D'Alembert, Volney and Diderot, are just as valid, even with decent infidels, as alchemy, magic, or the humoral pathology. Who cares (except in commiseration for his foolish soul) what such a one thinks of Christianity? Or the voice of complaisance toward our holy religion may issue from some back-shop or foul attic, where, among licentious verse and graphic abomination, the thumbed and smutched volumes, redolent of Birmingham or the collieries, bear the grosser names of Paine, Carlisle, or Holyoake. This is generally emigrant deism, and its converts among us are fished up from the filthiest pools, where drink and unthrift lie alongside of brutal ignorance or incorrigible stupidity. Shall I add to the list those apostates from Christianity, who, though bred in evangelical churches, never felt the power of grace, smarted under correction of their secret sins, found it their interest to prove that the murderer and the demon should be happy in heaven, kicked at the goads of reproof and overleaped the fence of mystery; the renegade Christians, who have betaken themselves to a scheme as much Mohammedan as Christian, to a Scripture without infallible truth, to a Cross without expiation, to a salvation without Christ? From any, from all of these, we reject the proffer of ostentatious aid. We would gladly give them of our stores; but save us from their patronage! Not by such attestation is heavenly Wisdom justified.

There is something like pusillanimity in the warmth with which certain professors of Christianity chuckle over every little good word doled forth in its behalf by men who scarcely know its tenets, and live in defiance of its commands; while the same weak friends of the cause overlook the testimony of millions, who have best known the reality of religion because they experienced it, and have yielded the strongest attestation by adhering to the faith. Infidelity shows no such throng of believers, confessors, dying saints and martyrs, as, with perpetual augmentation, have been avowing, age after age, the power of grace. These, these are the witnesses. When, with nervous trepidation, distrustful of your own cause, you betake you to the others, and pick up the paltry concessions of deists and heretics, it is as if you should call in a chance New Zealander or Esquimaux, who had descried the distant smoke of a propeller on his waste seas, to gain his testimony concerning the existence and value of a steam navigation which fills our harbour. Let them testify of what they know; of our heavenly Wisdom they know as little as "the eagle, and the ossifrage, and the ospray, and the owl," unclean birds all, sweeping over the desert where the tabernacle reposed, knew of the awful contents of the ark of the covenant. The testimony which such people give to religion, taken with its accompaniments, is often as horrible as it is ridiculous. A miserable suicide leaves his judgment that the Bible is true. The most misanthropic of all sensualists, Rousseau, to his elegant but poisonous confessions of lust and lying, adds a tribute to Jesus Christ, whom he prefers, O marvellous complaisance, to Socrates ! It is about a hundred years since Earl Ferrers, an English nobleman, was carried to the scaffold for his second murder. On his way the minister of religion tendered to him the admonitions and consolations which it is usual for aristocratic and plebeian felons to receive; but the school which taught him murder had also taught him deism: he haughtily rejected the good offices. But then, not to be too cruelly grand, and as if to spare the humbled feelings of Christianity, he deigned to say, that he believed in a God, and that he had always thought the Lord's Prayer a useful composition.* Such is the commendation which some are fain to chronicle, from the condescending admissions of absurd and immoral men. Let all such lie silent in their original worthlessness, while a healthful love of truth leads us to suspect and avoid organs to which the light of noon is repugnant. We do not require the tardy, reluctant tribute of minds which still reject our heavenly Master. Pilate and even Judas may yield testimony to innocence, and we own the power of conscience; but it is to the faithful eleven that Jesus says, "Ye shall be my witnesses." And this leads me to turn suddenly from the false witnesses to the true; from those who yield a reluctant, insufficient and insincere testimony, to those who speak in honour of the truth with heartiness and acclamation; from outside lookers-on to believing inmates and loving children. Let us, then, reflect on the meaning of these words which the Lord addresses to his people: YE ARE MY WITNESSES.

The truth to be considered and applied is, that all true Christians are witnesses for God. And here it is hardly requisite to premise, that there is a sense in which God asks no attestation. He is himself the infinite source of all authority and the fountain of honour. Were all systems of planets, with all their inhabitants, and every thinking, active creature, smitten and turned

* Walpole's Letters.

back into nothing, the self-existent, independent Jehovah would still be glorious, in the mutual comprehension of the Divine Persons, to all eternity. But the Most High, in the communicative flowing out of his love, has come forth in creation, for the very purpose of reflecting his rays upon the intelligent moral beings whom he formed by his power. Of all it may be said, "For thy glory they are, and were created." Of human subjects God declares: "This people have I formed for myself, they shall show forth my praise." Such is the grand intention of the method of grace. Souls are saved, that they may eternally laud and magnify the riches of divine excellency; "that he might make known the riches of his glory on the vessels of mercy, which he had afore prepared unto glory." Salvation, when consummate, will prove to have had this end, the exhibition of wisdom, power and love; "that in the ages to come, he might show the exceeding riches of his grace in his kindness toward us, through Christ Jesus." Indeed; this reverberation of God's praise is the office of all creatures, animate and inanimate, being what is fitly named his declarative glory. And all this declaration, whether vocal or silent, may be considered as a witness-bearing, which has this pre-eminence in children of God, that it is the tribute of holy love and gratitude. Every true believer, then, is a witness for God. In time and in eternity, he is a lamp kindling into brighter and yet brighter flame, in the sanctuary of his Lord. Early in his ministry, our Master taught this to his disciples;

"Ye are the light of the world;" "Shine," and "Glorify your Father which is in heaven." For this very purpose of bearing witness to the truth every believer was first called. And as Jesus, the Messiah, the elect of God, is the Chief Witness and pre-eminent glorifier of God, so all the members of this Head and followers of this leader, render a testimony according to their respective positions. "Ye are my witnesses, saith the Lord, and my servant whom I have chosen." But this testimony to God and his truth must not be left in its generality, but traced out a little further into some of its branching exemplifications; in order that we may see how complete, irrefragable and glorious is the witness borne to revelation and the gospel. True believers, then, are witnesses for God, by their believing, their profession, their example, and their suffering.

1. BY THEIR BELIEVING. To believe God's words is the very first act of adherence. Here the vital connexion is formed with God incarnate. At this point the rebel wheels into the ranks of service. The erring orb turns its lately darkened side towards the Sun of righteousness. What though the act be inward and invisible? God reads his own inscription on the soul: and who shall say that it is not read by higher created intelligences? Even among men, this light is not placed within the crystal globe of a soul to remain unseen. Acceptance of truth, especially of Jesus, the primeval truth, is inferior to no act of homage which the creature ever puts forth during all the career of grace. The chief

attestation given by any man is himself to believe. He "setteth to his seal," that God is true; he witnesses. It is his endorsement, or subscription. He avouches God to be his God, and passes over to his side. This is introduced allusively a few verses later: xliv. 5: "One shall say, I am the Lord's, and another shall call himself by the name of Jacob; and another shall subscribe with his hand unto the Lord, and surname himself by the name of Israel." He who has faith in the Gospel thereby becomes a witness for Christ. It is by the Spirit in the soul that believers are enabled to say: "And we have seen and do testify that the Father sent the Son to be the Saviour of the world."

2. Believers are witnesses for God, BY MEANS OF THEIR PROFESSION. This is literal, positive, and open witness-bearing. In Scripture it is often called confession, and those who brave perils in making this avowal are named confessors. "With the heart man believeth unto righteousness, and with the mouth confession is made unto salvation." In early times it was often, as indeed it sometimes is with us, a joint attestation, a "good confession," before many witnesses. This comes home tenderly to all such as have lately taken God to be their God, and sat down among his people. They then and there stood forth as witnesses. To this Paul alludes, saying, "Let us hold fast the profession [joint attestation] of our faith without wavering." All professing Christians since the world began have been so many witnesses for the Christian system. They voluntarily

come out from the world and take their position on the Lord's side. They avouch the Lord to be their God, and Jesus Christ to be their leader and captain of salvation. Of this testimony they are not ashamed. If religion is unpopular, and strict Christians in a minority; if social persecution, in the way of ridicule and calumny, arises; if false opinions, called liberal, but savouring of perverse progress, erroneous and heretical, have currency and sit in the heights of fashion; if consequently it costs something to be a disciple, and the professor must often be singular, conspicuous, and solitary; none of these things move him. As a witness would go into court joyfully and with open face to attest the character of a father or a friend, though all the world were on the other side, so the Christian is ready to stand up for his Redeemer. There is even a glorying, in the ingenuous soul, when adherence to a friend and vindication of a righteous cause involve some peril or obloquy. The majority of you, my brethren, are called to profess the name of Jesus, in a much more quiet and secure way. You rather gain than lose by appearing as Christians. Very different is your condition from that of early believers, who often signed their own death-warrant when they owned Christ before men. But you do as really witness for God, when you come into the fellowship of saints, and show the Lord's death till he come.

3. Disciples are witnesses for God by their EXAMPLE. Actions speak loudly for any cause. "By this," said our Saviour, "shall all men know that ye are my dis-

ciples, if ye keep my commandments." It is by letting our light shine that we glorify our Father which is in heaven. No words, however well chosen, repeated or earnest, no professions, however public, can avail so much for the honour of Christianity, as a pure and consistent life. In the early progress of the Gospel, this was the attestation which first struck, then attracted, and eventually convinced the Gentile observer. The truth, the peacefulness, the meekness, the fraternal affection, the charity of the new sect, won its way to the moral approbation even of enemies. This is a species of testimony which, from its nature, is continually on the increase. The more wide our field of observation and the closer our scrutiny, the more will instances of moral excellence, as fruits of faith in Christ, brighten on our vision, as new tracts of stars come into view in galaxies and nebulæ, under the penetrative power of the telescope. All believers are thus God's witnesses, by a holy life; and this to the confounding of infidelity, which can show no such seals. Our very familiarity with this class of facts deadens our susceptibility to their just force. We almost weary of seeing men made better by Christianity. But let us see how the account will read, if we reverse the statement, and imagine such things recorded of infidelity. Let me feign the history of such inverted revival, thus: A man well known as a liar, swindler, and profane swearer, has lately been convinced of the falsity of the Christian religion, and has consequently abandoned all his evil courses. A riotous, drunken ruffian, the scourge of his family and terror of his neighbourhood, has lately become quiet, pure, and temperate, and has closed his den of madness, all as the fruit of Deism, to which he has been converted. Two miserable debauchees ascribe their return to a life of virtue to having embraced the doctrine of universal salvation, and express great comfort in the belief that Judas Iscariot passed immediately into glory. An entire community has just sustained a transformation from litigious conflict and angry feud to concord and humanity, from yielding to the belief that there is no God.—You are startled, my brethren, and justly. Infidelity bears no such fruit and summons no such witnesses; while the religion of the Bible exhibits them with uniformity, splendour, and incalculable extent.

4. True Christians are witnesses for God by their SUFFERINGS. All Christian suffering is a kind of witness-bearing. It is the greatest consolation of saints under heavy trials, in long debilitating illnesses, and those retirements and straits which forbid active service, that they are all the while passively serving. Under the Cross they bear witness of God; attesting his justice, his faithfulness, his power, his wisdom, his covenant-gentleness; they bear witness of Jesus, that he hears the sigh of the humble, distils the dew of his grace, sustains the fainting head with his arm, tranquillizes and elevates by his Spirit, and shows himself altogether lovely. Suffering is witness-bearing, O believer,

when under pangs, or in painless intervals, when the clammy moisture and heaving breast and languid eye betray the wrestling just past, you are permitted and prompted to honour your God and Saviour. Not only men, but angels, nay God himself, regard such endurance, even in a single case; what shall we say of the gathering myriads, who for ages have been coming out of great tribulation, and ascending to the white robes and triumphal palaces of Zion? "Ye are my witnesses," will the King say to such, but especially to those who shall have sealed the confession of the truth with their own blood, Let not the overstrained eulogy and superstitious veneration of these by a corrupt Church lead us to deny the value of their testimony. A witness is callèd in Greek a MARTYR. We have borrowed the word, and made it sacred in our own tongue; for though it appears only twice in our version, in application to Stephen and Antipas, the very same word occurs repeatedly and is in the Greek translation of our text. "The noble army of martyrs" praise God, and should not be forgotten of men. Among external evidences, these avowals of men, who, at the risk of every thing earthly, and in contempt of every favour and reward, owned Christ at the stake, or in the face of ravenous beasts, abide conspicuous. In regard to the miracles of Christ and his apostles, as well as to the predictions uttered by these and afterwards fulfilled, the attestations of such original witnesses, at the instant of martyrdom, are beyond all price. We are forced to believe them. Every law of evidence and every principle of human nature must be violated, before we can doubt the numerous concurrent uncontradicted testimonies of those who could not have been mistaken, and who would not in such perils have deceived. All antiquity shows that the witness-bearing of both classes had a mighty effect in commanding the credence of Jews and Gentiles, on the spot and at the time. Nor was the validity of the miracles which were thus attested left to be settled by the intrinsic evidence of the truth which such miracles confirmed. This opinion, which has trickled in upon our theology from the corrupt springs of German latitudinarianism, and which would prove miracle by doctrine rather than doctrine by miracle, belongs to a system which, speciously gaining over our younger scholars, is carrying them over by squadrons to the camp of rationalism. The late eminently philosophical statesman, Mr. Gallatin, once said to me, alluding to the lax opinions of certain erroneous teachers: "They say, we believe *in spite* of the miracles; but I say I believe *because* of the miracles." And when we accredit the early martyrs and confessors, we build on the miracles and other supernatural sanctions which constitute the ground course of the evidential wall. To which we add, in another sense, all the suffering and dying witnesses of later ages.

Behold here, my brethren, in the faintest outline, something of the testimony which God receives from his people. To *them* you must go, if you would learn the grounds and import of Christianity. Only they can say, "We speak that which we know, and testify that we have seen." They can tell of a Saviour who has proved himself sufficient iu the day of trial, who has lifted them out of the swoon of despair, and breathed rapture into them with the kiss of peace. Their language will naturally be, Come and hear what the Lord hath done for our souls. They are not reluctant witnesses, but long for opportunities to report the greatness of the Divine love. Their number is incalculable. In all human tongues these attestations will be given. Out of all kindreds and peoples they will flock in concourse to the green and fragrant banks of the River of Life, to renew, amplify, and perpetuate that testimony which they began below. Go to them, ye doubters, and not to the ignorant and deluded sons of philosophy, falsely so called; go to them, and accept their record. They *know* that these things are so. They have believed; and believing have had the spirit of adoption. The things of religion are realities, ascertained to them by an infallible consciousness. It is the certainty of their assurance which gives earnestness to their unanimous declaration.

And *ye*, my fellow-witnesses for God, consider whom you attest, and what the office you discharge. The voice which shakes heaven and earth, says, "Ye are my witnesses!" Let the solemn vocation penetrate, and the heavenly sanction overshadow your minds; let other duties, callings, and privileges be merged in this. Looking back on all the way in which the Lord has led you, must not you speak good of his name? Love should constrain you to testify that nothing has failed of all that was promised. But you live in the midst of a crooked and perverse nation, among whom ye shine as lights in the world. Let the light be brilliant and unmistakable. Hold it high, so that none need ever ask twice whether you are on the Lord's side or not. However ardent may be the professions of some, at a season of general awakening, and how firm soever their attachment to Christ's church and ministers, observation shows that time works marvellous changes in stony-ground hearers. Such were the Galatians; warm converts, strenuous adherents, eager witnesses for a while. But listen how Paul addresses them: "Where is, then, the blessedness ye spake of? for I bear you record, that if it had been possible, ye would have plucked out your own eyes and have given them to me." Life, entire life, beloved servants of my Lord, is a period of witnessing. By act, by omission, by speech, by silence, whether you will or not, you are forever testifying. Hour by hour you are testifying, sometimes much more loudly than by words, either for or against your Master. You are doing that which leads others to conclude, either that Christ affords a satisfying portion, or that his service is annoying and wearisome. Here, surrounded by the partners of a common hope, and supported by a public opinion which honours the Gospel, you are prompt to appear on the side of truth.

It costs no sacrifice of profit, ease, or good name. But change the scene; go among the wicked, or even the gay. Enter the summer circle, at public resorts, where strict conformity to God's law is unknown; and allow me to ask, is your mind made up to be a witness for your Redeemer there also? Are you likely to be firm for Christ, when all the tide of opinion, business, pleasure, runs the other way; when to be a consistent disciple is to be pointed at and shunned; and when your testimony may be as unwelcome as it is solitary? For such Christianity, you need a courage which will never come to you except upon your knees. Though left as solitary as was your Lord, and like him beset with false witnesses, if you only have his Spirit, if his life flows into you, if, believing on and clinging to him, you have inward pulses which keep time with his heart; you will stand in the evil day, you will win souls, you will recommend the Gospel, you will live teaching and die witnessing. Amen.

XVIII.

THE CHURCH A TEMPLE.

THE CHURCH A TEMPLE.*

---

1 Peter ii. 5.

"Ye also, as lively stones, are built up a spiritual house."

It is difficult, if not impossible, for us to enter into the feelings of an ancient Israelite in regard to the temple at Jerusalem; yet unless we do so in some degree, we must lose the force of numerous figures in the New Testament, which seized upon the imagination of the Jew. To him, that structure was the best of all terrestrial things. It was at once the citadel of his commonwealth and the sanctuary of his Church. To this spot his face was turned in devotion, wherever he might wander on the earth's surface. Its walls contained all that he held most splendid in ceremonial and most sacred in mystery. In some sense it was the

* New York, April 3, 1854.

centre, not of Palestine only, but of the world, for his Lord had said, " My house shall be called a house of prayer for all nations." Its pomps and praises, the volume of its harmonies both vocal and instrumental, its bleeding and smoking propitiations, its odorous clouds of incense, its ablutions and sprinklings, its throngs of exalted worshippers, its festive processions, and its inaccessible mysterious shrine, all conspired to give it a hold on his admiration and his affections, such as no other material structure ever gained over human hearts. Hence the most available charge against our Lord Jesus, and that which was best fitted to make the populace infuriate, was that he had spoken contemptuously of the holy fabric. It was not unnatural, that in a period of formal religion, the minds of the people should have become knit to the external pile. No gleam of its higher mystery and spiritual intention had yet broken upon their worldly minds. Not yet had it been revealed that God is a Spirit, and that they who worship him must worship him in spirit and in truth, anywhere, everywhere, and not at Jerusalem or this mountain. And yet, from the beginning, God had been preparing his Church for better things, by means of this visible type, and clearing the way for the setting up of a house not made with hands. Even in the rudest stages of religious·discipline, all that is outward, palpable or formal, is in its nature temporary, and is used to symbolize something greater and lovelier, beyond the domain of sense. The day was rapidly approaching when this glorious architecture should be given to the flames, and when Israel should be without an earthly sanctuary. The vanishing of the typical system was foreshown, when the vail of the temple was rent in twain from the top to the bottom. Shortly after this, the Church began to take its new and Christian form. But those who came under this New Testament influence from out of Judaism, were steeped in associations derived from Hebrew rites. The apostles, therefore, themselves Jews, found it natural and important to address them in terms derived from the old economy; and hence we find no figures more abundant than those which are derived from the temple and its rites. In this instance, the mind of the apostle Peter, full of the strains of Old Testament psalmody, thinks of his adorable Redeemer as predicted in the 118th Psalm. The words of David are: "The stone which the builders refused is become the head stone of the corner." All in a glow with the image, his imagination under divine influence, proceeds to carry up a spiritual structure on this foundation, and to fill it with a worshipping spiritual Israel. So he breaks forth: "To whom coming, as unto a living stone, disallowed indeed of men, but chosen of God and precious, ye also as lively stones are built up a spiritual house, an holy priesthood, to offer up spiritual sacrifices acceptable to God by Jesus Christ." The warmth of Oriental style does not shrink from all that our severer rules might regard as a mixture of metaphors. The rapid transition of mind here certainly gives origin to a double figure; for the same persons who in one clause are called the temple, are in the next represented as the worshippers. Both temple and worshippers, in the type, were intended to show forth the Church of God, or the entire body of sanctified believers. From these words, therefore, I would invite you to consider with me the Church of the Lord Jesus Christ as a temple.

1. It is a SPIRITUAL HOUSE. The apostle Paul speaks of a house not made with hands, eternal in the heavens. Here also we may say with him, "that was not first which was spiritual, but that which is natural, and afterwards that which is spiritual." Such is the order of divine revelation to the human mind. We are led from the material to the immaterial. Common apprehensions fail to reach this; and there are many who never get beyond that which can be seen and felt. But in proportion as we gain insight into God's plan and are elevated by faith, we learn to value the things unseen, and awake to the knowledge of a vast and glorious spiritual universe, of which all that surrounds us is but the husk and emblem. Our Lord was continually engaged in lifting the minds of his disciples from all the glory of their darling shrine, to the wonders of an imperishable house. You remember that when they would have attracted his admiration to the buildings of the temple, he replied, "See ye not all these things? Verily I say unto you, there shall not be left here one stone upon another, that shall not be thrown down."

All was to make way for a masterpiece of spiritual architecture, which only the wise and the believing have eyes to behold.

2. It is very obvious that, of this spiritual temple, the "BUILDER AND MAKER IS GOD." It is for his glory and for his residence. The plan and the execution are his. In all ages of the world his eye has contemplated this structure, and his arm is carrying it forward. In the spiritual temple, God is pre-eminently doing his own work; manifesting his own perfections; exalting created intelligences to purity and happiness; and producing those heavenly virtues which are more precious than all the marble, gold, and gems of the earth, and which are wrought only by the Spirit of holiness.

3. Yet this spiritual temple, reared by the hand of the infinite Spirit, is nevertheless no shadowy edifice. It is in a high sense REAL, being composed of HUMAN BEINGS. Angels may contemplate the work and aid in it, but they form no part of it. "Ye," says our apostle to Christians, "ye, as lively (that is, living, animated) stones, are built up a spiritual house." Such is the value and dignity of a human soul, made in the image of God, redeemed by the Son, and dwelt in by the Spirit, that there is a consummate glory in a structure of which every component part is such a soul. In other places, the individual believer is represented as a temple of God; but here, by a change of figure, which beautifully and expressively brings forward the fellowship, multitude and union of believers, the whole are set be-

fore us as compacted into one perfect structure. The stones are no longer masses of granite, marble or porphyry, but men, redeemed and sanctified, and hereafter to be perfected and glorified. Every saint has his appointed place. The temple comprises all the righteous, who have been, are, and shall be to the end of time. We often think of believers, as separate existences, and sometimes of the Church on earth at a particular time; but we must also rise to the contemplation of the complete body, in which not one true servant of God is wanting, from righteous Abel to the last who shall be summoned to glory by the final trump.

4. The temple has a FOUNDATION. We need not wander far to find what it is. "Behold, I lay in Zion a chief corner-stone, elect, precious." "Other foundations can no man lay than that is laid, which is Jesus Christ." "Built upon the foundation of the apostles and prophets, Jesus Christ himself being the chief corner stone, in whom all the building fitly framed together groweth unto an holy temple in the Lord, in whom ye also are builded together for an habitation of God through the Spirit." It was meet that the Son of God should take humanity, in order that he might be the foundation of this human temple. It rests on him, for its coherence, beauty, grandeur and very existence. Its walls are cemented by his precious blood. Every lively stone in the pile bears his image, and is fashioned after the head stone of the corner. His truth is the basis of all faith in the Church. His righteousness is the ground

of all pardon, acceptance, and title to life. His Spirit prepares and adorns each individual member, brings him into the structure and keeps him there. Each soul, and all conjoined, rest and rely on Jesus Christ alone, as the source of strength, union, and perfection. The whole heavenly architecture is of him and for him, and his divine virtue is felt in every part of it, from the base to the summit.

5. THE WORK OF REARING THIS TEMPLE IS NOW GOING ON UPON EARTH. This is expressly said by Peter: "To whom coming, as living stones, ye also are built up;" that is, ye are now in the very process of being built up a spiritual house. It may be affirmed that our sinful world is permitted to remain chiefly, if not solely, for this very purpose, that the work of the living temple may go on. When a wise architect is about to frame a great edifice, he selects his site, designs his plan, and gathers his materials. From the guilty race of Adam God is perpetually choosing and calling those who shall be the living stones in his temple. Though the consummation is to be in another state, the busy process of preparation and erection is in this. When the temple of Solomon was to be reared, what hewings, shaping and transportation of cedars in the forests of Lebanon ; what excavations in the quarries of the vale ; what castings in the plain of Zarthan ; what moulding and carving of gold and silver among the artificers of Israel. All was looking towards the going up of the stately walls upon Moriah, without the sound of axe or hammer. Thus may

we gain an emblem of what is now in process among ourselves. Our state is altogether preparatory. Nothing has yet taken its real shape. All that we call the work of religion or of the Gospel among men, is only the getting out of the material, or the building of it into its place. Forgetting this, we frequently judge amiss of all that God is doing, and "quite mistake the scaffold for the pile." No wise critic will judge of a half-finished architecture. At such a stage much is temporary, much is obscure, all is incomplete. The beautiful idea of the artist lies hidden among a chaos of platforms, engines, and heaps of rubbish. Such is precisely the condition of the Church below. It is at best but a small part of the entire structure, which belongs to all ages, and which is to see an age when believers shall be increased, perhaps, as a thousand to one. Much that we behold is, after all, only scaffolding that shall be removed, or rubbish that shall be cast away. But meanwhile the work is going forward, and the walls, however slowly, are rising. Every thing in God's providence respecting the present world is made to lead to this. All preaching of the Word, diffusion of truth, conversion of sinners, and edification of saints, are means in God's hands for carrying up his structure. Prophets and apostles are humble instruments in the work. Thus Paul, a wise master-builder, says: "Ye are God's building. I have laid the foundation, and another buildeth thereon. Know ye not that ye are the temple of God, and that the Spirit of God dwelleth in you? If any man defile the temple of God, him shall God destroy; for the temple of God is holy, which temple are ye."

6. But we must go further. Not only is the work going on, but under the mighty hand of God the process is so conducted by the wise position, due adjustment, and manifold mutual relations of all the parts, as to procure that symmetry and perfection which is one day to be the admiration of the universe, who will see in it the brightest DISPLAY OF THE DIVINE PERFECTIONS. The plan is perfect, and, unlike human plans, is carried out with the absence of all defect and error. From the massive foundation to the humblest interior appendage, all belongs to one perfect draught; all exhibits one sublime idea. Every stone, timber, moulding, surface, tint and pinnacle, is just what was designed, in its proper place and just connexion. In every well-ordered building, there are parts which could not be anywhere else, without being useless, offensive, or hurtful. So in the "spiritual house," each of the "lively stones" is laid according to God's infallible design; each soul is built into its proper niche, each Christian that is born into the world appears at the right time and place, if not for his own highest exaltation and reward, yet for the grand result of the Divine fabric. Each has a fixed relation to all the rest, but chiefly to those which lie nearest. Of all the millions of converted souls, there is not one which has not his office and function in the extensive scheme; and though, strictly speaking, the Creator cannot be said to need any of his creatures, yet in

reference to the execution of his plan, each individual is demanded for the very position which he occupies. The structure does not rise "like an exhalation," suddenly and all at once, but by slow degrees. The times for each successive development in the Church are ordered by an infinite Wisdom; and while our impatience murmurs at the tardiness of Him with whom "a thousand years are as one day," every revolution, persecution, reformation and revival, falls out exactly at its predetermined instant, while "the building groweth unto a holy temple in the Lord." As part answers to part by a felicitous arrangement, each member contributes its appropriate service. The truth of God and the graces of his Spirit pervade the whole; and the religious advancement of the humblest believer tends to the general end; for every part is connected with Christ, "from whom the whole body, fitly joined together and compacted by that which every joint supplieth, according to the effectual working in the measure of every part, maketh increase of the body, unto the edifying of itself in love." Our views are necessarily limited to the growth of the Church in our own particular age, and even this demands a scope of observation wider than is given to most; but the Infinite Mind takes in the lapse of ages, contemplates periods yet more astonishing than any which have revolved, and sees the magnificent spiritual house, going up in stately proportions through them all.

As each renewed soul is just that which God has

made it, born in the country and the age which he foreknew, trained by providences which he designed, and removed to the upper world at his good pleasure, we may rest assured that Divine skill will never want proper instruments, and that no vacuity will exist in those temple-chambers, for lack of men or talents, when their hour has come. In surveying the past, we observe a beautiful fitness and an enchanting variety in the materials which have been already built into that part of the edifice which has thus far been reared. How unlike the corps of prophets to the corps of apostles; and how unlike the several individuals of each. We have Scripture authority for placing these among the most honourable and sustaining parts of the fabric, near the cornerstone; for we are " built upon the foundation of the apostles and prophets." Isaiah with his evangelic clarion, Jeremiah with his pastoral reed of sorrows, and David with his many-voiced harp, sometimes loud in notes of triumph and sometimes subdued to the voice of weeping, stand out with a marked individuality which becomes the more surprising, the more nearly we examine the distinctive features. They may be likened to those immense but goodly stones, carried up in courses, along the precipitous side of the valley, to form the bases for the temple of Solomon. The twelve apostles, including the last and, humanly speaking, the greatest, though brethren, how unlike! Who, for an instant, could mistake Paul for Peter, or either of them for John? They occupy salient angles of the great foundation, and lie nearest to the corner-stone, elect and precious. Some of their brethren, though not visible in the front which meets our eye, may have done equal service in the bearing up of the mass. Martyrs and confessors found their place, in succeeding ages, as the wall advanced; some as glorious for ornament as strong for use. When love needed a signal display, amidst the blood of martyrdom, we see it immortalized in an Ignatius and a Polycarp. When stalking heresy needed a front of steel to stand unmoved against all its columns, we find an "Athanasius against the world." When the language of Greece is to be elevated to new dignity by conveying the wonders of Christianity, we hear the golden eloquence of a Basil and a Chrysostom. When Roman philosophy had died out of the world, we behold it revived in an Augustine, the father of the fathers. Later down in ages, we catch glimpses even amidst Romish corruptions of a Bernard and a Kempis. The note of alarm is given to a sleeping carnal church, first by Wiclif, Huss and Jerome, then by Zwingle, Luther, Calvin, and Knox. But time would fail me, should I try to illustrate by particular instances the truth, that in God's building every variety of temper, genius, and talent finds its place, and that heavenly wisdom will never suffer any want of material for the sacred walls. Let it be for the encouragement of such among us as are conscious of no high powers, and who sometimes wonder for what service in Christ's Church we are fit, that in a great structure all the component portions are not equally great. There is not only the solid and the costly, the rock and timber; not only the precious and ornamental, the gold and silver; but likewise the humble and subsidiary, yea, even the otherwise valueless and the minute; for not even mortar and earth can be spared from the construction. The Great Builder has some lowly crevice in his house, which the meanest and feeblest of us may occupy. We may not be called to bear up buttresses, or to crown turrets, or to adorn the carved work of the sanctuary; but it should satisfy us, if in some remote recess and unknown shade, we fulfil the office which the Master has laid upon us.

The building of God, compared with which all human enterprises and structures are as nothing, goes on in a manner unobserved by men, in a mysterious silence, though often amidst surrounding turmoil and alarms. Divine Providence can turn to its own account events the most untoward and convulsions the most appalling. The blood of martyrs was the seed of the Church. The irruption over the Greek and Roman nations of the great barbaric hordes from the Indo-Germanic stock, laid open the way for the coalescence of Christianity with a new social and political element, to which we owe our language, our laws, our freedom, and our modern civilization. We read that the second temple went up "in troublous times." The wall of the Christian fabric has done so too. Dreadful and sinful as wars are, they are instruments in God's hand; and when we hear the hurtle of arms and the shriek of battle-fields, we may consider that Jehovah has not forgotten his temple; these sounds are but the blasts of his quarry or the crash of cedars in his forest of Lebanon. The conquests of Charlemagne and his successors carried the Gospel, more or less purely, into regions hitherto pagan. That great event of our day, as yet partially understood—the revolution in China—however it may result, shows how easily the high wall of separation might be broken down and the triumphant standards of Christianity carried in. And that great European conflict, for the crisis of which the whole civilized world is now waiting with breathless expectation, direful as must be its proximate effect, will undoubtedly in some way tend to the upbuilding of Christ's kingdom. "Surely the wrath of man shall praise thee; the remainder of wrath shalt thou restrain."

7. The living temple is to have an EXTENSION AND GLORY, even on our earth, such as has never yet been attained. How far the walls have thus far risen no man is competent to declare. But the work is daily advancing. Whatever some may find it convenient to assert, in favour of darling hypotheses, religion is in progress. To go no further back than the beginning of this century, which has been the era of Bible and Missionary associations and triumphs, we see an undeniable extension of the Christian area on earth. But the Scripture abounds with declarations of a latter day, the glory of which is yet future. "In the last days it shall

come to pass, that the mountain of the Lord's house shall be established in the top of the mountains, and it shall be exalted above the hills; and people shall flow unto it. And many nations shall come and say, Come and let us go up to the mountain of the Lord, and to the house of the God of Jacob." In a great edifice, the later stages of construction are those which most reveal the beauty of the conception. Therefore God addresses his Church: "The glory of Lebanon shall come unto thee, the fir-tree, the pine-tree, and the box together, to beautify the place of my sanctuary; and I will make the place of my feet glorious." Hasten on, O blessed day, when the resplendent towers of Zion shall catch the rising beams of the returning Sun of righteousness!

8. But let me not longer detain you from the truth, that for the completion of the living temple we must look to THE HEAVENLY STATE. Scripture metaphors and similitudes must not be so pressed as to urge a meaning out of every particular, nor must we be surprised if the parable does not show a perfect exactness in all its subdivisions. It has been said long ago, that similes and what they represent are often like circles; they touch only in a single point. If therefore we have thus far considered the spiritual house as going up in this world, we may by a slight variation of the image regard it still more precisely as attaining its real form and finish in the world to come. In this view, all that takes place here below is but the preparation of materials, the selection of the lively stones and the

goodly cedars, the excavation, hewing, felling, squaring, shaping and polishing; in expectation of being transported to the Jerusalem above. The home of the Church is not here. Here we have no continuing city, but we seek one to come. At no one period, even the brightest before the second coming, are all the members of Christ gathered together in one place. We often think and speak as if little was accomplished, because little is seen on earth. But we forget that only part of the living structure is here, and this a small part. Every moment, blessed souls, fitted by gracious discipline in this vale, by the axe and hammer and furnace of trial and the moulding hand of sanctification, are carried away in angelic arms, to be placed in the house above. This is only the preparatory state. Out of this mass God is gathering his elect and taking them to his temple. Are there not millions already in heaven? and are there not more countless millions yet to be gathered thither? Then, when the last redeemed one shall be caught up, to be added to the transcendent pile, "he shall bring forth the headstone thereof with shoutings, crying, Grace, grace unto it!" In the visions of the beloved disciple, we see the figure swelling in amplitude, and the house becomes a city, "the holy Jerusalem, descending out of heaven from God, having the glory of God, and her light like unto a stone most precious, even like a jasper-stone, clear as crystal; its wall having twelve gates, and at the gates twelve angels, and names written thereon, which are the names of the twelve tribes of Israel, every several gate of one pearl, and the street of the city pure gold, as it were transparent glass."

Let us awake, Christian brethren, to the reality of a spiritual structure, for which such preparations are making around us. We are in the midst of the labours which are to result in this great monument of divine wisdom, power, and love. What are our earthly palaces, what our civil and military marvels of architecture, what our toils and accumulations, compared with this building of God, which is to outlast the world? The people of this world, we know, are absolutely indifferent to the temple which is rising. They sneer at it as the antediluvians treated the ark; they are ignorant of it, as were the Tyrians and Zidonians of the first temple, even while unwittingly they aided it; or they oppose it, as the Samaritans did the second temple. Nevertheless, the foundation of God standeth sure, having this seal, the Lord knoweth them that are his. If the house is rejected, so was its corner-stone. Still it is ascending, and God's purposes are working themselves out. There is nothing which we can do in life so important as to contribute in some humble measure to the up-building of the Church. It is the only work of which the fruit cannot be lost. One soul, saved by our means, is a living stone added to the edifice. One soul made holier and better through our labours, is a new ornament to the unseen sanctuary. Not a toil, a self-denial, or a tear, shall fail of recognition; though lost to the view of men, "the day will reveal it." Open the eye of faith and behold God's great work of regeneration and salvation, which proceeds incessantly and successfully. The question is a solemn one: Am I in this temple or out of it? There is no middle ground. Have I come to Christ, the chosen precious corner-stone? Am I builded upon his truth, his righteousness, his person? Am I in union and communion with that multitude of saints, who, as lively stones, are knit together indissolubly in this sublime and increasing structure? Have I any good hope, through grace, that I shall be among the constituents of the heavenly city? The answer is important now; but the day is coming, when the answer shall be one of doom! If yea, lift up your head, and bid farewell to every anxious thought about inferior things. What are the loss or gain, the pain or joy, of threescore years and ten, when you look towards the things which are not seen, which are eternal! But if the answer be nay, pause this instant. All is at stake. Remaining thus without, all is lost, and forever. That headstone, however precious to them that believe, is no corner-stone to you; but "a stone of stumbling, and a rock of offence." "For whosoever falleth on this stone, shall be broken." Are we in our senses? Have men ever heard of their danger and their way of escape, that all should lie in so profound an apathy? God's temple will still be complete and glorious, though you should form no part of it. Much that seems (by church profession) to belong to the structure, is only an appendage or a seeming—"wood, hay, stubble." "The day shall declare it, for it shall be revealed by fire; and the fire shall try every man's work of what sort it is." And some who escape shall "hardly be saved," yea, "saved, so as by fire." May God own us, beloved, in that day! Amen.

XIX.

STRENGTH IN CHRIST

STRENGTH IN CHRIST.*

PHILIPPIANS iv. 13.

"I can do all things through Christ which strengtheneth me."

WHEN we consider that, next to that of the Lord himself, no biography of the New Testament is so fully given as that of the Apostle who uttered these words, we are led to infer that his life and character were meant to be closely studied, as affording the aid of example and incitement in the ordinary course of Christian duty. The variety of circumstances in which he is presented is remarkable, and gives occasion for the disclosure of every holy sentiment which belongs to the renewed nature, in its noblest and freest development. In his sorrows and his joys, his activity and his restraints, we see in Paul the moving power of an

* New York, New Year's Day, 1855.

inward principle, which overturned and renewed his whole being. Perhaps it is not going too far to say, that no mere man ever lived who has operated so extensively upon Christians in succeeding ages, in the way of example. Through him, though compassed about with infirmities, God seems to have chosen to show how true grace will work in a great diversity of conditions. In the Epistle now open before us, he is in those straits which sometimes make Christian equanimity difficult in our lower degrees of religious growth. But the maxim whereby he supports himself is one suited to a more general application, and suited like all high comprehensive truths to every state. The kind gift of his Philippian brethren had led him to touch delicately on his necessities; but he checks himself: "Not that I speak in respect of want; for I have learned (rare lesson) in whatsoever state I am, therewith to be content. (Gentile philosophy attempted the same result, but without success, for want of the principle which we are about to consider.) I know both how to be abased, and how to abound, (both difficult cases; for some have fallen by prosperity, whom Satan has vainly assaulted while poor.) Everywhere and in all things I am instructed (or, more exactly, I am initiated as into a mystery) both to be full and to be hungry, both to abound and to suffer need. I can do all things through Christ, which strengtheneth me."

Can there be presented a more appropriate sentiment for the year, or for every year?

There is, then, a strength in Christ, which so becomes the strength of the believer, that trusting in his Lord he may be equal to every demand of suffering or performance. Such is the proposition which I would unfold before you.

You will observe in the very expression an avowal of weakness. It is unlike the vaunting of Stoics and other sages, who, arrogant in their own resolved virtue, stood up to cope with every opponent that should affront them. Men of this temper abound, and their language is lofty. They are in armour of proof, and are mighty of will. Their nerve, resolution and purpose are not to be thwarted by any difficulty. The pride of a heroic morality holds them up. But he that trusteth in his own heart is a fool. And we have seen battle-fields strewed with the fallen, who have gone to the encounter of temptation without the aid of heaven. Such a champion, haughty and self-reliant, the youthful Saul had been, when his Pharisaic decision sustained itself against the angelic countenance of Stephen and the gentle power of Christ. But he had been lowered in his tone, that he might be exalted, and softened that he might become enduring. He had been brought into a conflict, in which he was fain to cry, "I know that in me, that is in my flesh, dwelleth no good thing; for to will is present with me, but how to perform that which is good I find not." In the desperation of this ordeal, he had burst forth, "O wretched man that I am! who shall deliver me from the body of this death?"

and rising to life, as he beheld his deliverer, had subjoined, "I thank God, through Jesus Christ our Lord." It was Christ, who was his strength; and in this perfect and communicable strength, he could do all things. Christ strengthened him; and Christ stands ready to strengthen the believer in our day.

Here as everywhere in the survey of experience, we are made to recognise the beautiful coherence of all divine truth, and to perceive how an inward sentiment of great value is based upon a solid doctrine of the system. The doctrine which acts as pedestal to the column, is that of Christ's union as head with the believer. "The head of every man is Christ." Never was this precious doctrine more nobly unfolded or more urgently pressed, than in the writings of Paul himself. The acts of the Redeemer are for the redeemed. He took their nature, assumed their liabilities, answered for their delinquency, procured their pardon, accomplished their justification, and abides in connexion with them, for all the manifold ends of their salvation. For them he was born, for them he lived, for them he died, for them he rose, for them he ascended, for them he intercedes and reigns. He is made to each of them, Wisdom, Righteousness, Sanctification and Redemption. The funded treasury of his merits, his wisdom and his might, are theirs. If he is strong—and "Thou Lord in the beginning hast laid the foundation of the earth, and the heavens are the work of thine hands"—it is a strength available for the very meanest of all his saints.

Observe how Paul, after saying, Col. ii. 9, "In him dwelleth all the fulness of the godhead bodily," immediately adds, "And ye are complete in him, which is the Head of all principality and power." There is, from those celestial and unseen fountains, a perpetual flow downwards to our world, where the heirs of the kingdom, amidst a thousand weaknesses, are struggling along towards the purchased possession. Of these, many a one, contemplating this reserve of power and deposit of wealth, has forgotten his thorn and the buffeting of Satan, and has exulted, "Most gladly, therefore, will I rather glory in my infirmities, that the power of Christ may rest upon me; therefore I take pleasure in infirmities, in reproaches, in necessities, in persecutions, in distresses, for Christ's sake; for when I am weak, then am I strong." Here, then, is the confession of weakness, but here also is the avowal of strength. And surely, O Christians, it is worth your inquiry, how you may find this strength and exercise this confidence, in those various conditions which await you in the remainder of life.

1. And here it seems most natural to make our beginning with the particular trial which drew these words from our apostle. It was that of poverty, or worldly embarrassment, which in every age has been the lot of the majority of mankind, and especially the majority of Christians. The fact that religion has wrought its chief wonders among the humble, and that God has chosen the poor of this world, "rich in faith," is too

clear to be questioned; but the reasons of the fact may not be so apparent. Among them may be these; first, that the infinite benevolence of God stoops with its comforts and supports to those who are most sunken, who suffer the greatest ills, and who are despised by the luxurious and magnificent. Therefore into ten thousand cottages and even hovels, the blessed Jesus, who was himself a poor man, has entered, to convey the "durable riches" of grace. And then, the humbling influence of penury and want, scanty fare which keeps daily fast, and sadness which ensures nightly vigils, the hardships of aching limbs, nakedness, uncertain lodging, wailing children, contempt of the lofty and oppression of the strong—this humbling discipline—fits the soul of man for that message which passes unheeded by the mansions of ease and self-importance. However it may be accounted for, the people of God, in the best periods of the Church, have often found themselves in a situation of straitened means. Moreover, the solicitude and fear of the heart may vex those who are far above the condition of degraded indigence or open mendicity. Clouds may overhang the morrow of the industrious father, the pallid widow, or the lonely relict of a once prosperous house; when channels run low, resources fail, as the barrel and the cruse seem near exhaustion. Times of commercial depression sometimes bring compulsory retrenchment into hundreds of Christian families at once. And poverty, my brethren, even in this wider sense, is a trial which it is hard to bear. Dependence is a yoke that galls the delicate sensibility. The heart of a good man may faint for a moment under the unexpected load. You, who never knew a day of hunger or shuddered at the knock of an obdurate creditor, would find your resolution brought to a rude test, if suddenly your household state should be reduced to the standard of the poor. The very apprehension of a reverse, so depressing and yet so common, brings the servant of God to the point of weakness; and after his first agitation, he proceeds to take account of his spiritual stock. How is it with the bank of faith? What hold is there on the treasure in heaven? Many a one, blessed be God, has been able to reply, in the terms of the Old Testament, "Although the fig-tree shall not blossom, neither shall fruit be in the vines; the labour of the olive shall fail, and the fields shall yield no meat; the flock shall be cut off from the fold, and there shall be no herd in the stalls; yet will I rejoice in Jehovah, I will joy in the God of my salvation." THE LORD GOD IS MY STRENGTH. Yes, the New Testament believer, seeing more clearly, will more triumphantly add, the Lord Jesus is my strength; I can do all things through Christ which strengtheneth me. I can be abased and can abound; I can be full and be happy. I have that part which cannot be taken away, bags that wax not old, investments that cannot be depreciated. My security is eternal in the heavens. My treasure and my heart are above. Having Christ, I have all things. Without him the wealth of kingdoms would but sink me to ruin; with him, I can be content upon a crust. My soul is strengthened to peace and acquiescence. He to whom I have committed the greater, will be surety for the less. "Is not the life more than meat, and the body than raiment?" I am firm in the persuasion that my Lord and Master, who has my love, will never allow me to sink under cares of this life. Thus the power of Christ is glorified in the experience of many a straitened but contented soul.

2. This case, then, of temporal necessity was that which drew out the believing and exultant affirmation of Paul. But the source of power and solace and assurance, is equally full for every instance of worldly solicitude. Let us look at one of the most familiar. As we are year by year journeying towards the certain termination of our course, in death, so we may be said to be dying daily. Each New Year's day marks another approach to dissolution. Even under the roses of health, the worm is at its fatal work. In some, the symptoms of mortality are striking and undeniable. To themselves and others, they appear as frail, decaying creatures. Sometimes there are vehement shocks of acute malady, which foreshadow the taking down of the shattered tent. Sometimes there is a train of weaknesses, aches, and despondencies, which keep the summons forever at the door. In such as attain old age, that period is but a long, incurable disease. Nothing more convicts man of his feebleness, than bodily distemper. A few nights of rolling and tossing in the sea

of pain, suffice to bring robust and stalwart health into puling infirmity. We do not find that earthly resources avail much in this contest. The blow that first strikes the body, presently lacerates the mind. "The spirit of a man will sustain his infirmity, but a wounded spirit who can bear?" Here, then, just where nature surrenders, is the point where grace triumphs. Such strength is given in every age of the church, every day, yea, this very moment. Take the extreme case, where death is certain and near. The Lord Jesus has not withdrawn his helpful arm. Nay, some of his chiefest condescensions are vouchsafed to those who have "the sentence of death" in themselves, that they should not trust in themselves, "but in God which raiseth the dead." Our benign Redeemer loves to hold up the sinking head of one whom he is about to release forever. "He giveth power to the faint: and to them that have no might he increaseth strength." In proportion as the promise of worldly good is abolished, the faithful soul grows mighty in the certainty and nearness of heavenly good; pledged to him in that divine Head, who bare our sicknesses and carried our sorrows, and who can be touched with a feeling of our infirmities. Nor dare I confine the enjoyment of Christ's strength to these particular classes of trial. Poverty and illness are, after all, not the most bitter and weakening of human woes. There are secret troubles, gaping wounds of the spirit, mortifications, disappointments and griefs, which are all the more fitted to cast down and to unman, when they cannot be revealed to the eye of vulgar examination, or ask the lips of forward condolence. Whatever the heart sinks under, causes a necessity for Christ's aid; and there it is! Amidst all the consciousness of sin, he who has entrusted his all to the freeness of the covenant, can be strong in the Lord and in the power of his might. "God is our refuge and strength, a very present help in trouble; therefore will not we fear, though the earth be removed, and though the mountains be carried into the midst of the sea." It is not the sufferer, it is the Saviour who is strong. "Their Redeemer is mighty; the Lord of hosts is his name." The cordial is suited to every case. The year can bring no exigency which the strength laid up in Christ shall not meet. Make it yours, beloved hearer; and let God's invitation resound in your heart, "For I the Lord thy God will hold thy right hand, saying unto thee, Fear not, I will help thee." Isa. xli. 13.

3. From temporal, let us go to spiritual troubles. There is a great conflict with sin, in which we need divine strength. Woe be unto us, if Christ does not help us here. It is a conflict in which every one of us will be engaged, either to conquer or be conquered. If Paul could rise and testify, he would declare that all his other contentions, not excepting his fighting with beasts at Ephesus, were nothing to this; and all true Christians have had a similar experience. The more advanced we are in holiness, the more shall we regard other trials, such as affect the body, or the property, or

the reputation, as not worthy to be named along with those which endanger the conscience. The greatest enemy we can possibly have, is he who makes us sin. The father of lies, who was a murderer from the beginning, has made his grand effort just here. His perpetual endeavour is to beguile or terrify the Christian into sin. He had the effrontery and diabolical madness to make an experiment with the Apostle and High Priest of our profession, in a threefold temptation. But the god of this world found that he had nothing in Jesus; no tinder in that bosom upon which his hellish sparks could kindle. His hopes are greater in tempting poor, fallen, partially sanctified humanity. Great are his successes for a time. If you call those Christians who have made high professions, he has caused thousands of Christians to fall; and he has humbled in the dust many of the real brotherhood, when, like David and Simon Peter, they have yielded themselves to his attacks. This invisible warfare is more fearful than the deadliest charge upon columns of a superior human foe. "For we wrestle not against flesh and blood, but against principalities, against powers, against the rulers of the darkness of this world, against spiritual wickedness in high places." The odds are fearful, if you look at your own native strength. I apprehend that the reason why some are not startled by this prospect, is, that they have more fear of suffering than of sinning; or perhaps they cherish a secret scepticism as to their own weakness. Either of these errors is fatal to progress in religion.

There is that before each of us, in the way of conflict and temptation, which will not only bring all our powers to the test, but will leave us defeated and utterly ruined, unless we have some strength greater than our own. And if we truly value holy obedience, we shall delight in the assurance that this battle is not to be fought by us alone. What will not the soldier dare, who is led by a brave and invincible commander? Such is ours. "Through God we shall do valiantly; for he it is that shall tread down our enemies." Ps. lx. 12. Not only have we Christ as a leader, but as the very source of our strength against sin, by our union with him, and the consequent effluence from Him to us of the Holy Spirit, the source of all light, purity and strength. It is belief of this, and trust in the covenant terms, which authorize the disciple to say, "I can do all things, through Christ which strengtheneth me." I can stand up in a struggle which would prostrate me in a moment, if my own power was all. This is the victory that overcometh the world, even our faith. I can pass unhurt through temptations also, for no temptation shall befall me but that which is common to man; and in Christ's name I will steadfastly resist the roaring lion, knowing that the same afflictions are accomplished in my brethren that are in the world. Christ's strength will be mine in the moment of sore trial.

4. It remains to say something about an obvious application of the words before us to the case of expected labours for God. In this we include every

thing which falls under the denomination of active obedience. For work, there must be strength. For Christian work, there must be spiritual strength. This does not exist in us by nature; nor even by grace and after renewal does it so exist, as to be a permanent stock, upon which we can draw, as something of our own. It is the plan of God that his redeemed people should feel their dependence at every step. They are not sufficient of themselves to think any thing as of themselves, but all their sufficiency is of God. This is true of the ordinary course of Christian performance. Every well-instructed disciple has discovered that he cannot walk for a single hour without the sustentation of the Divine arm. Those moments in which we are left a little to our own resources, are moments of darkness and grief, if not of disgrace and discomfiture. Satan desires to have us, that he may sift us as wheat, but Christ prays for us and succours us. He leads the safest, truest, happiest life, who most consciously leans upon the strength of the Redeemer, and takes each several step of the way, with his eye fixed on the Author and Finisher of his faith.

But if this is true of those labours which are ordinary, much more strikingly true is it of such as are extraordinary. Special demands of service are sometimes made. This is true in all branches of important worldly trust. Pride or temerity might smile at the grave view which an humble believer takes of new periods of life, new relations, new circumstances, new calling and office. He shrinks from what is laid upon him. As Moses: "Who am I, that I should go unto Pharaoh?" As Obadiah: "And now thou sayest, Go, tell thy lord, Behold Elijah is here; and he shall slay me." As Isaiah: "Woe is me, for I am undone." As Jeremiah; "Ah, Lord God! behold I cannot speak: for I am a child." As Ananias: "Lord, I have heard by many of this man, how much evil he hath done to thy saints at Jerusalem." When weakness is joined with unbelief, prospective labours are appalling. If we could enter into the secret experience of those Christian heroes who have achieved the greatest wonders for God, we should probably find that their mighty acts were not performed without some foregoing trepidation and sense of incompetency. Jacob weeps and wrestles before he is named a prince of God. The astonishing valour of Paul was a fruit of grace; and who knows how often the day of courage and endurance may have followed a night of agony? It is not only common, but it is good, to feel ourselves very weak in divine things. Then it is that we take hold of strength. Amidst floods of apprehension, the Psalmist cries: "When my heart is overwhelmed within me, lead me to the Rock that is higher than I!" Then when the self-distrusting one beholds the countenance of heavenly friendship turned full upon him, he knows on what to depend, and sings, "I can do all things, through Christ which strengtheneth me."

The careful examination of the text will show you

that it contains more than an acknowledgment of weakness; more than a persuasion that there is strength in another; it expresses the fixed purpose to go forward in duty, relying on Christ. It not only says, In myself I can do nothing, but In Christ I can do all things. And this is the very point of faith, to which we need to be brought; nor, till we are brought thither, shall we ever accomplish any high achievement in Christianity. We must feel that there is solid ground under our feet, before we can march confidently onward. This unwavering belief of the treasure laid up for us in Christ, is faith. It runs forward beyond the scope of sight; beyond all that has been traversed by actual experience. It takes God at his word, and rests on his assurance. Believing that he will call to no labours for which he does not furnish strength, it attempts much, and trusts mightily while attempting. The Christian, under these exercises of mind, does not put off the beginning of performance until the moment when he shall be sensible of Divine aid flowing in upon his soul, but puts forth endeavours now, in the assurance that consciousness of strength will accompany sincere effort. It is the only principle upon which rational obedience can be rendered. For if we never undertake a duty until all inward difficulties be removed, we only act over the part of him in Greek fable, who deferred crossing the river till all its waves should flow by. No; true courage and holy resolution will rather look the obstacle in the face, saying of it, even when most insuperable to the eye of nature: "I can do all things, through Christ which strengtheneth me."

And now, with the year before us, have we not, my Christian brethren, a watchword, with which to be diligent and undaunted for God? The ancient commanders used to cheer their soldiers on the eve of battle, by assurances that some of their favourite deities were descending to fight in the ranks; and the falsehood added vigour to their hearts and nerve to their arms. But in our soldiership we have the blessed truth to stimulate us, that the Captain of our salvation goes before us. Come prosperity or come pain, come wealth or bereavement, come health or sickness, come temptation or labour—if CHRIST be with us, all shall be well! And with us he is, and will be, if we are his people, and if his promise is true. We greatly err by making a sort of merit of our misgivings, and groaning over our weakness, as if this were pleasing to God; when, indeed, a high aspiring faith and unwavering confidence in God's aid for the future, is more welcome to him, and unspeakably more productive of obedience in us. If you have no satisfactory persuasion that the transforming work of grace has passed upon your souls, you have a great previous question to settle, and I implore you not to adjourn it. But if you have believed, you may make the words of the text your own, in prospect of the year. And O that, together, and as with one accord, we might go forward with these words blazoned on our shields! When the Lord Jesus was about to ascend to heaven, he gave a solemn commission to his original apostles, in which he assigned to them their work. But the commission was prefaced by these words: "All power is given unto me in heaven and in earth." It is this mediatorial power of the Lord our Master, this communicated power, resting in the Head, to which we as his members are privileged to resort. That strength is ours, if we lay hold of it by faith; which shows us again, what we are continually learning both in the Word and in experience, the value and necessity of faith; not only for first receiving Christ, but for walking in him. Just so much fortitude in affliction and courage in action have we, as we have faith. What we want for the year is more faith. The circumstances of some now present may be greatly and unexpectedly changed during the year. No preacher, no friend, no father, could expound to you the particular exigencies of the near future; and when the trial comes, you will feel that it is novel, and unlike all you have known before. For such junctures you cannot make special or detailed preparation. But here is a preparation which is sovereign, and universally applicable. Believe in the Lord Jesus, cast yourself on his arm, and appropriate his strength. Then, though it should be your lot to go down into the swellings of Jordan, you shall not be taken unawares. One of the most illustrious and triumphant deathbeds at which I have ever been summoned to minister, was that of a lovely Christian woman, of refined sensibility and timid disposition, who was suddenly smitten down in a strange city, on a journey far from friends, and out of the midst of apparently perfect health. And yet Christ was her strength and joy, and became her salvation; so that even the alarm of this strange surprise was wholly taken away from her.

In the history of the Church we meet with some striking instances of persons who have done extraordinary service, and had uncommon success, whose names are remembered with benediction, even in nations far asunder and for successive ages. These are the men of faith. They had learnt the secret of power. They dared much and endeavoured much, because they were backed and sustained by Christ's strength, which they acted on, and about which they had no misgivings. If you desire to be more useful than you have ever been, go to the field, as David against the Philistine, with a steady belief that your Lord will pour in the strength as certainly as you put forth the effort. Happy indeed will the New Year be to you, if you set about its tasks in this temper. Does the sinking of conscious weakness unnerve and subdue you? Turn yourself wholly over upon the Everlasting Arm. For some of you, beloved hearers, I have had and still have, peculiar anxieties for the changes which this very year may bring about. I have lived long enough to know, that great revolutions of mind and heart may be effected in a very brief period. "But I fear, lest by any means, as the serpent beguiled Eve through his subtilty, so your minds should be corrupted from the simplicity that is in Christ." However unlikely it may seem to you now—nay, however abhorrent it may be from all your present feelings—a few months or even weeks, under new influences, may suffice to carry you down the current of worldly and fashionable religion. The teachings to which you now listen with respect and docility, will have lost all charm, and the simplicity that is in Christ will have been exchanged for a polished but cold, an attractive but uninfluential, a philosophical but unevangelical strain, which shall fill the ear and entertain the intellect, and fascinate the imagination, but from which Jesus crucified shall be totally absent. How shall such a defection be prevented? How shall such instability be guarded? Only by being strong in the Lord. And O if, by intimate communion with him in devotional exercises, you are made to "grow in grace and the knowledge of our Lord Jesus Christ," then, and then only, will you be enabled to "stand in the evil day, and having done all, to stand." Now, beloved, having on this first Sabbath of the New Year sat together in the rest and refreshment of the sanctuary, as under a pleasant shade by the wayside, and being uncertain whether we shall ever meet thus again, or who among us shall, during this period, be called away; let us arise, and lift our burdens, and take up again the pilgrim staff, and set out anew upon our journey. We might utter the words of Moses: "If thy presence go not with me, carry us not up hence."

Ex. xxxiii. 15. The Lord has been with us; let us hope that he will not forsake us. As a church we can do all things, through Christ which strengtheneth us. We can cling together; we can grow; we can open our bosom to receive the young, the stranger, and the wanderer; we can abound in good offices and acts of charity; we can break forth to found new colonies for Christ; we can part with property, health, friends, yea, life itself, at the Master's call; we can drink deeply at the wells of truth, and derive nourishment from the bread of the Word; we can cast behind us old sins, and put on us the armour of light, letting our godly example shine on all around us; we can rejoice alway, and glory in tribulation also. All this, and more than this, can we do through him that strengtheneth our hearts. But without Him, branches separated from the Vine, we can do nothing.

XX.

YOUTH RENEWED IN AGE.

YOUTH RENEWED IN AGE.*

Isaiah xl. 31.

"But they that wait upon the Lord shall renew their strength; they shall mount up with wings as eagles; they shall run and not be weary; and they shall walk and not faint."

Compared with Psalm ciii. 5.

"Who satisfieth thy mouth with good things; so that thy youth is renewed like the eagle's."

Statues would be erected to the man who could disclose the secret of a happy Old Age. For while the most of mankind desire longevity, the judgment is equally universal that the decline of life is painful. The same law, however we may expound it, which binds over the entire race to dissolution, makes the avenues to death full of terror. The sentimentalism and poetry of our day, in a vain contest with the nature

* New York, January 20, 1850.

of things, would hang garlands over the grave, and educate the rising race in a persuasion that death has no horrors. But nature, how often soever driven out, persists in returning. We dread death; and we dread that old age which procrastinates it. Such is our dilemma. Viewed from the terrestrial side, the fearful object is seen aright. It is revelation, and grace confirmed to us by revelation, which clear the prospect. In what manner this is effected will be made apparent, if we consider these two statements included in our text. 1. That Old Age is naturally a time of weakness and trouble; but, 2. That Christian confidence and hope in God give freshness, strength and joy, even in the period of Old Age.

I. Old Age is naturally a time of weakness and trouble. We see it for ourselves; even if we have not begun to feel it. Till lifted out of the common track of opinion, every one looks on the aged as withdrawn from the path of happiness. Civilization and its refinements have undoubtedly elevated the condition of the aged, as truly as of the female sex. Yet even this is often no more than a delicate feigning; for if rank, wealth, place and power be abstracted, there is nothing reverential in such appellations as "the old man" and "the old woman." In this country, at least, we are on this head more Athenians than Lacedemonians. Of a surety we do not imitate the Hebrew, who is taught to rise up before the hoary head. Universally we attach to old age associations of debility and consequent with drawal from the arena of excitement and the bower of mirth. The old man's faculties are dim, and his susceptibilities are obtunded. He is left out of the programme of entertainment. If called to feasting, he is expected to say with Barzillai: "Can I hear any more the voice of singing men and singing women?" In a great number of instances, also, age is regarded as a disqualification for active service. And these results strike us more forcibly in those ruder states of society where nature presents its nude reality. All the history, all the fiction, all the observation of the world, ascribe to this stage of the human journey much of shadow, cloud, and obstruction. As it respects the fact, the case is not otherwise presented by Scripture. These are the days in which the weary one says: "I have no pleasure in them." If lengthened out, "yet is their strength labour and sorrow." "Surely every man walketh in a vain show; surely they are disquieted in vain; he heapeth up riches and knoweth not who shall gather them." In the prospect of such hours of gloom, the Psalmist prays: "Cast me not off in the time of old age; forsake me not when my strength faileth." When the youthful wish for long life, they seek they know not what. Age is solitary; the tritest figure is the most apt: the tree whose branches have been lopped off, till it stands a naked trunk. Such is the tax paid for longevity. Decline does not commonly arrive without a succession of warnings, enigmatically depicted in that strange oriental passage which closes the Ecclesiastes.

Limbs grow stiff; the repast is toilsome; articulate utterance is hindered; sight and hearing become obtuse; pains visit and revisit the frame, and at length make settlement. Caution waxes inordinate, and turns into timorous apprehension. Seasons of hilarity decrease, and the wintry nights are long. It requires something from another sphere than that of nature, to prevent despondency, suspicion and discontent. If the diseases which portend departure act on the physical functions, the sadness of a worldly Old Age is deplorable. If poverty or neglect or domestic disappointment be added to the loss of all life's pleasures and excitements, old age is a great and almost insupportable malady. Yet observation, in all varieties of condition, shows that the love of life abides in perfect vigour. We might expect that very weariness of living would make the old man prompt to go; but the ligament becomes only more tenacious. The wisest instructor we ever had used to say, and to say in old age, that natural decay produced no increase of readiness to depart. An eminent writer on Pastoral Theology reports, as of his own observation, that more than a hundred young persons, whose deathbeds he visited, passed away in peace; that the middle aged clung more closely to life; but that the most unwilling of all were the aged.* Even the crime of self-murder is perpetrated oftener by the young than the old. At no period does man hang on worldly

---

* "Erfahrungen am Kranken und Sterbebette;" von E. Kuendig. Basle, 1856.

things with a more tenacious clutch, than when they are all about to be rent away together. This very much levels the condition of rich and poor in old age. The wealthy sinner has that which he can no longer enjoy; yet never did he so yearningly gape for more. The ship is in the very harbour; yet the voyager is amassing fresh stores. It is a madness which constitutes part of the punishment of an irreligious life. The thirst of gain is insatiable. Comedy and satire in all languages have painted the same picture. Young enthusiasts think that when they shall be old and rich, they will diffuse blessedness on hundreds around them; and it is true this would tend to make the close of life delightful. But when they have reached the point, alas, the heart has grown old and is withered. Scores may have died who might have been claimants for aid; poor kinsfolk may have been long ago warned off by the chilly barrier; the doleful habitation may have its valves all opening inwards; and yet there is not enough. Just such a spot, in Gentile mythology, was the hell of Tantalus. Such old age is trouble and sorrow. So Solomon concludes; "There is one alone, and there is not a second; yea, he hath neither child nor brother: yet there is no end of all his labour: neither is his eye satisfied with riches; neither saith he, For whom do I labour, and bereave my soul of good? This also is vanity, yea, it is a sore travail." Ecc. iv. 8.

Even the true Christian, when his case is viewed without the solace of which we shall presently speak, sometimes passes through great trials in the latter portion of his life. To some the Valley of the Shadow of Death is long and dreary. Diversities of corporeal disability, family vexation, and mental agitation or depression, assault and weaken the resolution which has withstood repeated shocks. And I freely own, that if we could take no higher view of life than that which is admitted by the sceptical world, we should abandon the worn-out creature to his despair. He might, in lucid intervals of a partial belief, cry out to his Maker, "Why hast thou made all men in vain?" What can be more melancholy, than a soul about to migrate to an unknown state? There is something so contrary to nature in the forced attempts at gayety which sometimes disgrace aged people of the world, that society is prompt to manifest its disgust. The gravitation of native temperament prevails over all such affectations, mockeries and disguises. The solitary hour is honest, and it is dark. Outward mementoes are multiplied. Ah, in how many funeral processions must the survivor walk with sad decorum, himself a living sermon to all around! "Because man goeth to his long home, and the mourners go about the streets." No longer delighted to live, yet afraid to die, the worldly man who has survived his contemporaries, grows sullenly silent and keeps his own secret. For to whom shall he go with that complaint, which only serves to break the spell of his cherished delusion and reveal him to himself? Dear as his gold is, he would almost barter it all for a draught of that fountain of youth which Spanish adventure sought in tropical America. The poor disquieted sufferer is faint, and discovers, that so far as nature reaches, old age is a time of weakness and trouble.

II. Christian confidence and hope in God give freshness, strength and joy, even in the period of Old Age. "They that wait on Jehovah," or in modern English, they that wait for him, who evince their trust in his goodness and power by patiently awaiting the fulfilment of his promises, they, though no longer young (mark the contrast with v. 30), "shall renew their strength; they shall mount up on wings like eagles, they shall run and not be weary, and they shall walk and not faint." The same thought is in the thanksgiving of the one hundred and third Psalm, v. 5: "Bless Jehovah, O my soul, who satisfieth thy mouth with good things, so that thy youth is renewed like the eagle's." From both we may conclusively gather that Divine grace has influences to bestow which can counteract and often annul the debilitating tendencies of Old Age. We are not authorized, it is true, to teach that any degree of religious affection can turn back the shadow on the dial-plate, restore its auburn beauty to the gray head, or neutralize the physical causes of distress; though even here, such is the power of spirit over matter, that history shows marvels of an almost youthful gladness in blessed Christian old age. But we may and can assert, that he whose habits have been formed in a perpetual waiting upon God, receives a hallowed unction of grace, which, so to speak, makes him young again, or, more properly, keeps him from waxing old within. In the most rapid survey, we have considered some of the causes which make this season of life formidable. All ages have observed them; all philosophies have sought to destroy or lessen their force. The most accomplished of all Roman authors has left nothing more finished than his celebrated tract on Old Age. Short of the meridian beam of revelation and its reflections, nothing ever showed more nobly; yet the ray of its consolations is but a beautiful moonlight. In vain is the venerable Cato introduced to teach us secrets which Cato never knew. In this gem-like treatise Cicero refers the troubles of age to four classes. Old Age, so he tells us, is feared because (1) it withdraws from the affairs of life; because (2) it brings infirmity of body; because (3) it abridges or ends our pleasures; and (4) because it leads to death. Already, in treating of these several heads, much is said truly, ably, and to a certain extent satisfactorily, on the first and third topics; but on the last, there is nothing but melancholy conjecture. Even in regard to the other heads, of business, health and pleasure, the suggestions are infinitely below those known by the humblest Christian rustic. For what did this great and eloquent Roman know of the oil which grace pours into the sinking and almost expiring lamp?

It is not to be denied, when we come with candour to the investigation, that as a general truth, Old Age withdraws men from the employments of life, and seals up the active business years. In the great majority of instances, however, this retreat for labour is voluntarily sought long before the access of grave infirmity. Indeed, in prosperous communities, many retire too early, under a chimerical hope of enjoying an elegant repose, for which they have made no provision by mental culture and discipline of moral habits. There is, it is true, another sort of recession from productive labours, which we occasionally observe in old men, and which arises wholly from an unchastened selfishness. Let any one grow wealthy without the warming and expanding influences of benevolence, and he will more and more lose his interest in all that is going on in the world. Even wars and revolutions touch him only in their financial aspects, and the daily journal is to him not so much a courier of news, as a barometer of loss and gain. Without religion, the circle becomes more contracted. Friends have departed, by scores if not by hundreds. What cares he for mighty movements in behalf of humanity and holiness around him? What cares he for posterity, the country or the world, so that he can exalt his own gate, or die worth some round sum which floats before him as his heaven? In the same degree he wraps himself in his mantle, which is daily shrinking to his own poor dimensions. This is misery indeed. Take away the blessed sun, and every thing becomes wintry, frozen, all but dead: take away more blessed love, and the heart is dumb, cheerless, insulated, meanly poor, so that the Latins named such a one MISER. Let us leave him, shivering in his cave, overhung with icicles, and come out into the evening sunshine to consider the aged believer. He is like Mnason, "an old disciple." He still learns. The Greek story tells us that when Solon lay dying, and overheard some conversation on philosophy in his apartment, he raised his head and said, "Let me share in your conversation, for though I am dying I would still be learning." Ten thousand times has this been more reasonably exemplified in dying Christians, who consider the whole of this life as but the lowest form of the school into which they have been entered. And in regard to activity, while modes of service must vary with the bodily condition, we are bold to maintain that innumerable Christians now living are, in advanced life, impressing the whole engine of human affairs with as momentous a touch as at any previous stage of existence. If there is Wisdom, the proper jewel of age, and divine grace in its manifold actings, there need be no lack of influence. They still lift up the eagle pinion, and soar in such greatness as belongs to their nature. But the point to which we would ask more marked attention is this, that the aged believer, so far from being selfishly dead to what is going on in the world, is more vigilant and more in sympathy with all, than even in his days of youth. Blessed be God, we have seen this again and again. The man who waits on God, the man of faith and hope, the man of melting benevolence, looks through the loopholes of retreat upon a world whose vast and often terrific revolutions interest him chiefly as included in a cycle of providential arrangements calculated to develop and exhibit the glory of grace. His heart beats responsive to these. The news of Christ's kingdom is as dear to him as when he was vehemently active in the field. He looks down the ages by the lamp of prophecy, and beholds events which will take place when he shall have been long in paradise. This connects him with the cause of Christ on earth, and redeems him from that miserable dungeon-like seclusion of soul which wastes away the aged worldling. So far is it from being true that these portraitures are figments of religious imagination, that we have been led to the choice of the subject by knowledge and recollection of this very paradox in actual example, to wit, extreme old age made light, strong and happy, by community of interest in the progressive triumphs of philanthropy and missions.

When, according to the Talmudic fable, the eagle soars toward the sun, he renews the plumage of his former days. As the serene disciple withdraws himself from any personal agency in the entangling plans of life, he studies more profoundly what his Master is weaving into the web of history. No longer young, he has a heart which gushes in sympathy with the young. He cheers them on. He places the weapons in their hands. He takes from the wall his sword, shield, and helmet, and rejoices that God still has younger soldiers in the field. He lives his life over again in their achievements, and pictures to himself more signal victories after he shall have gone. Like the wounded hero Wolfe, he could even die more happy if the shout of victory should arouse his failing perception. Far from being shut up in morose neglectful selfishness, he glories that God's cause still lives and must prevail.

2. But, then, you retort, there is a sad infirmity, inseparable from Old Age. Piety, however exalted, will not remove this. Of all diseases this is proverbially the most incurable. Brethren, we might take the high ground, that godliness hath the promise of the life that now is; that temperance and other virtues prolong life and avert disease; that the righteous shall "see good days," and that religion is the best of all medicines. But fearing lest we should be charged with exaggeration by the inexperienced, we will pitch our cause on a lower plane, and rest content with declaring that Christian confidence and hope confer a strength which is perfectly compatible with all this bodily weakness, decay and pain. Christianity, my hearers, is a system of indemnities. It does not insure us exemption from all losses, but it guarantees that these shall be more than made up to us. True, the grand indemnification is at the recompense of the resurrection. But prelibations of glory are poured into the earthly vessels of grace. The quickening charm is not natural, but supernatural. Mark, in the twenty-eighth verse, how the eternal increate fount of good is pointed out; and

learn how the fulness of God, through a Mediator, becomes the available supply of man: "Hast thou not known? hast thou not heard, that the everlasting God, Jehovah, the Creator of the ends of the earth, fainteth not, neither is weary? There is no searching of his understanding. He giveth power *to the faint.*" Here is human infirmity brought into connection with Omnipotence. Here is the solution of Paul's enigma, "When I am weak, then am I strong." Here is Christ's cordial to the aged, "My strength is made perfect in weakness." But let us return to our prophet. He represents even blooming adolescence as desponding, while the feeble are made powerful by faith. "Even the youths shall faint and be weary, and the young men shall utterly fall; but they that wait on the Lord shall renew their strength."

In the return from Babylon the oldest were saddest; for they remembered the glory of the first house. Nehemiah, therefore, had peculiar reference to them, when he said to the weeping assembly, "Neither be ye sorry; for the joy of the Lord is your strength." Holy joy is a springhead of renewed youthfulness. The effects of grief and age are not unlike. How often have we seen a friend go into the house of mourning, young, and come out old? Such was David's experience, Ps. xxxii. 3: "My bones waxed old, through my moaning all the day long; for day and night thy hand was heavy upon me: my moisture is turned into the drought of summer." The cedars and palms of the sanctuary, planted in the house of the Lord, " shall still bring forth fruit in old age, they shall be fat and flourishing," Ps. xcii. Make a soul thoroughly glad, and you make it young. The effusion of divine joys has virtue to annul outward disabilities. For observe the perfect analogy of another passage concerning strength, Is. xxxv: " Strengthen ye the weak hands, and confirm the feeble knees : say to them that are of a fearful heart, Be strong, fear not!" "Then shall the lame man leap as an hart, and the tongue of the dumb shall sing." Such is grace, superseding nature, conciliating contraries, making the feeble mighty and giving youth to the aged. And O how greatly would our experience and observation of the gift be increased, if with higher faith and expectation we were waiting upon God !

.3. The antechamber of the Eternal abode is cold and appalling to nature. This makes Old Age unwelcome to the unprepared. This causes the wretched shifts by which they avert the thought of doom. So successful is the delusion, that the man of seventy plans for to-morrow as if he were not already in many senses dead. No man is so old, says Cicero, but that he thinks he may live another day. And so from day to day, as by stepping stones in the turbid stream, they totter on, till the sudden fall plunges them into eternity.

The fear of death, which on the young sometimes works salutary reflection, often becomes to the aged a motive for abstracting the thoughts from the hateful subject; and so they think of something else, and are damned. I dare not undertake to say, what may be the reflections of the old worldling, when he lies down for the last struggle, and finds that Eternity is dawning on his soul, and yet that he has not made the least provision for meeting his God. But I know, for I have often seen, how strong in faith and hope may be the old age of the true Christian. After all, it is celestial HOPE which sheds the dew of youth on his silver locks. His posture is that of waiting, as watchers expect the dawn. " More than they that watch for the morning." Fresh blood seems to course through those outworn arteries, as Hope waves the hand of indication towards perpetual spring and everlasting youth. Not in the mere elysian or Mohammedan sense, though we deny no attributes and enjoyments of that bodily complement of the soul which is to be raised in incorruption, in glory, in power, a spiritual body. But the fresh breath of knowledge, of reason, of truth, therefore of beauty, of love, of universal holiness, is wafted from those gardens to the ancient believer, as he worships, 'leaning on the top of his staff,' and sojourns a little in the land of Beulah. We have sometimes seen the clearness and vigour of former years come back. Call not that man old, who is full of joys and hallelujahs, and who is eager to drop the clog, shuffle off the mortal coil, and soar like a bird set free from the snare of the fowler. Call him old who is inveterate in sin; who never prays; who dares not think of death; who is without God and without hope, and on whose hoary head no blessing ever descends. The Simeon who has Christ in his arms, has in him a well of water springing; and so the true fountain of youth. All believing and sublime exercises of Christian experience have in them something as fresh as childhood. Once when I was supporting a very aged believer from the house of God, he turned to me and said: "I never felt younger, and I believe that promise is fulfilled in me, He 'satisfieth thy mouth with good things, so that thy youth is renewed like the eagle's.'" This persuasion, that true religion brings the soul into fellowship with all that is free, hopeful and advancing in earth, and all that is bright and perfect in heaven, led the most distinguished of late German theologians, Schleiermacher, to say, in the close of a long life: "The true Christian is always young."

The racy old English of John Bunyan best sets forth this stage of pilgrimage: "Here they heard continually the singing of birds, and saw every day the flowers appear in the earth, and heard the voice of the turtle in the land. In this country the sun shineth night and day. Here they were within sight of the city they were going to: also they met some of the inhabitants thereof; for in this land the shining ones commonly walked, because it was upon the borders of heaven. In this land also the contract between the Bride and the Bridegroom was renewed; yea, here, 'as the bridegroom rejoiceth over the bride, so doth their

God rejoice over them." My beloved brethren, we must be submissive to God's will, even if such an evening of life be not vouchsafed to us. Yet I will maintain, that it is of the nature of Christianity to produce such joys. The exceptions are not from grace, but from disturbing causes in our partially unsanctified hearts. Waiting on God is directly promotive of fresh and heavenly strength. The long continued practice and rooted habit of waiting upon God, in confidence and expectation, are the best preparative for a serene decline and a happy end.

If the sentiment of the world may be safely judged from its reflection in the mirror of the fictitious literature, which is seized with most avidity and reproduced in the greatest number of languages, then unquestionably the opinion is, that there is no happiness in evangelical piety; and an Old Age of religion is one of sourness, vindictiveness, and misanthropic woe. Let the picture of a Christian matron be painted by the matchless pencil of one, whose misfortune it must have been never to have beheld the original, and with whom devotion and hypocrisy are the same, and the lineaments are such as these: " Great need had the rigid woman of her mystical religion, veiled in gloom and darkness, with lightnings of cursing, vengeance, and destruction, flashing through the sable clouds." I quote from the ignorant and malignant travesty of Christian Old Age, which mars the most widely current story of the hour. And I quote it, because it will meet response in hundreds of thousands, who need the grace of Christ to avert these very storm-clouds of declining day. Let a holier literature prevail in the refined world, a literature which shall honour holy wedlock, family religion, and the Church of Christ, and we shall behold other portraitures of the wife or the widow upon whom evangelical truth has shed its dews of eventide.

You listen, my hearer, with the interest of one who expects to journey thitherward. But you will perhaps never reach that stage of the way. A small proportion attain to hoary hairs. Yet even for you, the topic is not devoid of interest. That which is good for Old Age is good for other conditions of sadness, which resemble it; for illness, disease, pain, solitude, reproach, poverty, or depression. When you shall have learnt to wait on the Lord, you shall tread all these under your feet, as ready to fly heavenward.

That which prepares for Old Age, prepares for the termination of life at any age. It is decreed that every human life shall close; and most close early. To go suddenly and unprepared into that shadow is fearful. Does not wisdom commend this familiar, trustful, filial waiting upon God? The judicious and eloquent SAURIN wished that he might in every sermon make some allusion to Death, because he had remarked how universally this consideration was affecting to the mind. The Father of our spirits meant that it should be thus. Endure the contemplation long enough to chill carnal ardours and dispel the juvenile mirage. Even in prosperity wait on the Lord.

It would be treachery in me to conceal altogether the woe and peril of a Christless Old Age. Horrid anomaly! So dead to this world's pleasures, so near to heaven or hell, and yet unconcerned. Tottering on his staff, the impenitent veteran in the camp of Satan blunders on, already half gone, and stupidly improvident as to the only means of dying well. O, poor old man! let me in affection and pity cry to you, seize on that only medicine which gives everlasting youth! Attach yourself, by acquiescing in his free redemption, to that Saviour whom we are authorized to offer to the worst and oldest.

THE END.

Ric Ergenbright Titles

The beautiful photograph that graces the cover of this volume of the sermons of J.W. Alexander was taken by Ric Ergenbright, a man who rejoices in the sovereign grace of God. He has published several volumes that combine the beauty of God's creation with the glory of His Word. We are delighted to offer the following for sale:

The Art of God
This award winning volume has been useful all over the world in spreading the glory of God's saving grace. Ric gives the story of God's grace in his life which is the backdrop of this breathtaking volume.

Think About These Things
This is the second volume in the *Art of God* trilogy, and in the words of John Piper, *"Here you will find (as always with Ric Ergenbright) the art of God wrapped in the Word of God."*

The Image of God
This is the third and final volume of the *Art of God* trilogy. This time Ric turns his camera to people, created in the image of God. People from all over the world are portrayed here with Scripture illuminating each photo.

Reflections
This is a devotional book unlike any you have seen. It takes Scripture, hymns and beautiful photography and leads you to see God, His world and His Word in a new way. There is room given for you to write down what you have learned that can be passed down to your posterity.

The Mercy of God and the Misery of Job
Ric joins his unique gift with John Piper to bring home the message of Job in a new and creative way. This book not only contains the words of Piper and the photos of Ergenbright, but it also has a cd of the book read by John Piper as well. This book will help you understand both the mercy of God and the misery of Job in new and profound ways.

Please visit his beautiful web site at **ricergenbright.com**

Some Other SGCB Classic Reprints

In addition to *A Shepherd's Heart* which you hold in your hand, we are delighted to list several other titles available from Solid Ground Christian Books, many for the first time in a century or more:

THEOLOGY ON FIRE: *Sermons from the Heart of J.A. Alexander*
THE ASSURANCE OF FAITH *by Louis Berkhof*
OPENING SCRIPTURE: *A Hermeneutical Manual* by Patrick Fairbairn
THE PASTOR IN THE SICK ROOM by John D. Wells
THE NATIONAL PREACHER: *Revival Sermons from the 2nd Great Awakening*
THE POOR MAN'S NT COMMENTARY by Robert Hawker
THE POOR MAN'S OT COMMENTARY by Robert Hawker
THE POOR MAN'S MORNING & EVENING PORTION by Robert Hawker
FIRST THINGS by Gardiner Spring
BIBLICAL & THEOLOGICAL STUDIES by Princeton Professors of 1912
THE POWER OF GOD UNTO SALVATION by B.B. Warfield
THE LORD OF GLORY by B.B. Warfield
CHRIST ON THE CROSS by John Stevenson
SERMONS TO THE NATURAL MAN by W.G.T. Shedd
SERMONS TO THE SPIRITUAL MAN by W.G.T. Shedd
HOMILETICS & PASTORAL THEOLOGY by W.G.T. Shedd
A PASTOR'S SKETCHES 1 & 2 by B.B. Warfield
CHRIST IN SONG: *Hymns of Immanuel from all ages* by Philip Schaff
THE PREACHER & HIS MODELS by James Stalker
IMAGO CHRISTI by James Stalker
LECTURES ON THE HISTORY OF PREACHING by John A. Broadus
A HISTORY OF PREACHING (2 VOLS.) by E.C. Dargan
THE SHORTER CATECHISM ILLUSTRATED by John Whitecross
THE CHURCH MEMBER'S GUIDE by John Angell James
THE SUNDAY SCHOOL TEACHER'S GUIDE by John Angell James
THE DEVOTIONAL LIFE OF THE SS TEACHER by J.R. Miller
And several more....

Call us Toll Free at **1-877-666-9469**
Visit us on the web at **http://solid-ground-books.com**

www.ingramcontent.com/pod-product-compliance
Lightning Source LLC
Chambersburg PA
CBHW020937180426
43194CB00038B/195